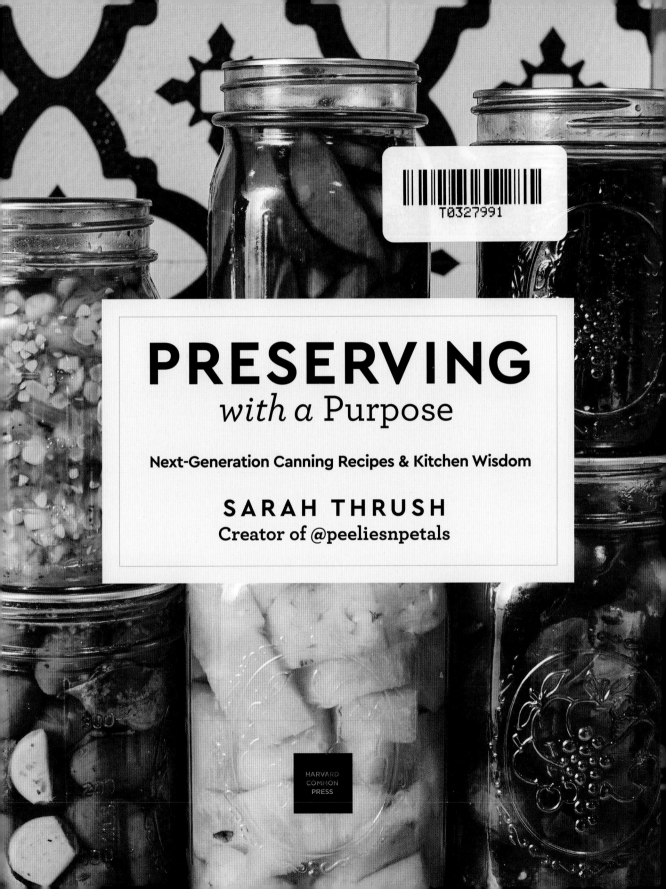

PRESERVING

with a Purpose

Next-Generation Canning Recipes & Kitchen Wisdom

SARAH THRUSH

Creator of @peeliesnpetals

HARVARD COMMON PRESS

Quarto.com

© 2024 Quarto Publishing Group USA Inc.
Text © 2024 Sarah Thrush

First Published in 2024 by The Harvard Common Press, an imprint of The Quarto Group,
100 Cummings Center, Suite 265-D, Beverly, MA 01915, USA.
T (978) 282-9590 F (978) 283-2742

The Harvard Common Press titles are also available at discount for retail, wholesale, promotional, and bulk purchase. For details, contact the Special Sales Manager by email at specialsales@quarto.com or by mail at The Quarto Group, Attn: Special Sales Manager, 100 Cummings Center, Suite 265-D, Beverly, MA 01915, USA.

28 27 26 25 24   1 2 3 4 5

ISBN: 978-0-7603-8707-8

Digital edition published in 2024
eISBN: 978-0-7603-8708-5

Library of Congress Control Number: 2024934661

Design: Laura Klynstra
Photography: Haas and Haas, except those from Shutterstock (pages 81, 93, 111, 131, 139, 203, 231, 253)

Printed in China

DISCLAIMER
Home food preservation and canning must be performed according to the most up-to-date safety standards. The reader is encouraged to rely on two primary sources for this information: 1) The latest published and online notices from national, regional, and local departments of food and agriculture, and extension services; and 2) The most-recent safety guidelines provided by the manufacturers of the *specific* canning and preserving supplies that each reader is using. The recipes and other instructions in this book have been safely tested by the author in her home kitchen, using her own equipment and supplies, in the course of writing this book, but they are not a replacement for the guidance given by the two sources named above. The author and publisher disclaim any liability incurred as a consequence of the use and application of any of the contents of this book.

To my mother, Patty, and grandmothers, Granny and MomMom,

I was listening.

To my children,

if you weren't, here it is.

CONTENTS

A Few Words from Sarah

"Food makes friends of us all."

———◆———

If I had one wish, it would be to have this as my epitaph.

One of my earliest and fondest memories was standing on a chair in the kitchen to watch my mother pour boiling grape jelly into jars and cover them with wax. I must have driven her nuts with all the questions I asked, but she never seemed frustrated as she passed down the knowledge she had gained from *her* mother.

I call myself a third-generation canner because my first memory is of canning with my grandmothers. My family has canning recipes that date back to the 1800s (I share some of them in the pages of this book). So how many generations back does my family's canning knowledge go? I don't really know.

I grew up in the late 1970s in a microcommunity on the border of Indiana and Illinois, just outside of Chicago. It's called "the Region," and it was there I encountered and became familiar with a diverse range of foods and cultures. We are known as Region Rats. "From a cultural standpoint, the Region is where the 'ethnic' slums of South Side Chicago [meet] 'white corn-fed hillbilly' Indiana, creating a very diverse and unique place that is by far better than any other location in Indiana." (Urban Dictionary, n.d.) The Region remains a true American melting pot of ethnic diversity.

The harsh winters in the Region meant regular blizzards and short growing seasons. My grandmothers were both survivors of the Great Depression and World War II, and I grew up with stories of Victory gardens and learning how to live a "waste not, want not" lifestyle. Stretching food resources, learning how to make something from nothing, and canning food to preserve the harvest were part of my education. My mother oversaw the planting, gardening, raising of animals, and preserving our bounties for the long winters ahead. This was the knowledge she kept and passed to me, as her mother and her mother's mother had done before her.

Beyond my family, there were people of all colors and nationalities in the Region. I wouldn't trade the imprints they left on me for anything. Inside the Region were other subcultures, like Little Mexico, where I hung out in the kitchens of my Hispanic friends' mothers, soaking up the methods and recipes for every dish prepared. While my friends were playing outside, I was spending time in a Puerto Rican or Polish kitchen, watching and learning, tasting, and asking questions. My best friend was Polish, and I had a regular seat at her family table. They lovingly called me "Sarah Sue" and took me in as their fifth daughter. And although I wasn't Catholic, I learned their dinner prayer and recited it alongside them, my eyes focused on the steaming pile of pierogies and sausage the whole time. These childhood experiences still influence me today.

As I grew into adulthood and started having children of my own, I quickly found myself struggling with food security. Had it not been for the knowledge instilled in me as a child, we would have gone hungry more than we did. I got to work growing food and canning it. I wasn't about to stand by idly waiting for someone to save us. After a few years tending my own garden, I no longer had to pretend I wasn't hungry while making sure my children had larger portions of food. Hopefully, a struggle they didn't even know existed until they read this book.

Soon, as we overcame our food insecurity, we had food on the shelves to eat. I vowed never to let myself get to that point again. But I did. After I lost my home, I lived out of a duffel bag for a year. With no job and nowhere to live, I was once again faced with the challenges of food insecurity. Each brought new solutions, like using community gardens and learning to make grilled cheese sandwiches with a clothes iron, but the common denominator that kept me going was my extensive knowledge of food preservation.

I wrote this book to share the knowledge I'm so fortunate to possess, and to preserve it for future generations. I want to help people gain the skills they need to maintain food security, something I believe is a basic human right.

Life is a never-ending series of challenges that test us mentally, physically, financially, and emotionally. We all encounter moments of suffering and struggle along the way. My own journey hasn't been easy, but throughout the challenges, one constant has been my lifeline: knowing how to survive.

I've carried my skills for food preservation everywhere with me. They've been a reliable tool kit to help me through mini-disasters and setbacks. My fervent wish is that, regardless of where you find yourself in life, the skills you acquire from this book will empower you with the knowledge and confidence to embrace a self-sufficient lifestyle. By mastering the art of food preservation, you'll not only gain the ability to provide for yourself and your loved ones; you'll also unlock the many rewards that come with self-sufficiency.

It's a journey of resilience and resourcefulness, and I'm excited to share it with you.

Sarah Thrush

CHAPTER 1

Preserving with Purpose

Canning with a Mission and Embracing the Whys of Preservation

Food is one of our most basic needs, yet there isn't a single place on this earth where food scarcity and insecurity are not present. Preserving food and making it available for use much longer than it would be otherwise can help counteract this problem.

If you're new to the idea of preserving food and canning—or are looking to expand your arsenal of food preservation knowledge and recipes—you should find this book useful. I come from generations of home canners and hope to pass these time-honored family traditions to others. What we grow, cook, and eat is a part of our cultural identity and helps us understand who we are and where we come from. Food is our past, present, and future, and it can make friends or foes of us all.

Today's families are turning to food preservation for many reasons, new and old. Since the Covid-19 pandemic, we've been faced with new challenges. Rising food prices, supply-chain disruptions, and lost income due to illness are just some of the reasons canning has made a comeback. We're looking to get back to the basics of living—food preservation is an integral part of that change.

Whether you grow your own food or buy it, I believe one of the most useful tools we have is the knowledge to preserve the food we have access to. If you own a refrigerator or freezer, you're already using food preservation techniques. *Canning is the natural next step.*

I often hear the common misconception that canning food is expensive. While there are some up-front costs, the truth is, canning can be quite economical and has been successfully practiced by poverty-stricken families and communities for centuries.

The most expensive food you'll ever buy is the food you throw away. Knowing how to preserve the food we have and to stretch its life is a survival skill. While canning isn't a new concept, it's one that continues to evolve as our technology and understanding of food preservation grows.

Preservation with a purpose means eating what you preserve and preserving what you eat. I hope this book will help you become comfortable with home canning, while offering you delicious new recipes. And, as a bonus, you'll gain food stability in an increasingly unstable world. I believe everyone deserves food security, and this book is meant to be my small contribution to helping you preserve your food with purpose.

I hope this book is well loved and well used by you. I envision your book full of your handwritten notes and Post-its peeking from the pages of your favorite recipes, tomato sauce thumbprints and blurred print from wet canning hands. I hope this book secures you as the future of the at-home canners and arms you with the tools you need to feed your family for generations to come.

Benefits of Canning

Canning offers numerous benefits and is suitable for a wide variety of people regardless of income, location, and lifestyle choices.

Physical and Mental Health

You choose what goes into the jar! No more guessing what the ingredients are on the food labels for products you buy in the store. This is especially helpful for those with food restrictions, allergies, special dietary needs, and lifestyle choices. There are also potential health benefits to home canning, including being able to preserve food without the use of artificial preservatives or additives.

More specific benefits that can help support you, mind and body, include the following.

* **Quality control.** Home canning gives you control over the quality of the ingredients used in your preserved foods. When you can your own food,

you can be sure it's free from contaminants and of a higher quality.

* **Tailored tastes.** Canning lets you preserve foods to match your personal taste preferences. You can adjust seasonings or add spices to create your desired flavor profile. When you preserve food at the peak of freshness, you can enjoy seasonal produce all year long.

* **Personal satisfaction and reward.** There's a sense of personal satisfaction and achievement with every jar you can. Standing in your pantry, you see beautifully vibrant foods waiting to be eaten. When you look at your tomatoes in a jar, knowing exactly where they came from, there's an internal sigh of relief. This sense of accomplishment and pride in your abilities has a positive effect on your mental health.

Financial Benefits

You've heard the saying "time is money"—you can save both with canning. On average, I save eight to ten thousand dollars a year by canning my family's food. You can start canning with any pot large enough to submerge your jars, making it economical for all.

* **Grocery prices.** The cost of food is rising, but canning can save your wallet. I take advantage of sales on fresh produce, canning what I buy for later use. When you grow your own food, the savings can be dramatic, and reducing the need for prepackaged and processed foods also saves you money.

* **Bulk buying.** You can reduce the cost per serving and save money on groceries by buying food in bulk or growing it yourself, then preserving it at home, instead of purchasing smaller quantities

of prepackaged foods. For example, by canning a large batch of tomato sauce from tomatoes in season (at their lowest cost), you can save time on future meal preparations and money instead of buying winter tomatoes (when they cost the most).

* **Time is money.** Meals can be made more quickly when using canned food. It's already prepared, ready to reheat and eat. You'll lower your trips to the grocery store and the time and effort required to purchase fresh food on a regular basis, another way to save time and money.

Waste Reduction

Home canning can also help cut the amount of food you throw away: you can preserve foods in quantities that meet your needs, rather than buying too much and then letting some of it spoil before you can use it. This can be beneficial for both personal and environmental reasons, as it helps to save money and resources.

* **Food waste.** By preserving food, we avoid throwing away spoiled or unused food. This in turn saves money on groceries and reduces your waste. You throw away 100 percent of your money every time you throw away moldy strawberries or wilted spinach. This makes canning purposeful in reducing wasted food and wasted money.

* **Packaging waste.** The glass jars and rings you can with are completely reusable. I have jars over a hundred years old that are still in rotation on my shelves. Every store-bought can and shrink-wrapped or packaged food item you buy ends up in a landfill (or, worse yet, in the ocean). Canning can be an effective way to reduce waste without excessive packaging waste.

* **Energy waste.** Canning allows you to batch-cook in larger quantities. Instead of making one chili meal for your family once a month, you can now preserve twelve jars of chili at once. This gives you twelve chili meals to enjoy throughout the year. Your stove takes the same amount of wood, propane, gas, or electricity, regardless of making one meal in a pot or twelve jars of meals in a canner. Canning reduces the resources needed to feed your family and can lower the costs of cooking.

Community Building

Canning offers a unique way to create community and help families bond. It's not just canning when we preserve our harvest and pass around recipes: We're learning from each other and making memories together. The shared labor of canning reinforces a sense of togetherness and tradition in an increasingly fast-paced world. In the act of preserving food, we also preserve our connections to each other.

Living Intentionally through Food

This is one of my favorite canning benefits: Home canning gives me a sense of personal satisfaction. I get a sense of accomplishment and connection with my heritage. Learning food preservation techniques and maintaining food security can help you live intentionally.

* **Engaging with your food.** Home canning is fun and rewarding. My mother calls it a "labor of love." It's a great way to learn new cooking skills and meet others who share a passion for home preservation.

* **Preserving cultural traditions.** Canning provides a sense of connection to my ancestors. I enjoy learning traditional canning methods and recipes passed down through the generations. This makes for a positive feeling of nostalgia, and that can help maintain our cultural traditions and carry them down to our children and grandchildren.

* **Food security.** Less reliance on food distribution chains and having shelf-stable food give you peace of mind, ensuring that your family will be fed. Food security includes physical and economic access to food while also extending its shelf life.

* **Emergency preparedness.** Emergency preparedness and food preservation are closely related. Canning can help soften the blow that can come with job loss, the impacts of inclement weather and power outages, or other emergencies. By being prepared for the unknown, we can funnel our attention to the bigger problems. No power? No problem! Your food will be shelf stable without refrigeration or freezing. You can help ensure your access to the food and resources you need by taking steps to prepare for emergencies.

CHAPTER 2

Food and Your Family

Planning Your Pantry

In this chapter, we will explore the details of pantry planning. I'll share my canning strategies and the supplies you need to create a well-prepared and purposeful pantry.

Food Planning: How Much Food Do You Need to Feed Your Family?

Step 1: *Assess Your Family's Needs*

The first step in successful meal planning is to track what your family is already eating. I keep a clipboard in the pantry with a list of all the food my family likes to eat. By tracking what we eat and how much we eat every day, I can easily see how much we eat in a week, a month, and a year. This helps us plan how much food we'll need to have on our shelves and what kinds of food I will need to grow or buy in order to preserve it.

My goal is to have enough individual ingredients to provide for a full year so our meals can be on hand from one harvest to the next. But you don't need to plan for the whole year when you start with smaller goals and see what's best for your situation.

Step 2: *Calculate Daily Caloric Requirements*

Calculate the daily caloric needs of each family member. On average, an adult requires around 2,000 calories a day. The needs for children and older adults may vary depending on their age and activity level.

Step 3: *Multiply by the Number of Days*

Determine how long you want to plan for, whether it's a week, a month, or a year. Multiply the daily caloric requirements by the number of days:

Meal Planning: The One Week, One Month, One Year Method

Meal planning is the next crucial step in pantry preparation. I use the "One Week, One Month, One Year Method," a strategic approach to feeding my family while building a purposeful pantry.

* The weekly meal plan helps me make efficient use of fresh ingredients and minimize food waste.

* The monthly plan provides for a well-prepared pantry that can handle fluctuations in my schedule and avoid last-minute grocery runs.

* The yearlong plan is the most effective part of this method. By considering a year's worth of food, I can stock my pantry with staples, canned goods, and other shelf-stable items. This approach supports our food security and promotes self-sufficiency and sustainability.

A purposeful pantry stocked for a year can help you gain peace of mind, knowing that you're prepared for unexpected situations while enjoying the freedom to create diverse meals.

Here's a breakdown of my One Week, One Month, One Year Method.

One Week

For a one-week plan, calculate the quantities of staple foods needed for balanced meals. Here's a sample for *one* person. Adjust this as needed for your family.

* Grains: 3 pounds total, e.g., 1.5 pounds (680 g) of rice, 1.5 pounds of pasta (680 g)

* Proteins: 3 pounds total, eg., 2 pounds (907 g) of meat of choice, 1 pound (454 g) of beans

* Vegetables: 2 pounds (907 g) of assorted vegetables

* Fruits: 2 pounds (907 g) of assorted fruits

* Dairy: 2 quarts (1.9 L) of assorted dairy, e.g., milk, cheese, or yogurt

* Fats and oils: ¼ cup (59 ml) of assorted oils, e.g., cooking oils

* Additional items: Spices, condiments, drinks, snacks, etc.

Here's a chart of food quantities that can be used as an example of how much a family of four needs for one week. I hope this helps you visualize how easily you can preserve food on your shelves to adopt the One Week, One Month, One Year Method in your home.

FOOD GROUP	QUANTITY FOR ONE WEEK
Grains (e.g., rice, pasta, bread)	14–16 cups (approx. 7-8 pounds)
Proteins (e.g., chicken, beans)	4–6 pounds
Vegetables (e.g., peas, carrots)	14–16 cups (approx. 7-8 pounds)
Fruits (e.g., apples, bananas)	14–16 pieces
Dairy (e.g., milk)	7–8 quarts (approx. 2 gallons)
Fats and oils (e.g., cooking oil, butter)	1–1.5 cups
Extras (e.g., spices, condiments)	As needed

SAMPLE WEEKLY MEAL PLAN

Here's a basic sample meal plan to help you visualize how the quantities mentioned above can be distributed over the week:

Breakfast

* Cereal, milk, and fruit (x4)

* Oatmeal with baked apples (x3)

Lunch

* Turkey and cheese sandwiches with veggie sticks (x3)

* Chicken salad with corn and cinnamon apples (x2)

* Beef stew with cornbread (x2)

Dinner

* Grilled chicken with steamed broccoli and rice (x4)

* Vegetarian chili with cornbread (x1)

* Spaghetti with tomato sauce and salad (x1)

* Beef stir-fry with mixed vegetables and brown rice (x1)

Snacks

* Greek yogurt with honey (x7)

* Apple slices with peanut butter (x7)

As noted, the quantities provided are basic estimates. The extras include spices, condiments, and any additions used for flavor. Adjust portion sizes based on the age and activity level of your family members. This plan doesn't account for beverages.

One Month

For one month, multiply the one-week quantities by four. For example:

* **Grains:** 6 pounds of rice, 6 pounds of pasta

* **Proteins:** 8 pounds of meat, 8 pounds of beans

* **Vegetables:** 8 pounds of mixed vegetables

* **Fruits:** 8 pounds of assorted fruits

* **Dairy:** 2 gallons (4 L) of milk

* **Fats and oils:** 1 cup (236 ml) of cooking oil

Here's an example of the jars my family of four consumes in one month.

CANNED VEGETABLES	QUANTITY FOR ONE MONTH
Green beans	12 jars
Corn	12 jars
Green peas	6 to 8 jars
Carrots	6 to 8 jars
Mixed vegetables	4 jars

CANNED FRUITS	QUANTITY FOR ONE MONTH
Peaches	6 to 8 jars
Pears	6 to 8 jars
Pineapple	4 to 6 jars
Mixed fruit	4 to 6 jars
Applesauce	6 to 8 jars

CANNED PROTEINS	QUANTITY FOR ONE MONTH
Canned tuna	10 to 12 jars
Canned chicken	8 jars
Canned beans	12 to 15 jars

CANNED TOMATO PRODUCTS	QUANTITY FOR ONE MONTH
Diced tomatoes	6 to 8 jars
Tomato sauce	4 to 6 jars
Tomato paste	2 to 3 jars
Canned pasta sauce	4 to 6 jars

CANNED SOUP AND BROTH	QUANTITY FOR ONE MONTH
Chicken or vegetable broth	8 jars
Canned soups	10 to 12 jars

CANNED EXTRAS	QUANTITY FOR ONE MONTH
Canned fruit juices	6 to 8 jars
Canned milk	4 to 6 jars

SAMPLE MONTHLY MEAL PLANS

This is a sample meal plan for a family of four for one week using the canned foods listed above. This is a very basic meal plan and can be adjusted for your family's needs. To extend this to a one-month plan, repeat every week or make two meal plans and rotate them every two weeks.

Day 1

* **Breakfast:** Cereal with peaches (canned fruit)

* **Lunch:** Tuna salad sandwiches (canned protein) with corn (canned vegetables)

* **Dinner:** Spaghetti with sauce (canned pasta sauce) and a side of green beans (canned vegetables)

Day 2

* **Breakfast:** Oatmeal with mixed fruit (canned fruit)

* **Lunch:** Chicken noodle soup (canned soup) with crackers or fresh bread bowls

* **Dinner:** Chili (canned soup) with green peas (canned vegetables)

Day 3

* **Breakfast:** Scrambled eggs with diced tomatoes (canned tomatoes) and potatoes (canned vegetables)

* **Lunch:** Grilled cheese sandwiches, tomato soup (canned soups), and pineapple (canned fruit)

* **Dinner:** Beef stew (canned soup) with carrots (canned vegetables)

Day 4

* **Breakfast:** Yogurt with applesauce (canned fruit)

* **Lunch:** Bean burritos with corn (canned vegetables) as a side

* **Dinner:** Sweet-and-sour chicken (canned meat) with pineapples (canned fruit) and mixed vegetables (canned vegetables) over rice

Day 5

* **Breakfast:** Cereal with peaches (canned fruits)

* **Lunch:** Turkey cheese sandwiches (canned protein) with vegetable soup (canned soup)

* **Dinner:** Ground beef tacos (canned protein) and ranch pinto beans (canned beans)

Day 6

* **Breakfast:** Blueberry muffins (canned fruit) and mixed fruit (canned fruit)

* **Lunch:** Tuna salad sandwiches (canned protein) with corn on the side (canned vegetables)

* **Dinner:** Chicken pot pie (canned protein) over mashed potatoes (canned vegetables) with green peas (canned vegetables)

Day 7

* **Breakfast:** Scrambled eggs with diced tomatoes (canned tomatoes)

* **Lunch:** Peanut butter and jam (canned fruit) sandwiches and pineapple (canned fruit)

* **Dinner:** Beef chili (canned soup) with carrots (canned vegetables)

Canning whole meals in a jar is another option to expand your purposeful pantry and give you a variety of quick meals to serve. When planning your canning menu, consider the meal-in-a-jar recipes found in this book.

These sample recipes, which we'll see later on, can help you plan your One Week, One Month, One Year menu.

* Burrito in a Jar (see page 194)

* Chicken Pot Pie (see page 154)

* Sweet-and-Sour Chicken (see page 206)

* Pork Carnitas (see page 204)

* Beef Stroganoff (see page 212)

* Cincinnati Chili (see page 186)

* Corned Beef Hash (see page 168)

* Zuppa Toscana (see page 221)

* Bourbon Chicken (see page 167)

* Sloppy Joes (see page 160)

* Beef Tacos (see page 192)

* Asian Orange Chicken (see page 205)

One Year

Planning for a year requires a more comprehensive approach. As you work out what to stock in your yearly pantry, it's vital to diversify your recipes and the methods of food preservation. Consider freeze-drying, freezing, fermenting, dehydrating, or other methods at your disposal, in addition to canning.

The easiest way to approach a one-year pantry is to decide on a rotating quarterly meal plan. To do this, I create a set of three-month meal plans and rotate them every four months. This helps us avoid food fatigue and stay away from repeating meals more than four times a year.

Keep your calculations simple. Consider canning two or three foods that your family eats regularly. For example, my family eats approximately two jars of corn and one jar of green beans per week. This is how I work out the amount I need to store as a year's supply:

2 jars corn per week x 52 weeks = 104 jars of corn

1 jar green beans per week x 52 weeks = 52 jars of green beans

Avoiding Food Fatigue

When planning for a year's supply of food, diversity is key in fighting food fatigue! This can be a real problem, which I learned firsthand as the "food mom" for drum corps.

For three months a year I would travel with a food truck, providing four meals a day for two hundred young adults competing around the country. The meals were repetitive and everyone quickly became bored with our food selections. It didn't take long to see the negative effect of the monotonous food options on morale.

If you've ever been on a ramen noodle budget, or have lived or worked where cafeteria food was the only option for every meal, you've experienced food fatigue. When planning for a year's supply of food, diversity is key in fighting food fatigue!

Planning to Can: Eating What You Can and Canning What You Eat

Canning is one of several great ways to preserve your food, but you should only can the foods you enjoy eating. It's not worth your time and resources growing and preserving foods that no one will eat.

In my house, food preservation goals encompass three key points:

* Reserve enough food to last from growing season to growing season. For example, in my climate corn is harvested in late August. By September, my corn shelf will be fully stocked for the year. By the following July, I will be down to my last couple of jars of corn as we get ready for the next harvest.

* Eat all preserved foods in rotation—"first in, first out"—so the oldest foods are consumed first and the newest foods are saved for last.

* Preserve foods we have in abundance before they go bad. Whether they come from a sale or after growing a bumper crop, preserving readily available food ensures that we can eat well all year.

Assess Your Produce

Identify the fruits and vegetables your family consumes regularly. For example, if your family enjoys tomatoes, beans, and peaches, focus on starting with these items for canning. I'm a huge advocate of small-batch canning, which is a great way to stock your shelves—you'll be surprised how quickly they fill up!

Use this guide to manage the food you want to preserve, organized in order of availability for freshness.

1. Home-grown produce represents the shortest time from vine to jar: you watch it grow, then you harvest it and can it for your shelves.

2. Local farmers or farmers' markets allow you to meet the producers and talk with them about what they're selling.

3. Food co-ops often carry foods produced by local farmers, which translates to less time in transportation and fresher foods.

4. Grocery stores offer foods that are the oldest, picked before they are ripe and, potentially, shipped from far away—even from overseas.

Equipment and Supplies

In canning, the initial investment in equipment and supplies is a one-time financial purchase. After purchasing canners and jars, you can reuse them for many years.

If you want to stretch your overall investment dollars, buy a pressure canner. This allows you to pressure cook and pressure-can and doubles as a water bath canner.

Another way to save money is to find jars and canning supplies at local resale shops.

Create a Canning Schedule

You may have heard the exclamation "Grab your Balls, it's canning season!" While cheeky (the "Balls" in question are Mason jars produced by the Ball Corporation), the expression reflects a real canning season or schedule that follows the cycle of harvests in a year.

Plan your canning schedule around the foods that are ready for harvest each month. While I preserve and can throughout the year, canning most often takes place during harvest months for produce.

Align your schedule with the harvest season of your chosen fruits and vegetables. When you have a schedule in place, you can begin to run your pantry like a well-oiled machine.

Sample Canning Schedule

Below is an example of my canning schedule based on my plant hardiness zone. I live in the Upper Peninsula of Michigan, which is known for long, cold winters: we can't grow any food outside for over six months. Because of this, it's essential to make the most of the available growing time we have.

Tailor your canning schedule to your plant hardiness zone.

Early Spring (March to April)

* **Seedlings indoors.** Begin your seeds for warm-season vegetables such as tomatoes and peppers. These will be transplanted outdoors after the last frost.

* **Cold-tolerant vegetables.** Plant cold-tolerant crops like peas, radishes, lettuce, and spinach directly in the garden as soon as the ground is thawed.

* **Asparagus.** Late April sees the first produce of the canning season when asparagus starts to bloom, and the canning season can kick off with pickled asparagus.

* **Tropical fruits.** Keep an eye out for supermarket sales on tropical produce for canning. Pineapples and other tropical fruits are usually at their lowest market price during April.

* **Ham.** Sales on this meat begin around Easter, so stock up while it's at its lowest price.

Late Spring (May to June)

* **Seedling transplant.** Once the threat of frost has passed (usually around June for us), transplant seedlings you have started indoors.

* **Rhubarb.** This hardy plant is often ready for harvest in late spring. You can make rhubarb preserves or can the leaves and stalks for later use. (Look for a strawberry rhubarb pie recipe on page 76.)

Early Summer (June to July)

* **Early crop harvest.** Begin harvesting early crops like peas, strawberries, and leafy greens.

* **Official start of canning season.** As you harvest fruits like strawberries and raspberries, start canning them as jams and jellies. If yields are limited at first, freeze your fruits until you have enough to begin canning.

* **Pickling.** As cucumbers become ready for harvest, consider pickling cucumbers to make dill pickles.

Mid-Summer (July to August)

* **Warm-season vegetables harvest.** Continue harvesting warm-season vegetables like tomatoes, peppers, and zucchini.

* **Salsa and tomato products.** This is the time to make tomato-based products like salsa, pasta sauce, and tomato preserves.

* **Fruit preserves.** Harvest and can fruits like peaches, plums, and apples as they become ripe.

* **Pickling.** Keep pickling your cucumbers and make other pickled vegetables like beets or green beans.

Late Summer (August to September)

* **More fruit preserves.** Continue canning fruits like pears, apples, and grapes.

* **Canning soups and stews.** As cooler weather approaches, consider canning soups, stews, and chili using your harvested vegetables.

* **Pickling.** Finish pickling any remaining vegetables.

* **Herb drying.** Harvest and dry herbs like basil, oregano, and thyme for winter use.

Early Fall (October)

* **Late-season harvest.** Gather any remaining vegetables from the garden before the first frost. This may include carrots, potatoes, and winter squash. Time to can your chow-chow and piccalilli (pages 104 and 106).

* **Applesauce and apple butter.** Make applesauce and apple butter with freshly harvested apples.

* **Game.** Hunting season brings an abundance of game meat to pressure-can.

Late Fall (November to December)

* **Winter preparation.** As winter approaches, take stock of your canned goods, making sure all jars are properly sealed and labeled. Store them in a cool, dark place.

* **Turkey.** Prices are at their lowest during these months. Keep an eye out for sale prices and purchase enough turkey to can for the year. Turkey is an amazing substitute for chicken recipes.

* **Spices and herbs.** Winter is also an excellent time to restock pickling spices and herbs for the upcoming canning season. Store shelves are restocked around this time. By stocking up in the winter, you'll beat the canning season rush when supply can't keep up with demand.

Throughout the Year

* **Herb preserving.** Dry or freeze herbs throughout the growing season to use in your recipes.

* **Meat canning.** If you hunt or raise livestock, consider canning meats like chicken, beef, or venison during the year.

* **Freezer cleanout.** Be sure to clean out your freezer, canning and preserving the year's bounties so you'll have space to refill for the next year.

Remember that specific timing may vary for individual growing conditions. Adapt this example schedule to suit your garden's unique characteristics and your family's preferences.

Properly canning and storing your preserved foods ensures a steady supply of homegrown goodness throughout the year, even in colder climates like mine.

Quantity Planning

Calculate the number of jars needed based on your family's consumption. For example, if you consume a quart of canned tomatoes per week, plan for fifty-two quart-sized jars of tomatoes for a year. You can do this for each type of food or recipe you want to stock in your pantry.

Jar Planner: How Many Jars Do You Need?

Every canner will give you this answer: there are never enough jars. Even when you think you have enough, you'll find yourself buying jars at garage sales and online marketplaces every time you see them. I like to keep around 200 empty jars in a closet for the "what-ifs" in life. *What if* my freezer breaks and I need to can everything in it? *What if* I get an extra deer during hunting season or I find a great deal on pork I can't pass up? An empty jar takes up the same amount of space as a full jar, so all of my empty jars have emergency water in them for the other what-ifs in life.

I'm not suggesting you run out and buy 500 jars today. In fact, most of my jars are used and have been acquired over long periods of time.

If you're just getting into canning, tell your family and friends about your new adventure. They might know someone who has canned and is no longer using their jars, or they may have a box or two they no longer need.

I've purchased hundreds of jars, for a fraction of the cost of new jars, from elderly women who once canned but no longer do so. I find "retired" canners love knowing that their jars will carry on feeding someone else's family for years to come. Friends and family can also help keep an eye out for jars and canning supplies for you. Before you know it, you'll have more than you need without having to purchase everything brand new.

The number of jars needed for a family of four can vary significantly depending on factors such as dietary preferences, the type of produce you want to preserve, and how often you consume home-canned goods.

STERILIZATION VS. SANITATION—THE MORE YOU KNOW

As we saw in the early chapters of this book, canning requires the right equipment and a strict adherence to safety guidelines to prevent foodborne illness. Before you begin, be sure that you've sanitized your canning jars, lids, and rings with hot soapy water and follow the manufacturer's instructions for your canning equipment.

You cannot sterilize canning equipment in an unsterile environment like a home kitchen. The word "sterilizing" is a misnomer; we should really call it "sanitizing." When we heat the jars for hot-pack recipes, we prepare the glass in order to avoid thermal shock, which can introduce hairline fractures and lead to glass breakage.

Here's a basic breakdown for how I calculate the quantity of jars I need.

* If I plan to can quarts of tomatoes for the year and use one quart-sized jar per week, I'll need fifty-two quart-sized jars.

* If I want to make chicken pot pie once a month, I need twelve quarts for that recipe.

I use this example for each type of food or recipe I want on my shelves. I write these down and add up how many jars I'll need in my inventory. This guideline assumes you will have a healthy mixture of other fresh or frozen foods in your meal planning. If your meal plan is to *only* eat your home canned meals, these numbers rise exponentially to meet the number of jars needed. After harvest season, when my pantry is full, we have between 800 and 1,000 jars of canned food on the shelves. We eat and rotate around 2,000 jars total per year for a family of four.

My goal is to always enter a harvest season with the shelves almost bare of produce ready to can the new season's bounties.

As a general guide, here's an estimate of the number of canning jars you might need to preserve a variety of foods for a family of four for a year.

* **Fruits.** Approximately thirty to fifty quart-sized jars; if you plan on canning fruit juice, add twenty to thirty quarts more.

* **Vegetables.** Approximately thirty to fifty quart-sized jars

* **Jams and jellies.** Twenty to forty pint-sized jars

* **Pickles and relishes.** Ten to twenty quart-sized jars

* **Sauces and salsas.** Twenty to thirty quart-sized jars

* **Meat.** Twenty to thirty quart-sized jars or more, depending on your consumption

* **Soup and broth.** Ten to twenty quart-sized jars

Remember that these are only general guidelines and can vary based on your family's eating habits. Some families may preserve more or less of certain foods, and it's important to adjust the quantities to meet your family's needs.

My family enjoys ready-made meals in a jar, fruits, and vegetables. We don't eat as many pickled foods, so we have less of those on the shelves. Your plant hardiness zone, availability of fresh produce, and the size of your garden can all influence the number of jars you'll need for home canning.

Jar Sizes Used in This Book

WHAT I CALL IT HERE	IMPERIAL MEASUREMENT	METRIC EQUIVALENT
Half pint jar	8 ounces	237-ml
Pint jar	16 ounces	474-ml
Quart jar	32 ounces	946-ml

CHAPTER 3

Mastering Canning Fundamentals

Canning Essentials and Equipment Know-How

❧

This chapter features a brief overview of two main types of canning, using water bath and pressure canning basics.

Water Bath Canning

Water bath canning is a traditional, reliable method for preserving high-acid foods safely. In this section, we will explore the science that makes water bath canning effective, the essential components of a water bath canner, a comprehensive list of foods suitable for this method, and an altitude chart to help you navigate canning at different elevations.

The Science Behind Water Bath Canning

Water bath canning relies on the science of food preservation, focusing on creating an environment that prevents the growth of harmful microorganisms. There are two scientific principles at play when preserving food with this method.

* **Acidity.** High-acid foods, with a pH level below 4.6, create an inhospitable environment for the growth of dangerous bacteria. The natural acidity of these foods acts as a preservative.

* **Heat processing.** This process involves submerging jars of food in boiling water. This accomplishes two critical tasks:

    * **Microbial destruction.** The high temperature of boiling water kills existing bacteria, yeasts, molds, and enzymes in the food, preventing spoilage.

    * **Vacuum sealing.** As the jars cool, a vacuum seal forms, preventing any recontamination and maintaining the food's quality during storage. This creates a hermetic environment to prevent oxygen from spoiling your food.

Anatomy of a Water Bath Canner

Understanding the components of a water bath canner is essential for safe and successful canning.

Large pot. The base of a water bath canner is a large, deep pot with a tight-fitting lid. It should be deep enough to allow for at least 1 to 2 inches (2.5 to 5 cm) of boiling water above the jars. Pressure canners can double as water bath canners as long as you do not lock the pressure canner lid.

Rack. Inside the pot, you'll find a rack or trivet that holds the canning jars above the pot's bottom. Elevating the jars ensures even heat distribution and prevents direct contact between the jars and the pot, which could lead to jar breakage. If you do not have a rack or trivet, you can use a kitchen towel at the bottom of the canner for the jars to sit on.

Jars and lids. Glass canning jars, typically quart or pint-sized, are used. Jars come in a variety of sizes, from 2 ounces to 1 gallon (29.6 ml to 3.8 L). Choose the correct size for your recipe, keeping your family's size in mind for correct portion sizes.

Lids also come in a variety of styles based on your geographical location and canning traditions for your area. Most jars in North America come with two-part metal lids: flat metal lids with a sealing compound and screw-on bands. You can also find lids in glass, one piece or reusable with rubber seal rings. In this book, instructions will refer to the two-piece lid system in the recipes.

Foods Safe for Water Bath Canning

Water bath canning is suitable for a variety of high-acid foods. Here are examples of foods you can safely preserve using this method.

* **Fruits and fruit juices.** Whole fruits and fruit preserves like jams and jellies

* **Tomatoes.** Whole or crushed tomatoes, tomato sauces, salsas, and tomato-based products with added acid (like lemon juice or vinegar)

* **Pickled vegetables.** Any vegetable with an acidic brine like vinegar

* **Chutneys.** Condiments made from fruits or vegetables, typically with added vinegar and spices

A NOTE ON PRESERVING LOW-ACID FOODS WITH THE WATER BATH CANNING METHOD

While preserving low-acid foods with water bath canning is common in many cultures and parts of the world today—in fact, it's known as "Amish canning" in North America—I don't practice it in my own home. Please do extensive research outside this book for details if you wish to use water bath canning for low-acid foods.

WATER BATH CANNING ALTITUDE CHART

Altitude significantly impacts the boiling point of water, which in turn affects the safety and success of water bath canning. Here's an altitude chart to guide your canning process.

FEET (METERS) ABOVE SEA LEVEL	INCREASE IN PROCESSING TIME
0 to 1,000 (0 to 304 m)	No increase required
1,001 to 3,000 (305 to 914 m)	5 minutes
3,001 to 6,000 (915 to 1,829 m)	10 minutes
6,001 to 8,000 (1,830 to 2,438 m)	15 minutes
8,001 to 10,000 (2,439 to 3,050 m)	20 minutes

Pressure Canning

Pressure canning is a crucial method for preservation of low-acid foods. In North America, pressure canners are readily available, and I highly recommend purchasing one to extend the foods available for canning in your home.

The Science Behind Pressure Canning

Pressure canning is founded on the principles of heat, pressure, and time, designed to eliminate harmful bacteria, molds, and enzymes in low-acid foods. Every recipe using this method has the three benchmarks listed below to make your food safe for storage with no refrigeration.

* **High temperature.** Unlike water bath canning, which operates at boiling point, pressure canning relies on higher temperatures achieved by pressurizing the canner. These elevated temperatures (usually around 240°F [116°C]) are essential to destroy microorganisms.

* **Pressure.** When water is heated in a sealed pressure canner, it builds up pressure, allowing the temperature to rise higher than water's boiling point.

* **Microbial inactivation.** The combination of high temperature and pressure inactivates harmful microorganisms, ensuring that low-acid foods remain safe for long-term storage.

Anatomy of a Pressure Canner

Understanding the key components of a pressure canner is vital for safe and successful canning. Here's a breakdown of the pressure canner's anatomy.

Pressure canner base. The base of the pressure canner is a large, sturdy pot with a tight-fitting lid. It is specially designed to withstand high pressure and the lid is designed to create a tight seal to the pressure canner pot.

Pressure gauge. Most modern pressure canners come equipped with a pressure gauge allowing you to monitor and control the pressure. This is also known as the dial gauge.

Weighted gauge. A self-regulating component of some pressure canners. Older models have a pet-cock, which is not self-regulating. If you have an older model with a pet-cock and want to upgrade it to self-regulating, these can be updated by removing the pet-cock and exchanging it with a vent pipe to hold a weighted gauge. Its primary function is to regulate and maintain the proper pressure inside the canner during the canning process.

Vent pipe or vent port. These components are responsible for releasing excess air from the canner as it builds pressure. The vent pipe is typically located on the lid, while the vent port is on the pot. They must be kept clean and unobstructed for proper venting.

Safety valve or over-pressurized plug. A safety valve is a crucial safety feature. It releases excess pressure if it exceeds safe levels, preventing potential accidents.

Wingnuts or locking lid handles. Ensures the canner lid is safely locked to the canner base.

O-ring. Some pressure canner models have a rubber or silicone ring under the base of the lid. These must be routinely oiled and replaced when worn. The O-ring ensures the canner lid fits tightly to the canner base, preventing steam from escaping from the canner.

Rack or shelf. Inside the canner, there is a rack/trivet/shelf that elevates the canning jars off the bottom, ensuring even heat distribution and preventing direct contact with the pot. In larger canners you may have two shelves, allowing you to double stack your jars.

PRESSURE CANNING ALTITUDE CHART

Elevation greatly affects the pressure canning process because it impacts the boiling point of water. To ensure safe canning, here's a pressure canning altitude chart.

FEET (METERS) ABOVE SEA LEVEL	WEIGHT TO USE (POUNDS OF PRESSURE)	DIAL-GAUGE READS (POUNDS OF PRESSURE)
0 to 1,000 (0 to 304 m)	10 Weight will jiggle	11
1,001 to 2,000 (305 to 609 m)	15 Weight will *not* jiggle	11
2,001 to 3,000 (610 to 914 m)	15 Weight will *not* jiggle	12
3,001 to 6,000 (915 to 1,829 m)	15 Weight will *not* jiggle	13
6,001 to 8,000 (1,830 to 2,438 m)	15 Weight will *not* jiggle	14
8,001 to 10,000 (2,439 to 3,050 m)	15 Weight *may* jiggle	15

By following this altitude chart, you can ensure that your pressure canning process effectively preserves your low-acid foods, making them safe and convenient for future consumption.

Foods Safe for Pressure Canning

Pressure canning is suitable for preserving low-acid foods. Once you have decided to start pressure canning, you open a whole new world of foods you can preserve! Here are some examples of foods you can safely preserve using this method:

* Vegetables
* Meat and game
* Soups and stews
* Seafood
* Beans and legumes
* Combination dishes

Pressure Canning: Your First Time

Read, reread, and reread again the canner's manual. If you don't have it, search for the make and model of your canner (often located on the bottom of the canner or the lid) on the internet. Most canning manufacturers offer free access to the manuals online, even for older canners.

A new pressure canner can be intimidating, but so was a car the first time you sat behind the wheel. First you must learn how to "drive" your pressure canner. That is, walking through the steps with your manual until you feel comfortable using the canner without guidance.

The good news is, once you memorize the steps, they are repetitive and rarely change!

I suggest canning jars of water for your canner's maiden voyage. That way you're not under any pressure (pun intended) to preserve food, or worried about wasting money on food should you make a mistake. Do as many of these trial runs with jars of water as you need to build your canning confidence. Even the jars of water can be useful, as sterilized water is great to have on hand for emergency drinking water or wound cleaning.

Canning Equipment and Supplies

There are several tools available to make your canning experience less work and more enjoyable. You may choose to invest in some or all of these accessories to enhance your canning experience.

* **Canning funnel.** This tool ensures that your food goes directly into the jar without touching the rim, which could interfere with the sealing process.

* **Jar lifter.** A jar lifter (or, as I lovingly call it, a "Ball grabber") is designed to safely lift hot canning jars in and out of boiling water. It provides a secure grip, reducing the risk of burns or dropped jars.

* **Lid wand or magnetic lid lifter.** If your lids require heating before use, this tool makes it easy to retrieve lids from hot water.

* **Bubble remover/debubbler tool.** This tool helps release any trapped air bubbles in the jar. My favorite debubbler is the economical wooden skewer. Do not use any metal, such as a butter knife, as it may interact with the liquid in the recipe and create more bubbles.

* **Headspace measuring tool.** Maintaining the correct headspace (the space between the food and the jar's rim) is crucial in canning. As you become a more seasoned canner, you will be able to measure headspace by the rings around the jar lip.

* **Timer(s).** A reliable timer is essential for keeping track of precise processing times. All canning recipes specify exact times, so having a timer on hand ensures accuracy.

* **Canning labels and markers.** Properly labeling your canned goods with the content, date of canning, and any other relevant information is essential for organization and food safety.

* **Jar storage and organization.** Shelving or storage racks designed for canning jars help keep your preserved foods well organized, allowing for easy access and rotation of your canned goods.

Storage

Proper storage conditions are crucial to ensure the safety and quality of home-canned foods. Here are the ideal storage conditions for home-canned foods.

* **Cool temperature.** Home-canned foods should be stored in a cool environment, ideally between 50°F (10°C) and 70°F (21°C). Avoid storing them in areas with extreme temperature fluctuations, like a garage or shed, as this can affect the quality and safety of the canned goods.

* **Darkness.** Keep canned goods away from direct light. Store them in a dark pantry or cupboard.

* **Dry environment.** Moisture can cause the lids to rust and compromise the seal on canned jars. Ensure that the storage area is dry and that the jars are not exposed to excessive humidity.

* **Good ventilation.** Make sure that air can circulate freely around the jars.

* **Stable shelves.** Use sturdy, stable shelves to store your home-canned foods. Avoid overloading shelves, as this can lead to breakage and create safety hazards. If you live in earthquake territory, be sure to secure a board or strap to the front of the shelves and wall brackets to the back.

* **Rotating stock.** Practice the "first in, first out" (FIFO) method. This means placing the newly canned jars at the back of the shelf and using the oldest ones first.

* **Labeling.** Clearly label each jar with its contents and the date it was canned. This helps you identify the contents and monitor the shelf life of the canned food. *Do not skip this step.* I've forgotten to label jars before, only to retrieve a jar later and have no idea if it's strawberry or raspberry jam. Label your jars!

* **Regular inspection.** Periodically inspect your canned goods. Once a month I do a light dusting of my jars and shelves. I use this brief chore to inspect the jars.

* **Elevation.** Elevate your stored canned goods slightly off the ground to prevent contact with potential pests or moisture from the floor. Although the food is in glass jars and can take a little abuse, you should make sure all your hard work stays intact.

* **Pest control.** Keep the storage area clean and free from pests. Use traps or deterrents to prevent insects or rodents from getting into your canned goods. Glass jars are almost impenetrable to pests, making them a great resource for long-term food storage.

* **Record keeping.** Maintain a record of the types and quantities of canned goods you have stored. This can help you manage your inventory effectively and use older items first. (See the note about "first in, first out" on page 39.)

Preserving the Goodness: Home Canned Goods' Shelf Life and Beyond

In the world of home canning, you've invested time, effort, and love into preserving the bounties of your garden or seasonal produce. But once those jars are sealed and stored away, how long can you expect your home-canned treasures to last?

Understanding Shelf Life

Shelf life is the duration for canned products to remain safe to eat and retain their desired quality,

such as taste, texture, and nutritional value. The shelf life of home-canned goods can vary depending on several factors. If a twenty-year-old jar of tomatoes is processed correctly and is still sealed, it should be safe to consume. The question is, do you really want to? The older the food, the more it has broken down in the jar. In our home, we eat everything in a one-to-three-year rotation for the best nutritional value and texture.

Here are factors to consider when thinking about how long you want to retain your canned goods.

* **Processing method.** The way you process your jars significantly affects shelf life. Heat processing, like water bath or pressure canning, is the key to creating a sealed, sterile environment that prevents spoilage. Proper processing helps extend shelf life.

* **Type of food.** Different foods have different shelf lives. Low-acid foods like vegetables, meats, and poultry generally have a longer shelf life than high-acid foods like fruits and tomatoes.

* **Quality of ingredients.** Starting with fresh, high-quality ingredients ensures a longer shelf life. Overripe or spoiled produce may reduce the overall life span of your canned goods.

* **Jar sealing.** A properly sealed jar is essential. Check the seals on your jars regularly, as a broken or compromised seal can lead to spoilage. Any jar I find unsealed is discarded: when in doubt, throw it out.

* **Storage conditions.** It also matters where and how you store your canned goods. Keep them in a cool, dry, dark place, away from direct sunlight, temperature fluctuations, and humidity.

* **Rings.** The rings used on the jars are a placeholder for processing. This means the ring is no longer needed once a jar lid has been sealed to the jar. I store all the jars without the rings, which ensures that any lid that comes unsealed remains unsealed. A jar that has lost its seal and is then resealed has become compromised and its contents should not be consumed.

What to Look for When Opening Jars

When the time comes to enjoy the fruits of your labor, here's what to look for when you open your home-canned jars.

* **Seal inspection.** Before opening, check the seal. Lift the jar by the lid before opening. The lid should remain sealed with the weight of the jar.

* **Smell.** Take a whiff of the contents as you open the jar. Spoiled food will often have a foul odor, which is a clear indication that you should discard it.

* **Visual examination.** Visually inspect the food for any signs of spoilage. Look for mold growth, unusual color changes, or an off-putting texture.

* **Hiss.** Sometimes, you'll hear a hissing or swooshing sound as you open the jar. This indicates that a vacuum seal was properly established, which is what you want.

* **Taste test.** Finally, taste a small amount. If the flavor is off or if the food has an unusual or unpleasant taste, discard it. Remember: when in doubt, throw it out!

CHAPTER 4

Overcoming Canning Challenges

Practical Problem Solving

—◆◆◆—

Canning can present challenges even to the most experienced canners. The more we practice canning, the more we learn. Let's look at some of the most commonly encountered canning issues and the practical solutions to help you overcome them.

Canner Conundrums

Pressure canners can be intimidating, especially if they require any problem solving. While a canner issue may be new to you, it has likely occurred before. Here are some of the common conundrums that may not be covered in your canner's user manual and how to fix them.

Pressure Fluctuations

Example: While pressure canning, you notice that the pressure frequently rises or drops unexpectedly, making it difficult to maintain a consistent canning process.

Solution:

* Note the air temperature where you are canning. Warm spaces can cause the canner to heat quicker while cool spaces cause it to lag. Make sure to keep the canner away from fans or open windows to reduce pressure fluctuations.

* Check the canner's gasket or seal for any damage or wear and replace it if necessary: steam may be escaping from the seal.

* Ensure that you have a steady heat source, adjusting as needed to maintain the recommended pressure. Your canner and your stove will have a relationship, with a "sweet spot" on your stove where the heat source is just right to maintain correct pressure.

* Make sure you have allowed the canner to vent for a full ten minutes to eliminate air before reaching full pressure. If you did not vent your canner, there may be air pockets inside the canner, causing pressure regulation issues. Turn off the canner, return to zero pressure, remove the weight, and start the canner again, venting for ten minutes.

Lid Sticking or Difficulty in Opening (All American Pressure Canners)

Example: After the canning process, you find it challenging to open the lid of your pressure canner. The lid is stuck to the canner pot.

Solution:

* Before using your pressure canner, be sure to oil the rim of the lid. See the owner's manual for your canner to review lubrication instructions. Re-oil the lid as needed to prevent sticking.

* Allow the canner to cool naturally after canning. Do not attempt to open the lid prematurely. Do not open the canner until the pressure gauge or dial reads zero and you can safely remove the weight or regulator.

* To pop open a sticky lid, I use a jar lifter or the back of a spoon. Place the jar lifter or spoon in between the canner lid and gently pop the lid open.

Leaking Steam

Example: During canning, you notice steam escaping from the sides, lid, or seal of your pressure canner.

Solution:

* Turn off the canner's heat source and wait for the pressure to reach zero. Remove the lid and add water back to the canner to reach the correct water line if any water loss is detected due to escaping steam.

* Tighten the lid securely but avoid over-tightening, which can cause excessive compression of the gasket.

* If your canner has an O-ring or gasket:

1. Look for any damage or signs of wear and replace if needed. I keep two extra gaskets for each canner in my supplies. There's nothing worse than having food in the canner and realizing your gasket has become defective midway through the canning session.

2. Ensure the gasket is correctly positioned and the canner lid is properly aligned. Sometimes the gasket can become twisted or folded over on itself.

Inaccurate Dial Gauge

Example: Your pressure canner's pressure gauge appears to be inaccurate, or condensation has gotten into the dial gauge, which makes it challenging to maintain the correct pressure.

Solution:

* Have your pressure gauge tested for accuracy every year by a reputable source or canning equipment provider. If you are in the United States, look for your county extension office. They often have free gauge testing for pressure canners.

* Replace your dial gauge if your dial gauge has condensation or has otherwise become defective.

Whistling or Unusual Sounds from the Pressure Canner

Example: You hear a high-pitched whistling noise coming from your pressure canner. Whistling noises during pressure canning are normally part of the process, but it's important to recognize any unusual sounds and to know how to manage them.

Solution:

If the noise coming from the canner is a high-pitched whistling or a noise you do not recognize:

1. Turn off the heat and walk away. Let the pressure canner fall to zero pressure before continuing.

2. Check the gasket for twists or worn spots. I've found that faulty gaskets are the most common reason for whistling.

3. Check your vent pipe. Hold the canner lid up to a light. You should be able to see the light all the way through the vent pipe. If the vent pipe is blocked, straighten a paper clip and clean out any debris inside the vent pipe.

In normal operation, as the pressure builds inside the canner, the weight begins to release steam in small, controlled bursts, causing some hissing sounds as it gently rocks. This is a sign that your canner is operating as intended and that the pressure is being regulated safely.

Jar and Lid Problems

There is nothing more frustrating in canning than when a jar breaks or a lid does not seal. It's important we recognize the difference between a product issue and issues in our own canning techniques so we can make the necessary adjustments. Always start with quality jars and lids, making sure to follow the manufacturer's instructions for best results.

Jar Lids Not Sealing Properly

Jars not sealing can be caused by many different issues, missteps, or defective products. In order to understand why a jar doesn't seal or stay sealed, approach the issue with an inquisitive mind and drill down to the cause.

Example: After the canning process, you discover that some of your jars haven't sealed correctly, leaving you with unsealed jars.

Solution:

* Examine the jar rims for cleanliness and make sure they are free from nicks or cracks. You can use a cotton ball to rub across the rim. Any nicks or cracks will catch on the cotton ball.

* Use new, undamaged lids for each canning session: lid quality matters! You may save three cents per lid by buying off brand, but lost food is more expensive than the extra cost you would pay for a reputable brand-name lid.

* Do not over- or undertighten rings. By overtightening rings, the flats will not seal. I use the phrase "finger light" instead of "finger-tight": place three fingers on the ring and tighten just until the ring engages and the jar spins.

* Remove air bubbles from the jar before canning. Air bubbles can cause large boils inside the jar, knocking the lid off the ring of the jar.

* Follow the recommended headspace for your recipe to allow for adequate sealing.

* Reprocess any unsealed jars with new lids within twenty-four hours after processing or place in the refrigerator and eat first.

Lid Unseals During Storage

Example: You've successfully sealed your jars, but the jar lid unseals on the pantry shelf.

Solution:

* Throw away the contents of the jar. Once a jar has been stored without refrigeration, an unsealed jar has been exposed to oxygen and microbes, making the contents unsafe for consumption.

* Check the temperature of your storage space. Large temperature fluctuations can cause lids to become unsealed.

Lid Buckles or Dents Outward During Processing

Example: You process your jars in the canner and, when you remove the jars, the lid of the jar has buckled or bent upwards.

Solution:

* The rings were too tight. Reprocess the jar with a new lid and add the ring slightly lighter than you had previously tightened it.

Rust or Corrosion on Jar Lids

Example: You notice rust or corrosion on the tops of the lids of your stored canned goods.

Solution:

* Ensure jars and lids are completely dry before storing them to prevent moisture buildup.

* Store jars in a cool, dry place with low humidity.

* Remove rings before storing. Moisture can get trapped between the lid and the ring.

Black Spots on the Underside of the Lid

Example: You open a jar of chicken and the underside of the lid has black spots. This is normal. Some foods deposit harmless natural chemical substances when canned. These black spots may seem alarming, but they have no effect on the safety of your food.

Solution:

* None; this cannot be circumvented and is normal with some recipes.

Rust Under the Lid

Example: You open a jar of tomatoes and you notice a rust spot on the underside of the lid.

Solution:

* Purchase lids from a reputable company with adequate coating. My favorites at the time of writing are lids produced by Superb. They use five coats of anticorrosive material on their lids, which is more than any other brand currently on the market. I've had no corrosion issues with them.

Siphoning Issues and the 10-10-10 Method

Siphoning can be a persistent challenge in home canning. This occurs when a portion of your product has seeped out of the jar, leaving a small amount of food residue around the seal. You may see siphoning at one of two points during the canning process: either in the canner during the cooldown phase or on your countertop after processing. Use my 10-10-10 method to effectively reduce the occurrence of this issue.

Example: You open the canner lid and the canning water is cloudy or colored with the jar liquids, or you remove the jars and they siphon on the countertop during cooling.

Solution:

* When filling your jars, make sure there's a proper headspace; this is usually ½ inch to 1 inch (1.3 to 2.5 cm) for most recipes. Overfilled jars can cause siphoning.

* Try using my 10-10-10 method. This is a technique I use to help prevent siphoning during water bath and pressure canning.

10-10-10 IN WATER BATH CANNING

Step 1: *10 minutes with the heat source off and lid on.* After completing the recommended processing time, turn off the heat source and leave the canner lid on for ten minutes.

Step 2: *10 minutes with the lid propped.* After the initial ten-minute rest with the heat off, prop the canner lid on a wooden spoon but do not remove it.

Step 3: *10 minutes with the lid off.* Finally, carefully remove the canner lid entirely and let the jars sit in the canner for an additional ten minutes before removing them. During this time, the jars continue to adjust to temperature changes, minimizing the risk of siphoning when they are finally removed from the canner to sit on the countertop or table overnight.

10-10-10 IN PRESSURE CANNING

Step 1: *10 minutes with the weight off.* After completing the recommended processing time, turn off the heat source and let the canner pressure fall to zero. Remove the weight and wait ten minutes.

Step 2: *Unlock the canner lid but do not remove it.* This step helps equalize the pressure inside and outside the jars, further reducing the likelihood of siphoning.

Step 3: *10 minutes with the lid off and jars in the canner.* Finally, carefully remove the canner lid entirely and let the jars sit in the canner for an additional ten minutes before removing them.

Note: Siphoning does not affect the safety of your food if properly canned. It will, however, cause any food above the lost-liquid line to darken over time.

Jam and Jelly Issues and Solutions

Jam and jelly issues can be extremely complex with a wide variety of causes and solutions. When I hear someone advise a new canner to start with jams and jellies, I cringe inside. There's an art to making these products, with many potential pitfalls, and it can take a lot of practice to get a good end result.

If you are new to canning, I suggest starting with fruits in syrups or fruit juices. You are far less likely to become discouraged with these than you may be with the complexity of jams and jellies.

Here are some of the more common issues with canning jams and jellies. To correct each issue, we must first look into its cause.

Testing Jam and Jelly for Gel Point

Making jam and jelly requires heating to a gel point, when the liquids turn into a thicker gel viscosity. The gel point is what gives jam and jelly their jiggle and is one of the more difficult steps to get correct when making them. This section will help you achieve the correct gel point with a few simple tests.

Spoon Test

Dip a cool metal spoon in the boiling jelly, then raise it at least a foot above the boiling pot, out of the steam, and turn the spoon horizontal so the syrup runs off the side. If the syrup forms two drops that flow together and fall off the spoon as one sheet, the jelly should be ready for canning.

Swipe Test

Dip a cool metal spoon in the boiling jelly. Lay the spoon on a plate, with the bowl side of the spoon facing up. Carefully and quickly run your finger through the center of the spoon in one swipe. If the jelly runs back together very slowly, the gel point has been reached. If it runs back together immediately, return to boiling.

Sheet Test

Pour a small amount of boiling jelly on a cold plate and put it in the freezer compartment of your refrigerator for one to two minutes. If the liquid gels, it should be done. Note: Turn off the burner while waiting for the result of this test to avoid overcooking your jelly.

Common Jam and Jelly Issues and Why They Happen

* **Jelly is cloudy:** Underripe fruit or fruit juice was not strained properly

* **Jelly/jam did not set firm:** Too much or too little juice or recipe was doubled

* **Jelly/jam set too firm or gummy:** Overcooked, too much pectin

* **Jelly/jam smells like alcohol/wine:** Improper seal, fermentation, or too little sugar

* **Fruit floating in jam:** Fruit not ripe or not cooked long enough

* **Weeping jelly (water on surface):** Too much acid, improper sealing

Reprocessing: My Jelly Didn't Set—Can I Reprocess It?

The answer is yes! Soft or syrupy jellies can sometimes be improved by reprocessing. It's best to do this only 4 to 6 cups (960 to 1,440 ml) at a time. If you have a large batch, reprocess your jelly in smaller batches. You can also use it as a fruit syrup if you don't want to reprocess.

Reprocess Using Powdered Pectin

1. Measure the jelly. For every quart of jelly, take ¼ cup (60 ml) sugar, ¼ cup (60 ml) water, and 4 teaspoons (20 ml) powdered pectin.

2. Create pectin water. Mix the pectin and water, and bring it to a boil.

3. Combine with jelly. Stir the pectin water into the jelly along with sugar, then mix thoroughly.

4. Boil. Over high heat, bring the mixture to a full rolling boil while stirring constantly. Boil hard for two minutes.

5. Remove and skim. Take the jelly off the heat, and skim off any foam.

6. Proceed to canning. Continue with your canning process.

Reprocess Using Liquid Pectin

1. Measure the jelly. For every quart of jelly, you'll need ¾ cup (177 ml) sugar, 2 tablespoons (30 ml) lemon juice, and 2 tablespoons (30 ml) liquid pectin.

2. Boil. Bring jelly to full boil over high heat, stirring.

3. Combine sugar, lemon juice, and liquid pectin with boiling jelly. Bring the mixture to a full rolling boil while stirring constantly. Boil hard for two minutes.

4. Remove and skim. Take the jelly off the heat, and skim off any foam.

5. Proceed to canning. Continue with your canning process.

Pomona's Pectin

Pomona's Pectin is a unique type of pectin known for its versatility. It's my go-to pectin for many recipes, and I use it in a few of the canning recipes in this book. I use this pectin when making flower-petal jellies and other low-pectin foods like corncob jelly. This pectin also works well in no-sugar/low-sugar recipes. What sets Pomona's Pectin apart is that it allows you to control the level of sweetness in your jams and jellies and achieve excellent gelling results without the traditional wait times.

Pomona's Pectin is different from other powder pectins because it comes with a small packet of calcium powder, which is mixed with water to create calcium water. This calcium water is a crucial component in the pectin, serving three essential purposes.

* **Gel activation.** Traditional pectin relies on sugar and acidity to activate the gelling process. Pomona's Pectin, on the other hand, uses calcium water to create the gel structure. This means you have greater control over the gelling process, even in low- or no-sugar recipes. It's especially useful for recipes involving fruits with low natural pectin content.

* **Versatility.** Calcium water allows you to make jams and jellies using a wide range of sweeteners, not just sugar. You can use honey, agave, or even alternative sweeteners while still achieving a perfect gel.

* **Customization.** You can adjust the amount of calcium water and pectin in your recipes to achieve the desired texture. This customization ensures that your jams and jellies are not too runny or overly firm.

CHAPTER 5

Water Bath Canning Recipes

Savor the Flavor

In the heart of every home kitchen, there's a symphony playing, the music of clinking jars and bubbling pots that provides accompaniment for the culinary dance of preserving food. The art of water bath canning directs that music.

This chapter will help you master water bath canning and understand ways to harness this method on your journey of creative food preservation.

This method of canning has seen a comeback in recent years. While we can enjoy canned foods that were standbys for our forebears, water bath canning is flexible enough to let us celebrate and incorporate new inventions into our repertoire. New takes on old favorites, like soda pop jelly and carrot cake jam, help us expand the diverse products we can store in our pantry.

The recipes in this chapter meld our ancestors' traditions with adaptation and innovation, spanning years and flavors on a single shelf. It brings me great joy to pass to you some of my family's oldest canning recipes. Delicate summer fruits are transformed into jewel-toned jams, pickled vegetables offer an explosion of vibrant tang, and a twist on a classic favorite becomes the warm hug of spiced Christmas pears.

Whether you're a seasoned canner or a novice just beginning to explore water bath canning, I hope you'll find ways to savor the fruits of your labor. Get ready to think outside the ordinary, listen to the music of your own creativity, and infuse your preserves with your song to craft homemade masterpieces that are distinctly yours.

Apple Ketchup

*Makes about
6 half pints*

Apple ketchup is a delicious twist on the classic condiment. Made with fresh apples, apple cider vinegar, and a blend of warm spices, this ketchup offers a piquant option for dipping fries, drizzling on grilled meats, or spreading on burgers or other sandwiches. You'll never want to go back to store-bought ketchup again!

---

4 cups (980 g) unsweetened applesauce: 8 to 12 apples (any variety you like) and 1 cup (236 ml) water; see homemade recipe option at right

1½ cups (240 g) minced onions

2 cups (472 ml) apple cider vinegar

1 cup (150 g) brown sugar

1 tablespoon (18 g) salt

1 teaspoon ground mustard

1 teaspoon black pepper

2 teaspoons (5 g) ground cinnamon

1 teaspoon ground ginger

CUSTOMIZING YOUR APPLE KETCHUP

✳ Spice it up. Customize the ketchup to your liking. To add heat, use a pinch of cayenne pepper or hot sauce.

✳ Texture. You can make chunky apple ketchup by skipping the blending and straining steps for a more rustic feel.

✳ Sweetness. Adjust the sugar content based on your preference. You can use honey or maple syrup as alternatives to brown sugar.

HOMEMADE APPLESAUCE

If using store-bought applesauce, skip to step 4.

1. Peel, core, and roughly chop the apples. Leave the peel on for added texture and nutrients if you prefer.

2. Place the chopped apples in a saucepan along with the water. Cover and cook over medium heat for 15 to 20 minutes, or until the apples are soft and easily mashed.

3. Use a potato masher or a blender to mash the cooked apples to your desired consistency. If using a blender, be careful not to overblend, as you want to avoid a completely smooth texture.

4. Add applesauce and remaining ingredients to a large pot and heat over medium heat for 30 to 40 minutes until mixture thickens.

CANNING (HOT PACK)

1. Heat jars in a large stockpot of water.

2. Ladle hot apple ketchup into hot jars, leaving ¼-inch (6 mm) headspace.

3. Wipe rims with vinegar, add lids and rings finger light.

4. Add jars to water bath canner and ensure the jars are covered with at least 1 inch (2.5 cm) of water.

5. Bring water to a full rolling boil and process 15 minutes for pints or half pints.

Green Tomato Ketchup

Makes approximately 4 to 6 pints or 8 to 12 half pints

Preparing green tomato ketchup is a great way to use up any tomatoes that may not ripen before the end of the growing season. It's perfect for dipping, spreading, or topping burgers and sandwiches.

6 pounds (2.7 kg) green tomatoes, peeled, cored, and chopped

2 onions, chopped

2 cups (472 ml) apple cider vinegar

1 tablespoon (18 g) salt

1 teaspoon ground cinnamon

½ teaspoon ground allspice

½ teaspoon ground cloves

1 cup (340 g) honey

1. In a large pot, combine the chopped green tomatoes and onions. Add the apple cider vinegar, salt, cinnamon, allspice, and cloves. Stir to combine and bring to a boil. Reduce the heat and simmer for 20 to 25 minutes, or until the vegetables are soft.

2. Remove the pot from the heat and allow it to cool slightly. Once cooled, purée the tomato mixture in a blender or food processor until smooth (see the sidebar "Ask Me How I Know," page 65).

3. Place a mesh strainer over a large bowl and strain the ketchup mixture. Discard the seeds and solids left behind in the strainer.

4. Return the puréed mixture to the pot and bring the mixture to a boil over medium-high heat. Reduce the heat and simmer for 1 to 1½ hours, or until the ketchup has thickened to your desired consistency. Stir occasionally to prevent sticking.

5. Once the ketchup has thickened, add the honey. Continue heating the mixture until the honey is well dissolved and incorporated into the ketchup.

CANNING (HOT PACK)

1. Heat jars in a large stockpot of water.

2. Ladle hot ketchup into hot jars, leaving ¼-inch (6 mm) headspace.

3. Wipe rims with vinegar, add lids and rings finger light.

4. Add jars to water bath canner, ensuring jars are covered with 1 to 2 inches (2.5 to 5 cm) of water.

5. Bring water to a full rolling boil and process 15 minutes for pints or half pints. Adjust processing times for altitude as needed.

Cucumber Ketchup

Makes about 4 pints or 8 half pints

If you're a fan of ketchup but want to try something new, you'll love this cucumber ketchup recipe. It's a great way to use up garden cucumbers and it offers a healthy alternative to traditional tomato-based ketchup.

8 cups (1.1 kg) cucumbers, peeled, deseeded, and chopped

2 cups (320 g) chopped onions

4 green bell peppers chopped

1½ cups (354 ml) water

3 cups (708 ml) white vinegar

2 cups (400 g) granulated sugar

4 tablespoons (36 g) mustard powder

1 tablespoon (7 g) ground cinnamon

1 teaspoon ground allspice

1 teaspoon ground cloves

1. In a medium saucepan, add cucumbers, onions, green bell peppers, and water. Cook until fork tender.

2. Blend mixture until smooth using an immersion blender. If using an upright blender, let the mixture cool slightly before blending for safety.

3. Strain the mixture through a fine-mesh sieve into a bowl, pressing on the solids to extract as much liquid as possible.

4. Return mixture to saucepan and add all remaining ingredients. Cook over medium heat until mixture has thickened or has reached desired consistency, about 20 minutes, stirring occasionally to prevent sticking.

CANNING (HOT PACK)

1. Heat jars in a large stockpot of water.

2. Ladle hot cucumber ketchup into hot jars, leaving ¼-inch (6 mm) headspace.

3. Wipe rims with vinegar, add lids and rings finger light.

4. Add jars to water bath canner and ensure the jars are covered with at least 1 inch (2.5 cm) of water.

5. Bring the canner water to a full rolling boil and process 15 minutes for pints or half pints.

Pizza Sauce:
An Amish Heirloom

Makes 12 to 14 half pints. Can be doubled with longer cook times.

I'm immensely grateful for the chance to pass along this treasured recipe, from my dear Amish friend who wishes to remain anonymous but has generously allowed me to share it here.

Canned Amish pizza sauce bursts with the robust flavors of Roma tomatoes, the essence of garlic, and a blend of herbs and spices. Remember that the water content of Roma tomatoes can vary, so the yield of this sauce may fluctuate slightly, as will the cook times needed to reduce the sauce.

---

15 pounds (6.8 kg) Roma tomatoes

8 tablespoons (120 ml) olive oil

1 head of garlic (approximately 10 to 12 cloves), minced

3 large onions, minced (about 3 cups/480 g)

3 tablespoons (39 g) granulated sugar (does not make sauce sweet, but balances acidity)

4 tablespoons (5.2 g) parsley

3 tablespoons (7.5 g) fresh basil

2 tablespoons (8 g) oregano

2 teaspoons (1.4 g) rosemary

2 teaspoons (12 g) salt

2 teaspoons (4 g) black pepper

1 tablespoon (15 ml) lemon juice per jar

1. Wash tomatoes, score an *X* on the bottom of each with a knife. In boiling water, drop tomatoes in batches for 30 seconds. Remove tomatoes from boiling water and place into a bowl of ice water. The skin should slip off. Remove tomato skin. Save skins for dehydrated tomato powders (see page 264).

2. Chop tomatoes and purée. You can use a blender, in batches, or purée in a large bowl with an immersion blender.

3. Add olive oil to a large stockpot and sauté the garlic and minced onions over medium heat until translucent.

4. Add tomato purée to the garlic and onions in the stockpot and stir to mix well.

5. Add sugar and spices to the sauce and bring sauce to a boil.

6. Reduce heat and cook sauce, uncovered, 2 to 4 hours on low, stirring occasionally.

   NOTE: The goal is to thicken the sauce and reduce it by half. The water content of the tomatoes will determine how long this takes. For double or triple batches, you can use an electric roaster pan set to 200°F (93°C).

7. When desired thickness is achieved and sauce is nearly ready, prepare your canning equipment. Place canning jars in a canning pot filled with water and bring it to a simmer (180°F/82°C) to heat the jars.

CANNING (HOT PACK)

1. Retrieve hot jars from canner.

2. Add 1 tablespoon (15 ml) lemon juice to each jar.

3. Place a canning funnel on top of a jar and ladle hot pizza sauce into jars, leaving ½-inch (1.25-cm) headspace.

4. Use a bubble remover tool to remove air bubbles. Add more pizza sauce or water to correct headspace if needed.

5. Wipe the jar rim with a clean, damp towel or a vinegar-dampened towel to remove any residue.

6. Place the lid on top of the jar and secure with a band, screwing it on until finger light.

7. Place the filled jar back into the canning pot using a canning rack. Ensure the jars are covered with at least 1 inch (2.5 cm) of water.

8. Bring the water to a boil and, once boiling, start the timer for 25 minutes for pints or half pints. Adjust processing times for altitude as needed.

My Family's Favorite Pasta Sauce

Makes approximately 8 to 10 quarts

I have so many great pasta sauce recipes, it was difficult to choose just one for this book. This is the one my whole family agrees is the best, in part because it can be used in many different dishes.

The number of pints this recipe will yield depends on several factors, such as the water content in your tomatoes and how much the sauce reduces during cooking. As a rough estimate, this recipe may produce approximately 8 to 10 quarts (1.2 to 2 kg) of tomato pasta sauce, but it's always good practice to have some extra canning jars on hand in case you end up with more sauce than expected.

25 pounds (11.4 kg) tomatoes

5 medium onions, chopped: approximately 7 cups (1.1 kg)

4 red bell peppers, chopped

1 green bell pepper, chopped

4 (6-ounce/195-g) cans tomato paste

¼ cup (60 ml) soy sauce

3 tablespoons (45 ml) Worcestershire sauce

⅔ cup (150 g) brown sugar, packed

8 tablespoons (144 g) to ¼ cup (72 g) salt, to taste

10 cloves garlic, chopped or minced

3 tablespoons (9 g) dried oregano

3 tablespoons (6 g) dried basil

2 teaspoons (2 g) red pepper flakes

2 bay leaves

1¼ cups (296 ml) lemon juice, reserved for jars

BLANCH AND PEEL TOMATOES

1. Bring a large pot of water to a boil.

2. Score an *X* on the bottom of each tomato.

3. Immerse tomatoes in boiling water for 1 minute, then transfer them to an ice water bath to cool.

4. Once cooled, peel the tomatoes, and cut into quarters.

PREPARE THE TOMATO SAUCE

1. Add onions and peppers to a food processor and pulse until finely chopped.

2. To a large stockpot, add tomatoes (with juices), onion and pepper mixture, and remaining ingredients minus lemon juice (reserve for jars).

3. Simmer the sauce, uncovered, 4 to 5 hours, or until it thickens to your desired consistency. Stir occasionally. Taste and add more salt or spices as needed.

4. If you prefer a thicker, smoother sauce, use an immersion blender to carefully blend the tomatoes until the texture becomes smooth. Alternatively, if you don't have an immersion blender, use a traditional blender to blend the sauce in manageable batches; this will achieve the same consistency.

5. Remove bay leaves.

(continued)

CANNING (HOT PACK)

1. When the sauce is almost finished simmering, prepare your canning equipment.

2. Place canning jars in a canning pot filled with water. Bring to a simmer (180°F/82°C) to heat the jars.

3. Remove a hot jar from the canning pot using a jar lifter.

4. Add 2 tablespoons (30 ml) lemon juice to the bottom of each quart jar or 1 tablespoon (15 ml) per pint.

5. Place a canning funnel on top and ladle hot tomato sauce into the jar, leaving ½-inch (1.25-cm) headspace.

6. Use a bubble remover tool to remove air bubbles and adjust headspace if necessary.

7. Wipe the jar rim with a clean, damp towel or vinegar-dampened towel to remove any residue.

8. Place lid on top of the jar and secure with a band, screwing it on until finger light.

9. Place the filled jars back into the canning pot using a canning rack. Ensure the jars are covered with at least 1 inch (2.5 cm) of water.

10. Bring the water to a boil and, once boiling, start timer: for pints, 35 minutes; for quarts, 40 minutes.

11. Adjust processing times for altitude as needed.

REPURPOSING YOUR TOMATO SKINS: SUSTAINABLE SCRAPS

Don't throw away the tomato skins! You can repurpose them into flavorful tomato powder. Saving and using your tomato skins can help you reduce waste while enhancing the taste of your dishes with this versatile and savory seasoning. See chapter 7 for a guide to dehydrating food scraps.

Teriyaki Sauce

Makes 5 to 6 half pints

This condiment is great for marinating, grilling, stir-frying, and more. For teriyaki sauce using clear jel as a thickening agent, below is a recipe to get you started.

Canning teriyaki sauce at home offers a range of benefits:

* Convenient. Canning teriyaki sauce means you won't need to make it from scratch every time a recipe calls for it.

* Cost-effective. Preparing your own teriyaki sauce allows you to buy ingredients in bulk and make larger batches, saving you money in the long run.

* Flexible. When canning teriyaki sauce, you can opt for healthier ingredients, such as reduced-sodium soy sauce or natural sweeteners, according to your preferences and dietary needs.

---

2 cups (472 ml) soy sauce

2 cups (472 ml) water

2 cups (400 g) granulated sugar

1½ cups (354 ml) vinegar (white or rice vinegar)

1 cup (236 ml) mirin (sweet rice wine)

2 tablespoons (12 g) minced fresh ginger

2 tablespoons (20 g) minced fresh garlic

1 teaspoon crushed red pepper flakes, to taste

¼ cup (60 ml) clear jel plus 1 cup (236 ml) cold water

1. Wash your canning jars, lids, and rings. You can do this by running them through the dishwasher or boiling them in a large pot of water. Keep the jars warm until you're ready to fill them.

2. In a large pot, combine the soy sauce, 2 cups (472 ml) of water, granulated sugar, vinegar, and mirin. Heat the mixture over medium heat, stirring to dissolve the sugar.

3. Stir in the minced ginger, minced garlic, and crushed red pepper flakes. Let the mixture simmer for about 10 minutes to allow the flavors to meld.

4. In a separate bowl, whisk together the clear jel and 1 cup (236 ml) of cold water until it's smooth and free of lumps.

5. Slowly pour the clear jel slurry into the simmering teriyaki sauce while stirring constantly. Continue to cook and stir until the sauce thickens to your desired consistency. This may take about 5 to 10 minutes.

6. If the sauce is too thin for your liking, add more clear jel 1 teaspoon at a time until desired consistency is achieved.

(continued)

CANNING (HOT PACK)

1. Place a canning funnel on top and ladle hot sauce into hot jars, leaving ½-inch (1.25-cm) headspace.

2. Wipe the jar rim with a clean, damp towel or vinegar-dampened towel to remove any residue.

3. Place lid on top of the jar and secure with a band, screwing it on until finger light.

4. Place the filled jars back into the canning pot. Ensure the jars are covered with at least 1 inch (2.5 cm) of water.

5. Bring the water to a boil and, once boiling, start the timer 15 minutes for half pints or pints. Adjust processing times for altitude as needed.

DISHES THAT USE TERIYAKI SAUCE

* Teriyaki chicken. Marinate chicken pieces in teriyaki sauce and grill or stir-fry.

* Teriyaki beef. Use the sauce to marinate beef strips, then stir-fry with vegetables and serve over rice or noodles.

* Teriyaki tofu. For a vegetarian option, marinate tofu cubes and pan-fry them with teriyaki sauce.

* Teriyaki salmon. Glaze salmon fillets with teriyaki sauce and bake or grill.

* Teriyaki vegetable stir-fry. Toss your favorite vegetables in teriyaki sauce for a quick side dish.

* Teriyaki bowl. Create a teriyaki bowl with rice, grilled protein (chicken, beef, or tofu), and a generous drizzle of teriyaki sauce. Top with sesame seeds and green onions.

WHAT IN THE WORLD IS CLEAR JEL?

Clear jel is a modified cornstarch that is safe to use as a thickener in canning because it doesn't break down during the canning process. If you don't have access to clear jel, leave it out and thicken your sauce with flour or cornstarch after opening the jar to use.

Clear jel is most often found in the canning section of retail stores, but not all stores carry it. Amish community grocery stores and online spice stores are a great place to buy clear jel in bulk at cheaper prices.

There are different types of clear jel. Any recipe that is heated, and all recipes in this book, use "clear jel, Cook Type."

*Sure-Jell (pectin) is **not** interchangeable with clear jel (modified cornstarch).*

Peruvian Sauce

Makes about 6 pints or 12 half pints

A delicious accompaniment to grilled meats, vegetables, or fish, this Peruvian sauce combines the zesty appeal of ripe tomatoes and apples with a hint of heat from the jalapeño pepper. This is a great recipe to use your end-of-summer tomatoes as the start-of-fall apples begin to ripen.

4 quarts (720 g) ripe red tomatoes (approximately 24 large), peeled, cored, and chopped

4 to 5 medium apples, peeled, cored, and chopped

3 medium onions, chopped

3 medium green bell peppers, chopped

1 garlic clove, minced

1 jalapeño pepper, seeded and chopped

3 cups (450 g) brown sugar

3 cups (708 ml) white vinegar

1 tablespoon (6 g) ground allspice

1 tablespoon (11 g) mustard seeds

1 teaspoon ground cinnamon

1 tablespoon (18 g) salt

1. In a large pot, combine the chopped tomatoes, apples, onions, bell peppers, garlic, jalapeño, and sugar. Cook slowly until thickened, about 1 hour. Stir frequently to prevent sticking.

2. Add white vinegar, spices, and salt and continue cooking for 45 to 60 minutes, or until desired consistency is achieved.

CANNING (HOT PACK)

1. Heat jars in a large stockpot of water.

2. Ladle hot Peruvian sauce into hot jars, leaving ¼-inch (6 mm) headspace.

3. Wipe rims with vinegar, add lids and rings finger light.

4. Add jars to water bath canner and ensure the jars are covered with at least 1 inch (2.5 cm) of water.

5. Bring canner to a full rolling boil and process 15 minutes for pints or half pints. Adjust processing time for altitude as needed.

ASK ME HOW I KNOW
"Use Caution When Blending Hot Ingredients"

Somewhere in Northwest Indiana is a home with orange, pumpkin-stained ceilings. No matter how many times I cleaned and painted the ceiling, the orange always bled through (apologies to the new owners). Steam expands quickly in a blender and can cause ingredients to splatter everywhere or even cause burns. To prevent this, fill the blender only one-third of the way up, vent the top, and cover with a folded kitchen towel while blending in short bursts. Blend any hot ingredients in small batches to prevent splattering—or be prepared to buy some ceiling paint.

Caramel Apple Pie Filling

Makes about 6 quarts or 12 pints

What's a more essential fall dessert than a slice of warm, homemade apple pie? Now, imagine having that delightful experience within arm's reach, ready to elevate your desserts and breakfasts at a moment's notice.

---

10 pounds (4.5 kg) apples, (about 20 cups/2.5 kg)

8 cups (1.9 L) water

Splash of lemon juice or 1 tablespoon (19 g) citric acid

2 cups (300 g) brown sugar

3½ cups (700 g) granulated sugar

1½ cups clear jel

1 tablespoon (7 g) cinnamon

1 teaspoon nutmeg

5 cups (1.2 L) apple cider

¾ cup (178 ml) lemon juice concentrate

1. Begin by peeling, coring, and slicing the apples. To prevent browning as you work through batches of fruit, place your slices in a bowl of water with a splash of lemon juice or citric acid.

2. In a large stockpot, combine the sugars, clear jel, and spices.

3. Gradually add the apple cider to the dry ingredients while whisking to ensure a smooth mixture.

4. Place the pot on the stove and bring the mixture to a boil. Continue cooking until it thickens, stirring frequently to prevent lumps.

5. Place canning jars in a canning pot filled with water. Bring to a simmer (180°F/82°C) to heat the jars while making the pie filling.

6. Once the filling has thickened, remove from heat. Add the lemon juice concentrate and mix thoroughly.

7. Drain the sliced apples from the water and gently fold them into the pie filling mixture until they are well coated and combined.

CANNING (HOT PACK)

1. Remove hot jars from the canning pot using a jar lifter.

2. Place a canning funnel on top of a jar.

3. Ladle hot pie filling into hot jars, leaving 1½-inch (4-cm) headspace. Pie fillings expand as they are being processed. Because of this, pay close attention to headspace to ensure jars do not siphon and cause sealing issues.

A WORD OF CAUTION

One word of caution about pie fillings: Pie fillings need extra space during the canning process, as they boil in the jars. Be sure to leave enough headspace to accommodate the product as it expands.

4. To ensure air bubbles are minimized, use a non-metal utensil to gently remove any bubbles from the jars. For optimal filling, follow a layering method. Begin by using a funnel to add a generous scoop of the mixture, then use a spatula to press down the apples within the jar, effectively eliminating any trapped air. Continue this layering process, gradually filling the jar from the bottom to the top. Try to limit formation of air bubbles as much as possible.

5. Wipe the jar rim with a clean, damp towel or vinegar-dampened towel to remove any residue.

6. Place lid on top of the jar and secure with a band, screwing it on until finger light.

7. Place the filled jars back into the canning pot. Ensure the jars are covered with at least 1 inch (2.5 cm) of water.

8. Bring the water to a boil and, once boiling, start timer: 15 minutes for pints or 20 minutes for quarts. Adjust processing time for your altitude as needed.

9. Use the 10-10-10 method in chapter 4 for cooling pie fillings.

SCRAPS TO SWEETNESS: APPLE SCRAP JELLY

In chapter 7 we explore the wonderful world of repurposing kitchen scraps, including turning apple peels and cores into a charming apple scrap jelly.

But sometimes you don't have enough kitchen scraps to use in a repurposing recipe. Plan ahead and you'll always have enough: instead of throwing away apple peels and cores, consider collecting them in a zip-top bag and storing them in the freezer. This simple step allows you to accumulate enough scraps over time, ensuring you have a substantial batch to create your apple scrap jelly when the moment is right.

Apple scrap jelly combines the joy of discovering hidden flavors in unexpected places with reducing kitchen waste and encouraging sustainability. It's a reminder that, with a little creativity, even kitchen scraps can be transformed into something useful. So start saving those apple scraps in your freezer and you'll be on your way to canning another delicious classic.

DISHES THAT USE CARAMEL APPLE PIE FILLING

* **Classic apple pie.** The most obvious use has to be as a filling for homemade apple pie. Pour it into your favorite pie crust, add a top layer, and bake to golden perfection. I use one quart of filling per pie.

* **Apple pasty.** Create quick and delicious apple pasties by placing a spoonful of filling on a small round pie pastry, then fold to cover the filling and crimp the edges. Bake until golden brown for a delightful treat that recalls the Upper Peninsula of Michigan.

* **Apple pancake topping.** Upgrade your breakfast by spooning this filling over a stack of pancakes or waffles. Add a dollop of whipped cream for extra indulgence.

* **Dessert crepes.** Fill crepes with this luscious filling, fold them into triangles, and dust with powdered sugar. A drizzle of caramel sauce takes it to the next level.

* **Apple-stuffed French toast.** Make your breakfast unforgettable by sandwiching slices of this filling between two pieces of French toast. It's a breakfast that feels like a decadent dessert.

* **Ice cream sundae.** Create an apple pie–inspired ice cream sundae by topping vanilla ice cream with warm caramel apple pie filling and a sprinkle of cinnamon.

* **Oatmeal or yogurt topping.** Add a spoonful to your morning oatmeal or yogurt for a delicious start to your day.

Luscious Lemon Pie Filling

Makes about 6 pints or 3 quarts

I love opening a jar of lemon pie filling in the dead of winter. Enjoying lemon pies and desserts while watching the snow fall outside helps us stave off those winter blues. We think of it as sunshine in a jar.

This lemony delight balances tart and sweet, perfectly capturing the essence of freshly squeezed lemons. It adds a zesty kick to your desserts or a burst of brightness to your savory dishes.

---

12 to 14 lemons, peeled and cut into chunks

9 cups (2.1 L) water

7 cups (1.4 kg) granulated sugar

2 cups (472 ml) clear jel

1. Blend the lemon chunks in a food processor or blender. Set aside the lemon rinds for making candied lemon rinds (see page 270).

2. Combine the lemon juice and pulp mixture with 8 cups (2 L) of water in a pan and bring to a boil.

3. Allow the mixture to boil for 15 minutes.

4. Place canning jars in a canning pot filled with water. Bring to a simmer (180°F/82°C) to heat the jars while making the pie filling.

5. Drain the lemon juice through a fine-mesh sieve or cheesecloth. This should yield approximately 9 cups (2.1 L) of lemon juice. You can save the lemon pulp for use in cakes, breads, or desserts.

6. Return the strained lemon juice to the pan and bring it back to a boil.

7. Stir in the sugar until it dissolves completely.

8. In a separate bowl, mix 1 cup (236 ml) of water with clear jel until there are no clumps, creating a smooth slurry mixture used to thicken the pie filling.

9. Slowly add the slurry mixture to the boiling lemon juice mixture and bring it back to a boil. Continue stirring until the mixture thickens. It may bubble, so be sure to stir the bubbles down as needed until it reaches your desired thickness. If necessary, you can add extra clear jel one tablespoon at a time until it achieves your desired consistency.

(continued)

CANNING (HOT PACK)

1. Remove hot jars from the canning pot using a jar lifter.

2. Place a canning funnel on top of a jar.

3. Ladle hot pie filling into hot jars, leaving 1-inch (2.5 cm) headspace. Pie fillings expand as they are being processed. For this reason, pay close attention to headspace to ensure jars do not siphon and cause sealing issues.

4. Wipe the jar rim with a clean, damp towel or vinegar-dampened towel to remove any residue.

5. Place lid on top of the jar and secure with a band, screwing it on until finger light.

6. Place the filled jars back into the canning pot. Ensure the jars are covered with at least 1 inch (2.5 cm) of water.

7. Bring the water to a boil and, once boiling, start timer: 10 minutes for pints, 15 minutes for quarts. Adjust processing times for your altitude as needed.

8. Use the 10-10-10 method described in chapter 4 for cooling pie fillings.

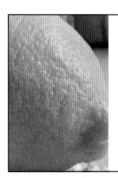

WHEN LIFE GIVES YOU LEMONS, MAKE CANDIED LEMON PEELS

In the spirit of reducing waste and maximizing every ingredient, consider making candied lemon peels from the peels you have left over from this recipe. Details are discussed on page 270.

Zapple Pie Filling: Mock Apple Pie

Makes about 5 quarts or 10 pints

Zapple pie filling is the master of disguise, a perfect ruse for apple pie lovers. They won't believe it, but it doesn't use a single apple.

Zucchinis can mimic the flavor and texture of traditional apple pie filling. Sometimes, the best flavors can come from the most unexpected places.

24 cups (2.9 kg) zucchini, peeled, deseeded, and thinly sliced

2 cups (472 ml) lemon juice

3 cups (600 g) granulated sugar

1½ cups (225 g) brown sugar

4½ teaspoons (22 ml) cream of tartar

2 tablespoons (14 g) cinnamon

1 teaspoon nutmeg

¾ teaspoon cardamom

¾ teaspoon ground cloves

¾ teaspoon ground allspice

1 teaspoon ground ginger

1½ to 2 cups (60 to 240 g) clear jel

1 tablespoon (15 ml) vanilla extract

1. Place canning jars in a canning pot filled with water and bring it to a simmer (180°F/82°C) to heat the jars.

2. Place zucchini and lemon juice in large stockpot and bring to a boil.

3. Reduce heat and simmer for 15 minutes, stirring until zucchini is soft.

4. In a separate bowl, combine sugars, spices, and 1½ cups of clear jel. Mix with a spoon.

5. Add dry ingredients to zucchini in stockpot and cook for 5 minutes until thick and bubbly. If mixture is too runny, add more clear jel, 1 tablespoon at a time. The pie filling will thicken with canning, so don't add too much. You can always add more thickener after opening the jar.

6. Remove from heat and stir in vanilla.

CANNING (HOT PACK)

1. Retrieve hot jars from canner.

2. Place a canning funnel on top of a jar and ladle pie filling into jars, leaving generous 1½-inch (4-cm) headspace. Pie fillings expand during canning, so be sure to pay attention to headspace to ensure a proper seal.

3. Use a bubble remover tool to remove air bubbles and adjust headspace if necessary. Use additional water to correct headspace if needed.

4. Wipe the jar rim with a clean, damp towel or a vinegar-dampened towel to remove any residue.

5. Place the lid on top of the jar and secure with a band, screwing it on until finger light.

6. Place the filled jars back into the canning pot using a canning rack. Ensure the jars are covered with at least 1 inch (2.5 cm) of water.

7. Bring the water to a boil and, once boiling, start timer: 30 minutes for pints or quarts. Adjust processing times for altitude as needed.

SAVVY FOOD SECURITY WITH ZUCCHINI

Whether you grow them in a sprawling garden or on a small balcony, zucchinis can thrive almost anywhere, making them a cost-effective addition to your home produce. There are always too many of them in my garden, but with canning I have a creative way to preserve them.

Incorporate your zucchini into a variety of dishes, from savory stir-fries to wholesome salads and, yes, even desserts like mock apple pie filling. You can also make zapplesauce, like the one shown in this photo. They absorb the flavors of whatever dish they're added to, making them a great addition for whatever meal you prepare.

With a little imagination, you can transform these versatile vegetables into delicious and budget-friendly meals, all while reaping the benefits of your green-thumb efforts.

Blueberry Spiced Pie Filling

I put a lot of thought into packing lunch for my husband, but there are times when I draw a blank. This homemade blueberry spiced pie filling is enough to inspire me to change up what I send in his lunch bag. With this filling, a modest container of cottage cheese becomes a gourmet delight, as the sweetly spiced blueberries blend with the creamy cheese to brighten his midday meal.

If you're a fan of blueberries, this filling is a great addition to any meal or snack. You also can spoon this filling over ice cream, yogurt, or pancakes, or use it as a filling for pies, tarts, or pastries. The filling is a must-have ingredient for your smoothies, too.

INGREDIENTS	SINGLE BATCH: 6 pints or 3 quarts	DOUBLE BATCH: 12 pints or 6 quarts	TRIPLE BATCH: 18 pints or 9 quarts
Blueberries	14 cups (2 kg)	28 cups (4 kg)	42 cups (6.1 kg)
Sugar	3⅓ cups (667 g)	6⅔ cups (1.3 kg)	10 cups (2 kg)
Clear jel	1⅓ cups (192 g)	2⅔ cups (384 g)	4 cups (288 g)
Lemon juice	¼ cup (60 ml)	½ cup (120 ml)	¾ cup (180 ml)
Ground nutmeg	1 teaspoon	2 teaspoons (4.4 g)	3 teaspoons (7 g)
Ground cinnamon	½ teaspoon	1 teaspoon	1½ teaspoons (3.1 g)
Reserved blueberry water	4 cups (948 ml)	8 cups (1.9 L)	12 cups (2.8 L)

1. Place canning jars in a canning pot filled with water and bring it to a simmer (180°F/82°C) to heat the jars.

2. Wash and remove stems from blueberries.

3. Fill a large stockpot halfway with water and bring water to a boil over high heat.

4. Add blueberries and cook for one minute.

5. Strain blueberries over a bowl, reserving 4 cups of the strained blueberry water.

6. To a large stockpot, add reserved blueberry water, sugar, clear jel, lemon juice, and spices. Bring sauce to a light boil, stirring constantly to prevent scorching.

7. Reduce heat and continue stirring. When sauce is thickened to pie filling consistency, remove from heat.

8. Gently fold in blueberries.

CANNING (HOT PACK)

1. Retrieve hot jars from canner.

2. Place a canning funnel on top of a jar and ladle hot blueberry pie filling into jars, leaving 1-inch (2.5 cm) headspace. Pie fillings tend to expand during canning, so pay close attention to correct headspace for this recipe.

3. Use a bubble remover tool to remove air bubbles. Add more filling or water to correct headspace if needed.

4. Wipe the jar rim with a clean, damp towel or a vinegar-dampened towel to remove any residue.

5. Place the lid on top of the jar and secure with a band, screwing it on until finger light.

6. Place the filled jar back into the canning pot using a canning rack and continue filling the remaining jars. Ensure the jars are covered with at least 1 inch (2.5 cm) of water.

7. Bring the water to a boil and, once boiling, start the timer for 30 minutes for pints or quarts. Adjust processing times for altitude as needed.

Strawberry Rhubarb Pie Filling

Makes about 4 pint jars. Recipe can be doubled or tripled.

Rhubarb season begins in late spring, and that's when I start pulling out my rhubarb canning recipes. This pie filling captures the tartness of fresh rhubarb throughout the year. I use it in pies and tarts, crisps, and cobblers. You can even get creative by incorporating it into your breakfast dishes or as a topping for ice cream.

7 cups (approximately 1½ pounds/ 681 g) rhubarb, cut into 1-inch (2.5 cm) pieces

3 large apples, peeled, cored, and chopped

2 cups (400 g) granulated sugar

¼ cup (60 ml) freshly squeezed orange juice

2 teaspoons (10 ml) orange zest

4 cups (580 g) strawberries, hulled and sliced in half

1. Place canning jars in a canning pot filled with water. Bring to a simmer (180°F/82°C) to heat the jars.

2. In a large stockpot, combine chopped rhubarb, apples, sugar, orange juice, and orange zest. Over medium heat, bring mixture to a boil, stirring often to prevent scorching.

3. Once a boil is reached, remove the pot cover and simmer for 15 minutes, or until rhubarb is soft. Continue stirring periodically to prevent burning.

4. Add strawberries and return to a hard boil for 5 minutes. Continue stirring while boiling.

CANNING (HOT PACK)

1. Remove a hot jar from the canning pot using a jar lifter.

2. Place a canning funnel on top and ladle hot pie filling into jars, leaving 1-inch (2.5 cm) headspace.

3. Use a bubble remover tool to remove air bubbles and adjust headspace if necessary.

4. Wipe the jar rim with a clean, damp towel or a vinegar-dampened towel to remove any residue.

5. Place the lid on top of the jar and secure with a band, screwing it on until finger light.

6. Place the filled jars back into the canning pot using a canning rack. Ensure the jars are covered with at least 1 inch (2.5 cm) of water.

7. Bring the water to a boil and, once boiling, start the timer for 15 minutes for pints. Adjust processing times for your altitude as needed.

Amaretto Pear Pie Filling

Makes about 7 quarts.

In late summer, we buy a few bushels of pears from local farmers and start experimenting with different recipes. This one features a subtle infusion of amaretto, an Italian liqueur that adds a touch of sophistication to preserves. If amaretto isn't your thing, feel free to skip it or consider brandy instead.

24 cups (2.6 kg) sliced pears (firm pears are best and peeling is optional) (see note below)

5½ cups (1.1 kg) sugar

1½ cups clear jel

2½ cups (290 ml) cold water

4 cups (944 ml) fruit juice (apple/pear/white grape)

1 cup (236 ml) amaretto liqueur

1 tablespoon (7 g) cinnamon

¾ teaspoon nutmeg

¾ cup (177 ml) lemon juice concentrate

The quantity of pears needed to make 24 cups (2.6 kg) of sliced pears will vary depending on the size and juiciness of the pears, as well as how tightly you pack the cups. Estimate about 12 to 15 pounds will yield roughly 24 cups of sliced pears.

1. Wash and cut pears into ½-inch (1.25-cm) sliced wedges. You can peel these before processing, but I find it's less work and the peels are soft and delightful after canning. Place cut pears in a bowl filled with cold water while you continue prepping all the fruit. A splash of lemon juice in the water helps prevent browning.

2. Prep all water bath canning equipment, jars, lids, and rings. Place canning jars in a large stockpot of boiling water. Keep them in hot water until ready to use.

3. In a large pot, combine sugar, clear jel, water, fruit juice, amaretto, and spices. Stir with a whisk over medium-high heat until mixture thickens to a pie filling consistency.

4. Add lemon juice and bring to boil for 1 minute, stirring constantly.

5. Remove pot from heat and fold in drained pear slices.

CANNING (HOT PACK)

1. Remove a hot jar from the canning pot using a jar lifter.

2. Place a canning funnel on top and ladle pie filling into the jar, leaving a *generous* 1½-inch (4-cm) headspace. Pie fillings need extra space during canning as they boil in the jars.

3. Wipe the jar rim with a clean, damp towel or a vinegar-dampened towel to remove any residue.

4. Place the lid on top of the jar and secure with a band, screwing it on until finger light.

5. Place the filled jar back into the canning pot using a canning rack and repeat canning steps until all jars are filled and in the canner.

6. Ensure the jars are covered with at least 1 inch (2.5 cm) of water.

7. Bring the water to a boil and, once boiling, start timer, using 25 minutes for quarts. Adjust processing times for your altitude.

Spiced Christmas Pears

Makes 10 to 12 pints

In our home, we lovingly refer to this recipe as Christmas Pears although we enjoy them all year long. This recipe embraces the holiday spirit and yields 10 to 12 pints (5 to 6 L) that are perfect for gifting, sharing, or savoring. The combination of pears, sugar, and cinnamon red-hot candies provides strong flavor and color: the vibrant pop of red from the candies makes jars of these delights stand out on your shelves.

1 tablespoon (15 ml) lemon juice

½ bushel pears (approximately 22 to 25 pounds/10 to 11.4 kg), peeled, cored, and sliced

2 cups (400 g) sugar

6 cups (1.4 L) water

1½ cups (240 g) cinnamon Red Hots candies

1. Begin by filling a large bowl halfway with cold water and add the lemon juice.

2. Place the pear slices in the lemon water to prevent browning.

3. While the pears soak, prepare your canning equipment. Place canning jars in a canning pot filled with water and bring it to a simmer (180°F/82°C) to heat the jars.

4. In a large saucepan, combine the sugar and 6 cups (1.4 L) of water. Bring this mixture to a boil, then reduce heat to a simmer. Stir until the sugar is completely dissolved.

CANNING (HOT PACK)

1. Remove a hot jar from the canning pot using a jar lifter.

2. Pack pears tightly into the jars, leaving ½-inch (1.25-cm) headspace.

3. Add ⅛ cup (20 g) of Red Hots to each canning jar.

4. Place a canning funnel on top and ladle hot syrup over pears, leaving ½-inch (1.25-cm) headspace.

5. Use a bubble remover tool to remove air bubbles and adjust headspace, if necessary.

6. Wipe the jar rim with a clean, damp towel or a vinegar-dampened towel to remove any residue.

7. Place the lid on top of the jar and secure with a band, screwing it on until finger light.

8. Place the filled jars back into the canning pot using a canning rack. Ensure the jars are covered with at least 1 inch (2.5 cm) of water.

9. Bring the water to a boil and, once boiling, start timer for 15 minutes (for pints). Adjust processing times for your altitude as needed.

WAYS TO USE CHRISTMAS PEARS

* **Holiday desserts.** Serve them as a festive topping for ice cream, yogurt, or cheesecake.

* **Side dishes.** Pair them with roast meats or poultry for a delightful side dish.

* **Gifts.** Include a jar of Christmas pears in a charming holiday gift basket with other homemade treats.

* **Charcuterie boards.** Add some spiced pears to your holiday charcuterie board for a pop of color and flavor.

Spiced Apple Rings

Makes about 7 pint jars or 3½ quarts. Recipe can be doubled or tripled.

There's a certain charm in preserving age-old family recipes that have been passed down through generations. For me, spiced apple rings hold a special place in my heart, since I inherited the recipe from my mother and grandmother. This delightful dish was a fixture at our family gatherings, especially during the holiday season.

8 cups (1.9 L) water

Splash of lemon juice or 1 tablespoon (19 g) citric acid

Approximately 20 large, firm apples

¾ cup (150 g) sugar

1¾ cups (280 g) cinnamon Red Hots candies

4 cups (944 ml) water

3½ teaspoons (7 g) whole cloves

1. To a large bowl, add 4 cups (1.9 L) of water and the lemon juice or citric acid.

2. Begin peeling, coring, and slicing the apples into ½-inch (1.25-cm) thick rings. The apples should resemble a flattened doughnut shape. A small melon baller makes easy work of coring whole apples. To prevent browning, drop the apple rings in the lemon juice/citric acid water as you work through them.

3. Heat sugar, Red Hots, and the remaining 4 cups (944 ml) of water in a saucepan to make cinnamon syrup.

4. Stir often with a metal spoon until the sugar and cinnamon candy are completely melted. Bring to a boil for 2 minutes.

5. Drain the apple rings and add to the syrup mixture. Toss gently to coat. Turn off heat and let apple syrup mixture sit for 15 minutes.

6. Place canning jars in a canning pot filled with water and bring it to a simmer (180°F/82°C) to heat the jars.

CANNING (HOT PACK)

1. Retrieve hot jars from canner.

2. Add ½ teaspoon whole cloves to the bottom of each jar.

3. Place a canning funnel on top of a jar and, using a slotted spoon, stack apple rings vertically into jars, leaving ½-inch (1.25-cm) headspace. The apple rings will be soft; do the best you can, it doesn't have to be perfect.

4. Ladle remaining hot syrup over apple rings, leaving ½-inch (1.25-cm) headspace.

5. Use a bubble remover tool to remove air bubbles and adjust headspace if necessary. If you don't have any spare syrup, add water to achieve correct headspace.

6. Wipe the jar rim with a clean, damp towel or a vinegar-dampened towel to remove any residue.

7. Place the lid on top of the jar and secure with a band, screwing it on until finger light.

8. Place the filled jars back into the canning pot using a canning rack. Ensure the jars are covered with at least 1 inch (2.5 cm) of water.

9. Bring the water to a boil and, once boiling, start timer: for pints, 15 minutes; for quarts, 20 minutes.

10. Adjust processing times for your altitude as needed.

Mock Pineapple

Makes 10 to 12 pints or 5 to 6 quarts

If you have zucchini in your garden, odds are your harvest is more prolific than you can handle (see page 73). With this recipe, you can transform zucchini into delicious mock pineapple. Use it in stir-fries, smoothies, or any dish that calls for tropical sweetness and zing.

16 cups zucchini, peeled; approximately 6 pounds (2.7 kg)

6 cups (1.4 L) canned, unsweetened pineapple juice

3 cups (600 g) granulated sugar

1½ cups (354 ml) bottled lemon juice

RECIPES TO USE MOCK PINEAPPLE

* **Pineapple upside-down cake.** Use it as a topping for a classic pineapple upside-down cake, replacing canned pineapple with your homemade mock version.

* **Hawaiian pizza.** Top your homemade pizza with zucchini pineapple and surprise everyone with your take on classic Hawaiian-style pizza.

* **Pineapple glazed ham.** Use as a glaze for your ham, giving your dish a touch of sweetness and tanginess.

1. Cut zucchini lengthwise in half and use a spoon to remove seeds and scrape any fibrous parts of the zucchini.

2. Cut zucchini into ½-inch (1.25-cm) cubes for chunk pineapple or shred for crushed pineapple.

3. Add zucchini to a large saucepan with remaining ingredients.

4. Bring everything to a boil, uncovered, for 1 minute. Reduce heat and simmer uncovered for 20 minutes, or until zucchini is soft and translucent.

5. Place canning jars in a canning pot filled with water and bring it to a simmer (180°F/82°C) to heat the jars.

CANNING (HOT PACK)

1. Retrieve hot jars from canner.

2. Place a canning funnel on top of a jar and ladle hot zucchini and juice mixture into jars, leaving ½-inch (1.25-cm) headspace.

3. Use a bubble remover tool to remove air bubbles. Add more juice to correct headspace if needed.

4. Wipe the jar rim with a clean, damp towel or a vinegar-dampened towel to remove any residue.

5. Place the lid on top of the jar and secure with a band, screwing it on until finger light.

6. Place the filled jar back into the canning pot using a canning rack. Ensure the jars are covered with at least 1 inch (2.5 cm) of water.

7. Bring the water to a boil and, once boiling, start the timer for 20 minutes for pints or 25 minutes for quarts. Adjust processing times for your altitude as needed.

Dilly or Silly Beans

Makes about 8 pints

This recipe lets you choose between the classic, dill-infused "Dilly Beans" or the spicy "Silly (Spicy Dill) Beans." Either way, you're in for fun and a great taste experience.

If you decide to can *both* recipes, be sure to mark the jars "Dilly" or "Silly," since they'll look the same on your pantry shelves.

The ingredients are simple, with fresh beans taking center stage, complemented by the blend of pickling salt, vinegar, and a generous helping of garlic. The true magic lies in the spices that give each recipe its distinctive personality.

---

4 pounds (1.8 kg) fresh green or yellow beans

4 cups (944 ml) white or apple cider vinegar

4 cups (944 ml) water

½ cup (64 g) pickling salt (you can substitute regular salt, but this will make your jars cloudy)

16 cloves garlic, whole

DILLY BEANS SPICES, PER PINT JAR

½ teaspoon red pepper flakes

1 to 2 fresh dill heads or 1 teaspoon dill seeds

SILLY (SPICY DILL) SPICES

1 teaspoon mustard seeds

1 teaspoon black peppercorns

½ teaspoon red pepper flakes

2 allspice berries

1 teaspoon dill seeds

1. Wash and trim ends from green beans. Cut beans into 5-inch (13-cm) lengths to fit upright in the jars.

2. Combine vinegar, water, and salt in a large saucepan, bringing the brine to a boil until salt is completely dissolved. Remove from heat.

3. Put two garlic cloves plus the spices into each pint jar.

4. Pack beans upright into jars, leaving ½-inch (1.25-cm) headspace.

5. Place canning jars in a canning pot filled with water and bring it to a simmer (180°F/82°C) to heat the jars.

CANNING (RAW PACK)

1. Retrieve hot jars from canner.

2. Place a canning funnel on top and ladle pickling brine into hot jars, leaving ½-inch (1.25-cm) headspace.

3. Wipe the jar rim with a clean, damp towel or vinegar-dampened towel to remove any residue.

4. Place lid on top of the jar and secure with a band, screwing it on until finger light.

5. Place the filled jars back into the canning pot. Ensure the jars are covered with at least 1 inch (2.5 cm) of water.

6. Bring the water to a boil and, once boiling, start the timer for 5 minutes for half pints or pints. Adjust processing time for altitude as needed.

Pickled Garlic

*Makes about
7 half-pint jars*

This water bath canning recipe answers the perennial question, "How can I preserve garlic?" You'll go from ordinary cloves to spicy condiment in about an hour. And with pickled garlic on hand, you'll be able to rev up your dishes without peeling garlic each time you cook.

Quickly add a burst of flavor to salads, pizzas, and sandwiches. If you want some heat, a sprinkle of crushed red pepper flakes in the jars will do the trick.

---

14 cups (3.3 L) water plus 4⅔ cups (1.1 L) water

7 cups (952 g) peeled garlic cloves (approximately 18 to 20 heads of garlic)

4⅔ cups (1.1 L) white vinegar

1 cup (340 g) honey

7 teaspoons (42 g) salt (optional)

3½ teaspoons (7 g) whole allspice

3½ teaspoons (6 g) coriander seeds

3½ teaspoons (5 g) oregano

7 bay leaves (1 per jar)

1. Place canning jars in a canning pot filled with water. Bring to a simmer (180°F/82°C) to heat the jars while making the brine.

2. In a medium pot, bring 14 cups (3.3 L) of water to a boil. Add peeled garlic cloves and cook for 3 minutes. Turn off heat, leaving garlic in the pot, and proceed to making the brine.

3. To make the brine, combine 4⅔ cups (1.1 L) of water, vinegar, honey, and pickling spices in a medium saucepan and simmer until honey is dissolved.

4. Using a colander, strain garlic from the water and proceed to canning.

CANNING (HOT PACK)

1. Remove a hot jar from the canning pot using a jar lifter.

2. Place a canning funnel on top and pack the hot jars with hot garlic cloves to ½-inch (1.25-cm) headspace.

3. Add one bay leaf to each jar.

4. Ladle hot brine into the jar over the garlic, leaving ½-inch (1.25-cm) headspace.

5. Use a bubble remover tool to remove air bubbles and add more brine to adjust headspace if necessary.

6. Wipe the jar rim with a clean, damp towel or a vinegar-dampened towel to remove any residue.

7. Place the lid on top of the jar and secure with a band, screwing it on until finger light.

8. Place the filled jars back into the canning pot using a canning rack. Ensure the jars are covered with at least 1 inch (2.5 cm) of water.

9. Bring the water to a boil and, once boiling, start the timer: 35 minutes for half pints. Adjust processing time for your altitude as needed.

GARLIC BLUES

Preserved garlic can change in your jars from white to various shades of blue or green. Totally normal! The color change is a natural reaction between garlic's sulfur compounds and the acid in the pickling solution. This can be more noticeable in younger garlic that has residual chlorophyll. While the discoloration may not be visually appealing, it doesn't affect the product's taste or edibility. If you want to minimize this reaction, use mature garlic cloves, briefly blanch the garlic before pickling, or use distilled water in your pickling solution.

Pickled Black Walnuts

Yields vary depending on how the walnuts shrink during sunning.

The original canning instructions I have for this 1831 recipe are vague and hard to decipher. That didn't stop me, as I couldn't pass up the chance to make my own version of this nearly forgotten delicacy. After cracking the recipe's code—and going through a lot of disposable gloves—I was able to lay bare its secrets.

Traditional pickled black walnuts include nutmeat as well as the husk and shell. They make an exquisite addition to cheese platters and can be great in salads, sandwiches, or alongside roast meats.

As for their taste, think of the rich, earthy flavor of walnuts infused with a bite of vinegar, subtly enhanced with aromatic spices. The closest thing I can compare it to is steak with a tangy steak sauce.

Approximately 100 small black walnuts

Salt brine: 1 gallon (3.8 L) water + 3 cups (708 ml) salt (you'll make this brine 4 times; in other words, use 4 gallons (15 L) water + 12 cups (3 L) salt total)

½ gallon (1.8 L) white vinegar

½ gallon (1.8 L) malt vinegar

1 cup (200 g) granulated sugar

24 whole cloves

24 whole peppercorns

12 blades of mace (if this is unavailable, 12 teaspoons [26 g] of ground nutmeg can be substituted, though you will not achieve the precise flavor profile)

STEP 1: FERMENTATION AND SUNNING (11 DAYS)

NOTE: This recipe requires an eight-day fermentation process plus three days of "sunning" the walnuts. Sunning dries out the nuts in the sun, removing excess moisture and intensifying flavors. If it rains, move the walnuts inside until wet weather passes, then resume the sunning process.

1. **Day 1.** Wearing gloves, pierce walnut husks with a fork 2 to 3 times per nut. Make saltwater brine (1 gallon [3.8 L]) water + 3 cups [900 g] salt) in buckets or large pots and soak walnuts in saltwater brine overnight.

2. **Day 2.** Drain and discard brine, cover in new saltwater brine (1 gallon [3.8 L] water + 3 cups [900 g] salt), and soak overnight.

3. **Day 3.** Drain and discard brine, cover in new saltwater brine (1 gallon [3.8 L] water + 3 cups [900 g] salt), and soak nuts in this brine on days 3, 4, and 5.

4. **Day 6.** Drain and discard brine, cover in new saltwater brine (1 gallon [3.8 L] water + 3 cups [900 g] salt), and soak nuts in this brine on days 6, 7, and 8.

5. **Day 9.** Drain and discard brine, place on parchment-lined cookie sheets, and set out in the sun for days 9 to 11, allowing the sunned walnuts to blacken.

NOTE: Your walnuts will turn black by the end of this process. Anything the walnuts touch will be stained black forever. I use the same stained buckets, cookie sheets, clothes, shoes, and so on every year. Wear gloves at all times when working on this recipe.

STEP 2 : PICKLING (7 DAYS)

1. **Day 12.** Pack walnuts in quart jars. The number of jars needed will vary greatly depending on the size and quantity of your walnuts.

2. In a large pot, combine white vinegar, malt vinegar, sugar, cloves, peppercorns, and mace. Bring to boil, stirring often until sugar is dissolved.

3. Pour pickling brine into jars over walnuts. If you're short on brine, top off with extra vinegar. Add lids and set aside.

4. **Days 12 to 14.** Allow walnuts to sit in pickling brine.

5. **Day 15.** Pour off pickling brine from jars into large stockpot. Reboil the pickling brine and pour back over the walnuts in the jar. Add lids and rings.

6. **Days 15 to 17.** Allow walnuts to sit in pickling brine.

7. **Day 18.** Pour off pickling brine from jars into large stockpot. Reboil the pickling brine and pour back over the walnuts in the jar. Add lids and rings.

You're done! Your pickled walnuts will be ready to eat in thirty days and will be shelf stable in your pantry for one year.

A BIT MORE ABOUT BLACK WALNUTS

Black walnuts should be harvested in early summer while they're still green, before the shell forms or wildlife snacks on them.

To see if the walnuts are worthy of pickling, put on some waterproof gloves and grab a heavy-gauge needle. You should be able to pierce the outer husk, through the soft shell, and into the nut on both sides. If there is any resistance, the shell has begun to form inside the husk and the walnut cannot be pickled.

Pickling walnuts is an exercise in patience. The process takes several weeks, demanding dedication and a willingness to embrace the stains that may come from working with these dark jewels. But the reward is a jar of pickled walnuts made from a historical recipe and, more importantly, they taste great.

Preserved Lemons

*Single recipe makes
1 quart*

If you live in a citrus-growing region, you may have access to more than enough lemons in the summer months. Tuck this centuries-old recipe in your back pocket and preserve your fruits for use during the winter months.

As the salt works its magic to ferment and preserve the lemons, the lemons' bitter pith and rinds soften, the flesh and juice turn into a luscious syrup, and the entire fruit's flavor profile intensifies. At the end of the process, everything you've preserved is edible—and delicious.

INGREDIENTS ARE PER QUART JAR

6 to 10 lemons

¼ cup (60 ml) lemon juice, if needed

Optional spices: 1 teaspoon whole black peppercorns, 1 teaspoon whole coriander seeds, 1 bay leaf, ¼ teaspoon red pepper flakes

6 to 10 teaspoons (108 to 180 g) kosher salt

1. Clean jars in hot soapy water and dry.

2. Scrub lemons in hot water.

3. Place optional spices (if using) in the bottom of the jar.

4. Cut ½ inch (1.25 cm) off the end of each lemon to give two flat ends.

5. Score lemon into an *X*, leaving the 4 quarters attached at the base.

6. Using your hands, gently open the four quarters like a flower blooming and pack with 1 teaspoon salt.

7. Place lemon in the jar with the cut side of the lemon facing upward.

8. Repeat the scoring and salting of the remaining lemons, stacking one on top of another inside the jar.

9. Use a pestle or wooden spoon to pack as tightly as possible, pressing the lemons into the jar.

10. Once the lemons are packed to the top of the jar, pour any remaining salt in the jar. If the lemons are not completely submerged in lemon juice, top off the jar with the additional lemon juice.

11. Cover the jar with a lid and set in a sunny window for 14 days.

12. Every day, turn the jar upside down to ensure all lemons are covered in juice. As the lemons shrink, make sure they're submerged in the lemon juice. Open jar periodically to release any fermentation gas and press lemons in the juice to keep them from growing mold during fermentation.

13. Allow the lemons to marinate for about a month to completely develop their flavor before using.

14. The jar can be stored in a cool pantry or refrigerator for up to a year.

WAYS TO USE PRESERVED LEMONS

* **As a garnish.** Elevate tartines with thinly sliced preserved lemons and a drizzle of olive oil. Their tart, salty notes perfectly complement creamy ingredients like soft cheese or avocado on toast. They also make a striking garnish for hummus.

* **As a seasoning.** Preserved lemons work wonders in salad dressings and vinaigrettes. Add them to your meat marinades to infuse a bright, citrusy essence.

* **As a condiment** (probably my favorite). Eat them straight from the jar! You can also mix them into accompaniments like chimichurri sauce, olive tapenades, and salsas.

Corn Relish

Makes 7 to 8 pints or 14 to 16 half pints

Bring a burst of my Hoosier roots to your cantry! A beloved tradition in the heart of Indiana, this Corn Relish combines the freshness of sweet corn with a kick of traditional salsa ingredients. A celebration of the Midwest harvest, and a delightful companion for a wide range of dishes, or tasty straight from the jar.

Enjoy this relish as a vibrant topping for grilled meats, a zesty addition to tacos, or a flavorful dip for your favorite chips. Be sure to let the relish rest for 2 to 4 weeks after canning to allow the vinegar to mellow fully.

---

10 ears of corn, shucked and kernels cut off the cob (see note below), approximately 7 cups (1 kg)

1 large onion, chopped

2 large red bell peppers, chopped

1 large green bell pepper, chopped

8 celery stalks, chopped

4 cups (944 ml) apple cider vinegar

2 cups (400 g) granulated sugar

4 to 5 whole allspice berries

2 teaspoons (12 g) celery salt

1 tablespoon (9 g) ground mustard

NOTE: *To easily cut the corn off of the cob, I set a Bundt pan right-side up on a table, then I place the shucked corncob in the center hole of the Bundt pan. Slice the kernels away, as close to the cob as possible, allowing the kernels to be captured in the Bundt pan bowl.*

1. In a large stockpot, add all ingredients.

2. Bring corn relish to a boil, stirring until all the sugar is dissolved.

3. Reduce heat and simmer corn relish, uncovered, for 20 minutes, stirring occasionally.

4. Place canning jars in a canning pot filled with water and bring it to a simmer (180°F/82°C) to heat the jars.

CANNING (HOT PACK)

1. Retrieve hot jars from canner.

2. Place a canning funnel on top of a jar and ladle hot corn relish into jars, leaving ½-inch (1.25-cm) headspace. Ladle vinegar brine over corn as needed to fill jars to ½-inch (1.25-cm) headspace.

3. Use a bubble remover tool to remove air bubbles. Add more vinegar brine or vinegar to correct headspace if needed.

4. Wipe the jar rim with a clean, damp towel or a vinegar-dampened towel to remove any residue.

5. Place the lid on top of the jar and secure with a band, screwing it on until finger light.

6. Place the filled jars back into the canning pot using a canning rack. Ensure the jars are covered with at least 1 inch (2.5 cm) of water.

7. Bring the water to a boil and, once boiling, start the timer for 10 minutes for pints or half pints. Adjust processing time for altitude as needed.

CANNED CORN: A CORNERSTONE OF FOOD SECURITY

Growing up in Indiana, I saw how my family embraced cherished corn as a staple food. Most of us kids worked our first summer job as corn de-tasslers. This humble (but ubiquitous) grain had a permanent place at our table and we used various canning recipes to preserve it for the winter months.

Canned corn isn't just an added touch in your pantry: it's a cornerstone of food security. Corn and other vegetables are easy to incorporate into your One Week, One Month, One Year pantry planning.

In my family, we enjoy one jar of corn a week, which we've found is the perfect balance with other vegetables in our meal repertoire. This means that, during late summer's harvest, I'm busy canning up to fifty-two jars of corn. This approach takes us from one growing season to the next, meeting our year-round need for corn without a lapse.

Atomic Frog Balls

Makes approximately 18 pints or 9 quarts

We're talking about Brussels sprouts here, but prepared in such a way to make them stand out, however you eat them. This recipe takes the nutritious base vegetable and adds an explosion of flavor combining the aromatic notes of garlic and ginger with a zesty kick of Korean red pepper.

A member of the cabbage family, Brussels sprouts are nature's little packages of deliciousness, ready to be transformed into something extraordinary.

If your children snub their noses at the sight of Brussels sprouts, the unusual but appealing taste of "Atomic Frog Balls" might just be enough to get them eating their veggies again. And the recipe's funny name is a selling point for picky eaters.

12 pounds (5.4 kg) Brussels sprouts

3 teaspoons (10 g) minced onions

6 teaspoons (20 g) minced garlic

6 cups (1.4 L) water

3 cups (708 ml) rice vinegar

4½ cups (1.1 L) white vinegar

3 tablespoons (45 ml) soy sauce

1½ cups (300 g) granulated sugar

3 teaspoons (2.6 g) Korean gochugaru red pepper

3 teaspoons (5.5 g) ground ginger

3 tablespoons (54 g) salt

1. Place canning jars in a canning pot filled with water and bring it to a simmer (180°F/82°C) to heat the jars.

2. Wash and cut Brussels sprouts in half. Set aside in a bowl.

3. In a large stockpot, combine all remaining ingredients to create pickling brine.

4. Bring brine mixture to a boil, stirring well until all sugar is dissolved and spices are well incorporated. Boil for 3 minutes.

CANNING (HOT PACK)

1. Retrieve hot jars from canner.

2. Pack Brussels sprouts in jars, leaving ½-inch (1.25-cm) headspace.

3. Ladle hot brine over Brussels sprouts, leaving ½-inch (1.25-cm) headspace.

4. Use a bubble remover tool to remove air bubbles and adjust headspace if necessary. If you don't have any spare brine, add vinegar to achieve correct headspace.

5. Wipe the jar rim with a clean, damp towel or a vinegar-dampened towel to remove any residue.

6. Place the lid on top of the jar and secure with a band, screwing it on until finger light.

7. Place the filled jars back into the canning pot using a canning rack. Ensure the jars are covered with at least 1 inch (2.5 cm) of water.

8. Bring the water to a boil and, once boiling, start the timer: 15 minutes for pints, 20 minutes for quarts. Adjust processing time for altitude as needed.

9. If you have excess brine, you can water-bath-can the brine in a separate jar alongside the Atomic Frog Balls. This brine can be used later for meat marinades or pickling other produce.

NOTE: *Patience is key when it comes to enjoying the full flavor profile of Atomic Frog Balls. I recommend waiting 4 to 6 weeks before opening a jar to experience the best taste.*

Bread-and-Butter Pickles

Makes 6 to 7 pints. Recipe can be doubled or tripled.

Bread-and-butter pickles bring the crunch. Create your own batch of this classic pickle style, perfect for sandwiches, burgers, or simply a mouthwatering snack. The key ingredients are fresh pickling cucumbers and thinly sliced onions, joined by a blend of spices that infuse these pickles with a burst of flavor.

5 pounds (2.3 kg) pickling cucumbers (Kirby), sliced ¼ inch (6 mm) thick (about 16 cups)

2 pounds (908 g) onions, thinly sliced (about 6 cups)

⅓ cup (96 g) pickling salt

3½ cups (826 ml) white or apple cider vinegar

4 cups (800 g) granulated sugar

10 peeled whole garlic cloves

2 tablespoons (22 g) mustard seeds

1½ teaspoons (6 g) celery seeds

1 teaspoon red pepper flakes (optional, for heat)

⅛ teaspoon ground cloves

1 teaspoon turmeric

¾ teaspoon Pickle Crisp Granules (optional)

1. In a large bowl, combine sliced cucumbers, onions, and salt. Toss everything together, then cover the bowl and refrigerate for at least 3 hours, up to 12 hours.

2. After refrigeration, drain the mixture in a colander. Rinse thoroughly under running water for about 2 minutes, then allow to drain.

3. Place canning jars in a canning pot filled with water and bring it to a simmer (180°F/82°C) to heat the jars.

4. In a separate medium-sized stockpot, combine the vinegar, sugar, garlic, mustard and celery seeds, red pepper flakes (if using), cloves, and turmeric. Heat this mixture over high heat until it comes to a boil.

5. Add the cucumber and onion mixture to the pot, stirring to combine, then bring it all back to a boil for 1 minute. Turn off the heat.

CANNING (HOT PACK)

1. Remove hot jars from the canning pot using a jar lifter.

2. If using Pickle Crisp Granules, add ⅛ teaspoon to jar.

3. Place a canning funnel on top of a jar.

4. Using a slotted spoon, pack food solids (cucumbers, onions, garlic) into the jar, leaving 2-inch (5-cm) headspace.

5. Ladle hot pickle brine liquid over the vegetables in the jars, leaving ½-inch (1.25-cm) headspace.

6. Debubble the jars, leaving ½-inch (1.25-cm) headspace. Add more brine or vinegar to jars if needed to achieve the correct headspace.

7. Wipe the jar rim with a clean, damp towel or vinegar-dampened towel to remove any residue.

8. Place lid on top of the jar and secure with a band, screwing it on until finger light.

9. Place the filled jars back into the canning pot. Ensure the jars are covered with at least 1 inch (2.5 cm) of water.

10. Bring the water to a boil and, once boiling, start the timer: 10 minutes for pints. Adjust processing time for altitude as needed.

CANNING CRISP CUKES

For pickle enthusiasts who want a crunch in every bite, these tricks will help your pickles keep their crispness.

* Begin with the freshest cucumbers you can find. Pick them straight from the vine in the morning, before the sun can deplete their natural moisture.

* Make sure to remove the cucumber's blossom end, as it can contain enzymes that might affect the texture of the pickles.

* Add two grape leaves on top of your cucumbers before canning: this will help preserve your pickles' crispness.

* For an extra boost and added crunch, consider using a product like Pickle Crisp Granules, which contain calcium chloride.

Patty's Pickled Asparagus

Makes about 12 quart jars

This cherished family recipe brings back memories of my childhood, where every jar held the essence of homegrown goodness. My mother's pickled asparagus is still one of my favorite pickling recipes. Patty's Pickled Asparagus isn't just a condiment—it's a piece of my history and, I hope, a beloved addition to your table.

---

20 pounds (9.1 kg) asparagus

13 cups (3.1 L) white vinegar

13 cups (3.1 L) water

¾ cup pickling salt (216 g) (can substitute table salt but liquid may become cloudy)

2 to 4 cups (400 to 800 g) granulated sugar, depending on desired sweetness

3 teaspoons (11 g) celery seeds

3 to 4 heads of garlic (36 cloves), 3 cloves per quart jar

½ cup (73 g) mustard seeds, 2 teaspoons (7 g) per quart jar

½ cup (53 g) dill seeds, 2 teaspoons (7 g) per quart jar

Optional heat: ½ teaspoon red pepper flakes per quart jar

1. Wash asparagus spears thoroughly and trim the stem end 1 inch (2.5 cm) shorter than the height of your canning jars. Be sure to remove any tough or woody ends.

2. Place canning jars in a canning pot filled with water. Bring to a simmer (180°F/82°C) to heat the jars while making the brine.

3. In a large pot, combine the white vinegar, water, pickling salt, and sugar. Stir well until the salt and sugar dissolve. Bring the mixture to a boil over medium-high heat.

4. Remove a hot jar from the canning pot using a jar lifter.

5. In each quart-sized jar, place 3 cloves of garlic, 2 teaspoons (7 g) of mustard seeds, and 2 teaspoons (7 g) of dill seeds.

6. Pack the prepared asparagus spears vertically into the jars, leaving ½ inch (1.3 cm) of headspace at the top. I pack these asparagus tips down into the jar with the stem end up, as it's easier to retrieve the asparagus from the jar this way. Lay the jar on its side while packing to use all the space in the jar and pack it tightly.

   NOTE: *For this recipe, using fresh asparagus will give you the best results. To check for freshness, snap the asparagus in half. If there is a clean snap, the asparagus is fresh and will retain its crunch better over time.*

CANNING (HOT PACK)

1. Place a canning funnel on top and ladle hot brine over asparagus into the jar, leaving ½-inch (1.25-cm) headspace.

2. Use a bubble remover tool to remove air bubbles and add more brine to adjust headspace if necessary.

3. Wipe the jar rim with a clean, damp towel or a vinegar-dampened towel to remove any residue.

4. Place the lid on top of the jar and secure with a band, screwing it on until finger light.

5. Place the filled jars back into the canning pot using a canning rack. Ensure the jars are covered with at least 1 inch (2.5 cm) of water.

6. Bring the water to a boil and, once boiling, start the timer, 10 minutes for quarts. Adjust processing time for altitude as needed.

ASPARAGUS: LET THE CANNING SEASON BEGIN

Asparagus is one of the first produce foods in a calendar year you can add to your canning planner. Asparagus typically becomes available in the spring; the exact timing for asparagus season can vary depending on your location and climate conditions. If you're purchasing asparagus, the lowest market prices will be in the spring months.

This recipe can be halved, doubled, or tripled, depending on the amount of asparagus you can obtain. Adjust the quantities as needed based on the number of jars you plan to put in your cantry.

Bruschetta in a Jar

Makes 5 to 6 pints

I love effortless recipes that make you think they're gourmet, like this bruschetta. It has all the flavor of classic bruschetta—with ripe tomatoes, fresh basil, garlic, and a touch of balsamic vinegar—preserved in a jar. This recipe works as a quick appetizer or a flavorful addition to pasta.

4 cups (944 ml) water

1 cup (236 ml) white vinegar

½ cup (118 ml) balsamic vinegar

1 cup (200 g) granulated sugar

1 tablespoon (18 g) salt

Cherry tomatoes, approximately 3 pounds (1.4 kg)

SEASONINGS PER PINT JAR

3 fresh basil leaves or 1 teaspoon dried basil

½ teaspoon dried oregano

1 sprig of dill or 1 teaspoon dill seeds

2 peeled whole garlic cloves

½ teaspoon coriander seeds

½ teaspoon mustard seeds

4 to 5 whole peppercorns

Patience pays off. Allow this recipe to rest in the jar for 2 to 4 weeks after processing. During this time, the tomatoes will swell as they absorb the sugar and vinegar.

1. Place canning jars in a canning pot filled with water. Bring to a simmer (180°F/82°C) to heat the jars while making the brine.

2. Make the brine by combining water, vinegars, sugar, and salt in a medium pot over medium heat. Boil brine for 3 to 4 minutes until sugar is dissolved.

3. Remove brine from heat.

CANNING (HOT PACK)

1. Remove a hot jar from the canning pot using a jar lifter.

2. Place a canning funnel on top and pack tomatoes into jars, leaving 1-inch (2.5-cm) headspace.

3. Add the seasonings to the jar.

4. Ladle hot brine over the tomatoes in the jar, leaving ½-inch (1.25-cm) headspace.

5. Use a bubble remover tool to remove air bubbles and add more brine to adjust headspace if necessary.

6. Wipe the jar rim with a clean, damp towel or a vinegar-dampened towel to remove any residue.

7. Place the lid on top of the jar and secure with a band, screwing it on until finger light.

8. Place the filled jar back into the canning pot using a canning rack. Repeat steps 1 to 7 until all jars are filled and in the water bath canner.

9. Ensure the jars are covered with at least 1 inch (2.5 cm) of water. Bring the water to a boil and, once boiling, start the timer: 10 minutes for pints, 15 minutes for quarts. Adjust processing time for altitude.

Pickled Peaches

Pickled Peaches are far more than just a preserved delicacy. They embody generations of cherished memories. I vividly recall the days when we would argue over who would be the lucky one to savor the pickled peach pit found within my grandma's jar of pickled peaches. Whether served as a side or atop succulent chicken, flaky fish, or tender pork, these peaches add a touch of Southern elegance to your meals. Their complex flavor profile includes apple cider vinegar, sugars, fragrant cloves, and the fresh clingstone peaches themselves. Adding cinnamon sticks introduces a warm note—other spices like ginger or star anise will bring even more boldness, if desired.

---

4 to 6 pounds (908 g to 2.7 kg) fresh clingstone peaches

1 cup (236 ml) apple cider vinegar

1 cup (236 ml) water

2 cups (400 g) granulated sugar

2 cups (300 g) brown sugar

2 tablespoons (12 g) whole cloves

5 to 6 cinnamon sticks, 3-inch (8-cm) long pieces

1. Choose 1 of 3 methods to prepare your peaches. For each, decide to peel your fruit or leave it unpeeled before proceeding.

METHOD 1, QUARTERED: MORE IN THE JAR

1. Cut and quarter peaches, removing peach pit. This method allows more peaches to be packed into the jars (which means you may need more peaches than the recipe ingredients listed). Place cut peaches in a bowl of cold water with a splash of lemon juice to keep from browning during preparation.

METHOD 2, HALVED: GRANDMA'S TRADITIONAL

1. Cut peaches in half, leaving peach pit in one half of the peach. You'll be able to fit 2 to 3 peaches in a quart jar with this method. Place cut peaches in a bowl of cold water with a splash of lemon juice to keep from browning during preparation.

METHOD 3, WHOLE: SOUTHERN APPROACH

1. Leave peaches whole. Can 2 peaches per quart jar.

2. Place canning jars in a canning pot filled with water and bring it to a simmer (180°F/82°C) to heat the jars.

3. In a separate large stockpot, bring apple cider vinegar, water, sugars, and cloves to a boil. Boil the pickling brine for 5 minutes, or until the brine has syrupy consistency.

4. Reduce heat to medium and place peaches in the boiling syrup. Simmer peaches for 5 minutes if using method 1 or 2 (cut peaches). Simmer peaches for 10 minutes using method 3 (whole peaches).

CANNING (HOT PACK)

1. Remove a hot jar from the canning pot using a jar lifter.

2. Place a canning funnel on top of jar.

3. Using a slotted spoon, spoon hot peaches into hot jar, leaving ½-inch (1.25-cm) headspace.

4. Place one cinnamon stick into the jar with the peaches.

5. Using a ladle, ladle hot brine (including cloves) over the peaches in the jar.

6. Use a bubble remover tool to remove air bubbles and add vinegar to adjust headspace if necessary.

7. Wipe the jar rim with a clean, damp towel or a vinegar-dampened towel to remove any residue.

8. Place the lid on top of the jar and secure with a band, screwing it on until finger light.

9. Place the filled jar back into the canning pot using a canning rack and repeat until all jars are filled and in the canner.

10. Ensure the jars are covered with at least 1 inch (2.5 cm) of water. Bring the water to a boil and, once boiling, start timer: 25 minutes for quarts. Adjust processing time for altitude.

IN A PICKLE: PEACH PITS

While peach pits may contain small amounts of cyanide if consumed, the pickling and heating process neutralizes any potential harm: that means your pickled peaches will be safe to enjoy. Likewise, the peach pit in whole peaches won't leach any dangerous compounds into the brine and can be left in if desired, per the National Center for Home Food Preservation.

Remove the pit before serving, not for consumption.

Candied Jalapeños

Makes approximately 5 to 6 half-pint jars

Have you ever found yourself with a recipe so irresistible that it defies your own taste preferences? For me, that's precisely what Candied Jalapeños represent. While I'm not typically a huge fan of jalapeños, this recipe is an exception. They strike a balance of spiciness and sweetness that hits all the right notes.

3 pounds (1.4 kg) jalapeños

2 cups (472 ml) apple cider vinegar

6 cups (1.2 kg) granulated sugar

½ teaspoon turmeric

1 teaspoon garlic powder

1 teaspoon red pepper flakes

SERVING SUGGESTIONS

* Spread over cream cheese and pair with crackers.

* Give your hamburgers and hot dogs a sweet and spicy kick.

* Incorporate into salsas.

* Add to casseroles for an unexpected burst of flavor.

* Enjoy with warm, fluffy cornbread for an enticing contrast of textures.

* Stir into chili to lend an extra dimension of flavor.

* Use as a topping for deviled eggs.

* Drizzle over ice cream to balance the heat with a sweet, cool finish.

1. Using gloved hands, slice washed jalapeños into ½-inch (1.25-cm) rings. No need to remove seeds.

2. In a pot, bring all the ingredients except for the jalapeños to a boil. This will be your brine.

3. Once boiling, let brine cook for 7 minutes, then reduce the heat to a simmer.

4. Meanwhile, place canning jars in a canning pot filled with water. Bring to a simmer (180°F/82°C) to heat the jars while brine is heating.

5. Add the sliced jalapeños to the simmering mixture, stir to coat, and cook for an additional 4 minutes.

CANNING (HOT PACK)

1. Remove the hot jars from the canning pot using a jar lifter.

2. Place a canning funnel on top and, using a slotted spoon, carefully remove the jalapeños from the mixture and place them into half-pint or pint jars, leaving ½-inch (1.25-cm) headspace.

3. Return the remaining brine to a vigorous boil and continue boiling for an additional 6 minutes.

4. Remove the brine from the heat and carefully ladle it over the jalapeños in the jars, leaving ½-inch (1.25-cm) headspace.

5. Use a bubble remover tool to remove air bubbles and adjust headspace if necessary.

6. Wipe the jar rim with a clean, damp towel or a vinegar-dampened towel to remove any residue.

7. Place the lid on top of the jar and secure with a band, screwing it on until finger light.

8. Place the filled jars back into the canning pot.

9. Ensure the jars are covered with at least 1 inch (2.5 cm) of water. Bring the water to a boil and, once boiling, start the timer for 15 minutes for half pints or pints. Adjust processing time for altitude.

NOTE: This recipe will have extra brine, but don't throw it away! You can save the brine for other dishes. To do this, place the brine by itself in a jar and water-bath-can alongside your candied jalapeños for 15 minutes. Use the same canning process for the brine as you did for the candied jalapeños.

See chapter 7 for spicy peanut brittle, another use for the brine.

HOME-CANNED FOODS: IS THAT NORMAL?

It's normal for foods like jalapeños to shrink and float to the top of the jar during the canning processing. The peppers will soak up the brine and relax in the jars over time. The contents may appear to be half jalapeños and half brine, but this will change: the longer the jars sit on the shelf, the more liquid will be absorbed by the peppers (which means they'll also become sweeter). Wait 4 to 6 weeks before cracking open a jar.

Southern Chow-Chow

Makes approximately 6 to 8 pints (see note)

This recipe comes from my Southern grandmother's recipe box. It's a staple in Southern cuisine, known for its zesty blend of cabbage, peppers, and spices. A versatile condiment, it adds a burst of flavor to everything from hot dogs and sandwiches to beans and collard greens.

1 head of cabbage, finely chopped, approximately 8 cups

4 cups (720 g) cored and chopped green tomatoes

4 cups (720 g) cored and chopped ripe red tomatoes

8 cups (1.28 kg) finely chopped onions

3 green bell peppers, deseeded and chopped

3 red bell peppers, deseeded and chopped

1 head cauliflower, finely chopped

6 tablespoons (108 g) sea salt

1 pound (455 g) dark brown sugar

1 tablespoon ground mustard

1 tablespoon celery seeds

1 tablespoon turmeric

½ tablespoon curry powder

1½ tablespoon black pepper

4 cups (960 ml) white vinegar

NOTE: *The amount of jars you need will vary greatly depending on the size of vegetables, so have extra jars on hand.*

1. In a non-reactive bowl, like glass or stainless steel, mix all vegetables.

2. Add salt and toss to coat vegetables.

3. Cover bowl and refrigerate overnight. Salt will pull the water from the vegetables.

4. The next day, drain salt water from vegetables. Rinse vegetables with water and drain. Rinse and drain a second time. This removes the salt.

5. In a large stockpot, mix remaining ingredients. Add vegetables and simmer for 20 minutes.

6. While chow-chow is heating, prepare your canning equipment.

7. Place canning jars in a canning pot filled with water. Bring to a simmer (180°F/82°C) to heat the jars while making the brine.

CANNING (HOT PACK)

1. Remove a hot jar from the canning pot using a jar lifter.

2. Place a canning funnel on top and ladle hot chow-chow into the jar, leaving ½-inch (1.25-cm) headspace.

3. Use a bubble remover tool to remove air bubbles and adjust headspace if necessary.

4. Wipe the jar rim with a clean, damp towel or a vinegar-dampened towel to remove any residue.

5. Place the lid on top of the jar and secure with a band, screwing it on until finger light.

6. Place the filled jar back into the canning pot using a canning rack and repeat steps 1 to 6 until all jars are filled and in the canner.

7. Ensure the jars are covered with at least 1 inch (2.5 cm) of water. Bring the water to a boil and, once boiling, start the timer: 10 minutes for pints. Adjust processing time for altitude as needed.

Piccalilli: Sharp or Sweet

Makes 6 to 8 pints

Piccalilli is a British relish featuring a delightful medley of vegetables. The choice of ingredients will vary according to the region, so customize the recipe according to availability and your own taste. Two common variants are zesty "sharp heat" or soothing "sweet mild" piccalilli, so you can tailor your jars to the profile you like.

Use piccalilli to add a punch to sandwiches or as a side for hearty British favorites like ploughman's lunches and cheese boards. Many recipes use it as their secret ingredient, and it's the perfect partner for meats, cheeses, and savory dishes.

1¼ pounds (570 g) cucumbers, peeled and chopped

1¼ pounds (570 g) green beans, snapped into 2-inch (5-cm) pieces

1¼ pounds (570 g) cauliflower florets, chopped

1¼ pounds (570 g) green tomatoes, cored and chopped

1 pound (455 g) onion, chopped

½ to 1 cup (150 to 300 g) salt

CHOOSE YOUR SPICES
Sharp Heat

1 tablespoon (6.8 g) turmeric

3 tablespoons (27 g) ground mustard

3 tablespoons (17 g) ground ginger

1½ tablespoons (13.5 g) clear jel

3½ cups plus ½ cup (826 ml plus 118 ml) white vinegar

1 cup (200 g) granulated sugar

1. In a deep bowl, layer chopped vegetables and sprinkle liberally with salt.

2. Repeat until all vegetables are layered and salted.

3. Cover and let sit unrefrigerated 8 to 10 hours or overnight.

4. Drain vegetables and rinse in cold water, removing all salt.

5. Select sharp heat or sweet mild spices from the ingredients list and add to a large stockpot.

6. In a small bowl, add clear jel to ½ cup (118 ml) vinegar and stir until you have a smooth slurry. Set aside.

7. Place canning jars in a canning pot filled with water and bring it to a simmer (180°F/82°C) to heat the jars. Have extra jars available as the yield depends heavily on the cut of the vegetables.

8. Add remaining vinegar and sugar to the spices. Over medium heat, bring to a simmer, stirring occasionally until all sugar is dissolved.

9. Add all vegetables to the stockpot and turn heat to high. Bring the stockpot to a boil for 5 to 6 minutes until vegetables start to soften but are not yet mushy.

10. Add clear jel slurry and return to boil for 2 minutes.

Sweet Mild

1 tablespoon (6.8 g) turmeric

1 tablespoon (9 g) ground mustard

3 tablespoons (17 g) ground ginger

5½ cups plus ½ cup (1.3 L plus 118 ml) white vinegar

3 tablespoons (27 g) clear jel

1½ cups (300 g) granulated sugar

CANNING (HOT PACK)

1. Remove a hot jar from the canning pot using a jar lifter.

2. Place a canning funnel on top and ladle hot piccalilli into the jar, leaving ½-inch (1.25-cm) headspace.

3. Use a bubble remover tool to remove air bubbles and add vinegar to adjust headspace if necessary.

4. Wipe the jar rim with a clean, damp towel or a vinegar-dampened towel to remove any residue.

5. Place the lid on top of the jar and secure with a band, screwing it on until finger light.

6. Place the filled jar back into the canning pot using a canning rack and repeat until all jars are filled and in the canner.

7. Ensure the jars are covered with at least 1 inch (2.5 cm) of water. Bring the water to a boil and, once boiling, start the timer: 5 minutes for pints or half pints. Adjust processing time for altitude.

Zingy Zucchini Relish

Makes about 4 pints. This recipe can be doubled or tripled.

By the beginning of fall I have so many zucchinis I can't even give them away. I even leave them on other people's doorsteps, making me the tooth fairy of zucchinis and Santa Claus of squash.

Over the years I've come up with a lot of creative ways to preserve this prolific crop (to the relief of my neighbors). This is one of my go-to recipes to add a little zing to our meals.

---

10 cups (1.24 kg) green or yellow zucchini/squash, peeled and chopped

3 jalapeño peppers, seeded

4 cups (640 g) chopped sweet onions

2 red bell peppers, seeded and chopped

4 tablespoons (72 g) salt

6 cups (1.4 L) apple cider vinegar

3½ cups (700 g) granulated sugar

1 teaspoon ground mustard

1 teaspoon nutmeg

1 teaspoon turmeric

1. Place vegetables in a strainer, sprinkle with 1 tablespoon of salt, and toss to evenly coat. Leave strainer over sink or bowl for 30 minutes for vegetables to release some of their water content.

2. Prepare the relish brine by adding remaining ingredients to a large stockpot and bringing to a boil. Stir often until sugar is fully dissolved.

3. Add vegetables to the brine and return to a boil for 20 minutes.

4. Place canning jars in a canning pot filled with water. Bring to a simmer (180°F/82°C) to heat the jars while making the brine.

CANNING (HOT PACK)

1. Remove a hot jar from the canning pot using a jar lifter.

2. Place a canning funnel on top and ladle hot relish into the jar, leaving ½-inch (1.25-cm) headspace.

3. Use a bubble remover tool to remove air bubbles and adjust headspace if necessary.

4. Wipe the jar rim with a clean, damp towel or a vinegar-dampened towel to remove any residue.

5. Place the lid on top of the jar and secure with a band, screwing it on until finger light.

6. Place the filled jar back into the canning pot using a canning rack and repeat steps 1 through 6 until all jars are filled and in the canner.

7. Ensure the jars are covered with at least 1 inch (2.5 cm) of water. Bring the water to a boil and, once boiling, start timer: 10 minutes for half pints or pints. Adjust processing time for altitude.

Sweet Peach Mango Salsa

Makes approximately 8 to 12 half-pint jars or 4 to 6 pint jars

This sweet peach mango salsa is one of my personal favorites: the fresh fruits add a natural sweetness to balance the heat from the jalapeños or habaneros. The addition of zesty orange bell peppers, red onions, and a burst of fresh lime makes this salsa a flavor explosion.

Serve this salsa as a topping for grilled chicken or fish, a flavorful dip for tortilla chips, or a unique twist on tacos.

Note that the total volume of ingredients, without accounting for any reduction during cooking, is around 12 cups, which is the equivalent of 6 pints. The amount of product with the reduction during cooking makes jar estimation difficult. That means you should have extra jars on hand, just in case.

---

4 firm fresh peaches, peeled (if desired) and diced; approximately 6 cups (1 kg)

3 firm ripe fresh mangoes, peeled and diced; approximately 2 cups (350 g)

4 fresh jalapeños or 1 habanero, deseeded and diced

2 orange bell peppers, deseeded and diced, approximately 1½ cups (225 g)

1 red onion, diced; approximately 1½ cups (240 g) diced fine

2 tablespoons (20 g) minced garlic

1 fresh lime, juice and zest

1½ cups (354 ml) white vinegar

1 cup (200 g) granulated sugar

½ teaspoon salt

1. In a large bowl, add peaches, mangoes, jalapeños or habanero, bell peppers, onion, and garlic. Stir and set aside.

2. Place canning jars in a canning pot filled with water. Bring to a simmer (180°F/82°C) to heat the jars.

3. In a large stockpot, bring lime juice and zest, vinegar, sugar, and salt to a simmer until sugar is dissolved and ingredients are well mixed.

4. Add produce to vinegar brine and bring to a boil for 1 minute.

CANNING (HOT PACK)

1. Remove a hot jar from the canning pot using a jar lifter.

2. Place a canning funnel on top of jar and ladle hot salsa into hot jar, leaving ½-inch (1.25-cm) headspace.

3. Debubble the jar, leaving ½-inch (1.25-cm) headspace. Add vinegar to jar if needed to achieve the correct headspace.

4. Wipe the jar rim with a clean, damp towel or a vinegar-dampened towel to remove any residue.

5. Place the lid on top of the jar and secure with a band, screwing it on until finger light.

6. Place the filled jar back into the canner and repeat canning steps until all jars are filled and in the canner.

7. Ensure the jars are covered with at least 1 inch (2.5 cm) of water.

8. Bring the water to a boil and, once boiling, start the timer for 15 minutes for half pints or pints. Adjust processing time for altitude.

Cowboy Salsa

*Makes approximately
6 to 8 pints or
3 to 4 quarts*

Also known as black bean and corn salsa, this take on Tex-Mex relish is a hearty recipe you can tailor to your preferences. Try adding more jalapeños for an extra kick, using presoaked dried beans instead for a rustic touch, or even taking it up a notch with roasted corn on the cob to import a deeper flavor profile.

Use this salsa as a vegetarian taco filler, spoon it over loaded nachos, use a jar in your favorite chili, or, my favorite, scoop it up in a tortilla chip.

8 cups (1.4 kg) tomatoes, chopped

2 cups (320 g) chopped red onion

4 to 5 jalapeños, chopped

1 cup (150 g) green bell pepper, chopped

8 garlic cloves, minced

1 bunch fresh cilantro, chopped

1 (15-ounce [439 g] can) black beans, drained and rinsed

2 cups (450 g) whole kernel corn

1 (15-ounce [425 g] can) tomato sauce

1 (12-ounce [340 g] can) tomato paste

¾ cup (175 ml) apple cider vinegar

½ cup (120 ml) lime juice

1 teaspoon cumin

1 tablespoon (18 g) salt (optional)

½ teaspoon black pepper

1. Place tomatoes, onion, jalapeños, bell pepper, garlic, and cilantro in a large stockpot.

2. Place black beans and corn into the stockpot.

3. Add remaining ingredients to the stockpot and stir well.

4. Bring the stockpot to a boil over medium heat and simmer for 30 minutes, stirring often to keep from scorching.

5. Place canning jars in a canning pot filled with water. Bring to a simmer (180°F/82°C) to heat the jars.

CANNING (HOT PACK)

1. Remove a hot jar from the canning pot using a jar lifter.

2. Place a canning funnel on top and ladle hot salsa into the jar, leaving ½-inch (1.25-cm) headspace.

3. Use a bubble remover tool to remove air bubbles and adjust headspace if necessary.

4. Wipe the jar rim with a clean, damp towel or a vinegar-dampened towel to remove any residue.

5. Place the lid on top of the jar and secure with a band, screwing it on until finger light.

6. Place the filled jar back into the canning pot using a canning rack and repeat until all jars are filled and in the canner.

7. Ensure the jars are covered with at least 1 inch (2.5 cm) of water. Bring the water to a boil and, once boiling, start timer: for pints, 30 minutes; for quarts, 35 minutes. Adjust processing time for altitude.

Jalapeño Tomatoes: Mock RO*TEL

Makes approximately 8 to 10 pints

At my house we can't get enough of "Mock RO*TEL" jalapeño tomatoes. Turns out we go through over sixty jars a year, so the odds are good you'll find this salsa on our table most nights.

It's a delightful twist on the classic, store-bought version. I prefer my own version, since it offers the vibrant taste of freshly harvested tomatoes, the perfect balance of spicy jalapeños, and a touch of sweetness to create a perfect balance of flavors.

You can do so much with Mock RO*TEL, from adding a jar to a chili for a fiery kick to elevating a simple cheese dip into a crowd-pleasing sensation. It also makes a delicious base for salsa, a zesty topping for nachos, or a standout ingredient in tacos.

This recipe can be doubled, tripled, quadrupled. When I have more tomatoes than I know what to do with in the summer, I large-batch-can this recipe to ensure we have a year-round supply.

---

12 to 13 pounds (5.5 to 5.9 kg) tomatoes, cored and chopped

8 jalapeños, deseeded and chopped (for extremely spicy do not remove seeds)

2 large bell peppers, chopped

1 large onion, diced

¾ cup (175 ml) apple cider vinegar

¼ cup (50 g) granulated sugar

1½ tablespoons (27 g) salt

8 to 10 tablespoons (120 to 150 ml) lemon juice (1 tablespoon [15 ml] per jar)

1. Add all the vegetables to a large stockpot.

2. Add vinegar, sugar, and salt to the stockpot and bring to a boil, stirring occasionally.

3. Reduce heat and simmer for 45 minutes uncovered.

4. Place canning jars in a canning pot filled with water. Bring to a simmer (180°F/82°C) to heat the jars.

CANNING (HOT PACK)

1. Remove a hot jar from the canning pot using a jar lifter.

2. Add 1 tablespoon of lemon juice to each pint jar.

3. Place a canning funnel on top and ladle hot jalapeño tomatoes into the jar, leaving 1/2-inch (1.25-cm) headspace.

4. Use a bubble remover tool to remove air bubbles and adjust headspace if necessary.

5. Wipe the jar rim with a clean, damp towel or a vinegar-dampened towel to remove any residue.

6. Place the lid on top of the jar and secure with a band, screwing it on until finger light.

7. Place the filled jar back into the canning pot using a canning rack and repeat until all jars are filled and in the canner.

8. Ensure the jars are covered with at least 1 inch (2.5 cm) of water. Bring the water to a boil and, once boiling, start the timer for 15 minutes for pints. Adjust processing time for altitude.

GARDENING WITH A PURPOSE

As you plan your garden, consider dedicating part of it for a specific purpose. You might set aside a section for growing ingredients to go into RO*TEL or other salsas. Planting by ingredient for recipes will maximize your growing space and brings into focus the kinds of canned product you'll add to your cantry.

Here are some reasons gardening with a purpose makes sense.

* Recipe-centered. Tailor your garden to match your favorite recipes, so you grow precisely what you need.

* Efficiency. When you plant by intention, you minimize waste and maximize your harvest. No more wondering about what to do with excess produce.

* Canning confidence. With a garden dedicated to your canning recipes, you'll know you have the right ingredients on hand for preserving your homemade delicacies.

* Space optimization. Even if you have limited growing space, a single RO*TEL or salsa garden bed can yield essential ingredients for your cantry.

Suggested Vegetables for Your Salsa Garden Bed

* Tomatoes
* Jalapeños
* Bell peppers
* Onions
* Cilantro
* Garlic
* Cayenne peppers

Chunky Tomato Salsa

Makes about 6 pints or 3 quarts

Combine ripe tomatoes, crisp bell peppers, zesty onions, and a burst of cilantro for this simple yet mouthwatering salsa.

10 cups (about 4½ pounds/1.8 kg) peeled, chopped, cored tomatoes

5 cups (750 g) chopped green bell peppers

5 cups (800 g) chopped onions

1 cup (135 g) deseeded and chopped jalapeños

3 cloves garlic, finely chopped

4 tablespoons (16 g) fresh cilantro, finely chopped

1 tablespoon (18 g) salt

1¼ cups (296 ml) apple cider vinegar

NOTE: You'll need three pots for this recipe: 1 medium to large pot for boiling tomatoes to remove their skins (can be a smaller pot if worked in batches); 1 medium to large pot for boiling the salsa; and 1 large water bath canning pot.

1. Boil water in a pot.

2. Cut a small *X* on the bottom of each tomato. Add tomatoes in batches to boiling water and boil for 3 minutes. Remove tomatoes and add to a bowl of cold water to cool. Once cooled, peel, chop, and core tomatoes.

3. Add all veggies and remaining ingredients to a large stockpot and mix well.

4. Bring salsa ingredients to boil, reduce stove heat, and simmer at a low boil for 10 minutes.

5. While salsa is heating, prepare your canning equipment.

6. Place canning jars in a canning pot filled with water. Bring to a simmer (180°F/82°C) to heat the jars while making the salsa.

CANNING (HOT PACK)

1. Remove a hot jar from the canning pot using a jar lifter.

2. Place a canning funnel on top and ladle hot salsa into the jar, leaving ½-inch (1.25-cm) headspace.

3. Use a bubble remover tool to remove air bubbles and adjust headspace if necessary.

4. Wipe the jar rim with a clean, damp towel or a vinegar-dampened towel to remove any residue.

5. Place the lid on top of the jar and secure with a band, screwing it on until finger light.

6. Place the filled jar back into the canning pot using a canning rack and repeat steps 1 to 6 until all jars are filled and in the canner.

7. Ensure the jars are covered with at least 1 inch (2.5 cm) of water. Bring the water to a boil and, once boiling, start timer: for pints, 15 minutes; for quarts, 20 minutes. Adjust processing time for altitude.

Watermelon Lemonade Concentrate

Makes 2 to 3 quarts or 6 to 8 pints of concentrate

Want to capture the purest flavors of sun-ripened watermelons and zesty lemons and pour it right into your glass on a hot summer day? This is the recipe for you.

Making this concentrate is one way to make the most of a bumper crop. Dilute the preserved concentrate with an equal amount of water (or more if you prefer a milder flavor). It's great as slushies or frozen as popsicles, or take it for a spin in your favorite adult beverage.

---

1 medium-sized watermelon

4 cups (944 ml) lemon juice, about 12 to 16 large lemons

6 cups (1.2 kg) granulated sugar

The number of watermelons needed to make 6 cups (1.4 L) of watermelon purée will depend on their size and juiciness, but, in general, you'll be able to get by with one medium-sized watermelon. If your watermelons are smaller or less juicy, you may need more than one to reach the desired amount. It's always a good idea to have a little extra on hand, just in case.

1. Prepare water bath canning equipment. Wash canning jars, lids, and bands. Place the jars in a large pot of simmering water to keep them hot until you're ready to fill them.

2. Wash and cut the watermelon into chunks, removing rinds and any seeds if necessary. Place the watermelon chunks in a blender and purée until smooth. You should have approximately 6 cups (1.4 L) of watermelon purée.

3. In a large pot, combine the watermelon purée, fresh lemon juice, and sugar. Stir well to thoroughly combine all the ingredients. Heat mixture over medium heat until the sugar is completely dissolved and the mixture is well combined. Do not bring to a boil; you only need to dissolve the sugar.

CANNING (HOT PACK)

1. Remove a hot jar from the canning pot using a jar lifter.

2. Place a canning funnel on top and ladle liquid into the jar, leaving ¼-inch (6 mm) headspace.

3. Wipe the jar rim with a clean, damp towel or a vinegar-dampened towel to remove any residue.

4. Place the lid on top of the jar and secure with a band, screwing it on until finger light.

5. Place the filled jar back into the canning pot using a canning rack and repeat canning steps until all jars are filled and in the canner.

6. Ensure the jars are covered with at least 1 inch (2.5 cm) of water. Bring the water to a boil and, once boiling, start the timer: 15 minutes, for pints or quarts. Adjust processing time for altitude.

NO-WASTE WATERMELON

In the pursuit of reducing kitchen waste, we look to see if every part of an ingredient can be utilized for culinary creativity. When it comes to preserving watermelon, not only is it a flavorful endeavor, but it's also an eco-conscious one. Here's how you can fully embrace the "no waste" philosophy with this recipe.

* Shake it up. After canning watermelon, it's perfectly normal for the purée and lemon juice to separate as the jars cool and sit on your pantry shelf. If this happens, give the jar a gentle shake and the contents will mix together again.

* Save those rinds. Collecting the watermelon's juicy red flesh is just the beginning: Watermelon rinds are often discarded, but they can be transformed into treats. See chapter 7 for ways to turn them into candied watermelon.

Granny's Tomato Juice

Makes approximately 7 quarts

Granny's homemade tomato juice recipe has been passed down through generations and will transport you to a simpler time. Savor this juice in the morning or use it as the base for a special dish you whip up. It'll carry the warmth and comfort of my Granny's kitchen, wherever you enjoy it.

It may look like the final salt content in the end product is high, but it's actually relatively moderate. In fact, each jar of this recipe, which amounts to 4 cups (944 ml), contains roughly 1 teaspoon of salt. This equates to just ¼ teaspoon per cup, a comparable level to what you'd find in commercial tomato juice.

The role of salt in this recipe is primarily for enhancing flavor, and it can be entirely omitted without compromising the safety of the final product. For those seeking a low-sodium option, you can substitute the salts with powdered celery, onion, or garlic.

Approximately 23 pounds (10.5 kg) fresh tomatoes, cored

2 teaspoons (26 g) salt (optional)

1 tablespoon (7.5 g) celery salt or powder

1 teaspoon onion salt or powder

1 teaspoon garlic salt or powder

¾ cup plus 2 tablespoons (210 ml) lemon juice (equates to 2 tablespoons [30 ml] per quart jar)

1. Working in batches, cut 5 to 6 tomatoes at a time into quarters and place in a large bowl.

2. Using a potato masher, mash the tomatoes to quick release the juices.

3. In a large stockpot, add mashed tomatoes. Continue quartering the remaining tomatoes, adding them to the stockpot.

4. Bring mashed and quartered tomatoes to a simmer over medium heat, stirring often. Cook until tomatoes are soft and juice is released, approximately 10 minutes.

5. Place cooked tomatoes in a Foley mill and process to remove skins and seeds. Work in batches until all the tomatoes have been run through the mill, reserving the juice.

6. If you like a thicker tomato juice, run the tomato pulp through the food mill a second time until all juices have been separated away from the pulp.

7. Place canning jars in a canning pot filled with water and bring it to a simmer (180°F/82°C) to heat the jars.

8. Return tomato juice to the large stockpot. Add salt spices or powders to juice. Return to simmer for 5 minutes, stirring well.

CANNING (HOT PACK)

1. Remove hot jars from the canning pot using a jar lifter.

2. Place a canning funnel on top of a jar.

3. Add 2 tablespoons (30 ml) lemon juice to the bottom of each quart jar.

4. Ladle hot tomato juice into hot jars, leaving ½-inch (1.25-cm) headspace.

5. Wipe the jar rim with a clean, damp towel or vinegar-dampened towel to remove any residue.

6. Place lid on top of the jar and secure with a band, screwing it on until finger light.

7. Place the filled jars back into the canning pot. Ensure the jars are covered with at least 1 inch (2.5 cm) of water.

8. Bring the water to a boil and, once boiling, start the timer for 40 minutes for quarts. Adjust processing time for altitude as needed.

NOTE: Canned tomato juice will separate after processing, with the red tomato contents on top and water on the bottom. Shake jar before opening to mix the contents back together.

UPCYCLING TOMATO PULP

When making homemade tomato-based dishes, you'll often find yourself with leftover tomato pulp. Instead of tossing the pulp, consider repurposing it to create your own version of Lawry's seasoning. You'll reduce food waste while adding to your spice options. Find the recipe on page 265.

Triple-Berry Lemonade Concentrate

Makes approximately 6 to 7 pint jars of concentrate

Triple-berry lemonade combines berry juice with a zap of freshly squeezed lemon juice. Try different berry combinations: blackberries, mulberries, and lingonberries are all great for this. Every pint jar of concentrate yields a half gallon of lemonade. If you're looking for low-sugar options, add less sugar or sugar substitutes to your desired level of sweetness. You can also turn this into vibrant fruit purée popsicles or, for mature audiences, you can add a splash to your favorite adult beverage.

6 cups (830 g) mixed berries, for example:

* 2 cups (290 g) blueberries

* 2 cups (250 g) raspberries

* 2 cups (290 g) strawberries

4 cups (944 ml) lemon juice, about 12 to 16 large lemons

3 cups (600 g) granulated sugar or sugar substitutes, to taste

This is a concentrated drink. When you're ready to use what you've preserved, pour one jar into a large pitcher and add three equal jars of water, ginger ale, tonic water, or your chosen liquid to dilute.

1. Place canning jars in a canning pot filled with water. Bring to a simmer (180°F/82°C) to heat the jars.

2. Wash the fruit and remove any stems or hulls.

3. Working in batches, purée blueberries, raspberries, and strawberries in a blender or food processor until smooth.

4. If you do not want any seeds in your juice, press pulp through a fine-mesh sieve (optional).

5. Place puréed fruits into a large stockpot.

6. Add lemon juice and sugar to fruit purée, stirring on low until sugar is dissolved.

7. Remove from heat and skim off foam.

CANNING (HOT PACK)

1. Remove hot jars from the canning pot using a jar lifter.

2. Place a canning funnel on top of a jar and ladle hot juice into hot jars, leaving ¼-inch (6 mm) headspace.

3. Wipe the jar rim with a clean, damp towel or vinegar-dampened towel to remove any residue.

4. Place lid on top of the jar and secure with a band, screwing it on until finger light.

5. Place the filled jars back into the canning pot. Ensure the jars are covered with at least 1 inch (2.5 cm) of water.

6. Bring the water to a boil and, once boiling, start the timer: 15 minutes for pints. Adjust processing time for altitude.

Sweet Tea Concentrate

Makes approximately 6 to 8 pints

Maybe it's because most of my family comes from the South, but sweet tea is a must in our homes. Having canned tea concentrate on hand means a refreshing glass of tea is yours, anytime, anywhere.

10 cups (2.4 L) water

50 tea bags, single-serve size

3 tablespoons (45 ml) lemon juice

6 to 8 cups (1.2 to 1.6 kg) granulated sugar or 4 cups (1.4 kg) honey, to taste

1. Place canning jars in a canning pot filled with water. Bring to a simmer (180°F/82°C) to heat the jars.

2. In a second large pot, boil the water. Add the tea bags and steep for 5 minutes.

3. Remove the tea bags and add lemon juice and sugar or honey.

4. Return to a boil for 1 minute, stirring until sugar is dissolved.

CANNING (HOT PACK)

1. Remove a hot jar from the canning pot using a jar lifter.

2. Place a canning funnel on top of jar and ladle hot tea concentrate into hot jar, leaving 1/8-inch (3 mm) headspace.

3. Wipe the jar rim with a clean, damp towel or a vinegar-dampened towel to remove any residue.

4. Place the lid on top of the jar and secure with a band, screwing it on until finger light.

5. Place the filled jar back into the canner and repeat canning steps until all jars are filled and in the canner.

6. Ensure the jars are covered with at least 1 inch (2.5 cm) of water.

7. Bring the water to a boil and, once boiling, start the timer for 10 minutes for pints. Adjust processing time for altitude.

NOTE: To use tea concentrate, pour 1 pint of tea concentrate into a gallon pitcher or jug and fill the rest of the pitcher with water. Chill and enjoy!

Cranberry Juice

Making your own cranberry juice is simple and requires no special equipment. The flavor of homemade cranberry juice is superior to its store-bought counterpart. I have posted this beginner-friendly recipe on social media tutorial videos with over 10 million views.

PER QUART JAR

Water to fill each jar (approximately 3 cups [708 ml])

1¾ cups (175 g) cranberries

¼ cup (50 g) sugar (You can also use less, none, sugar substitutes, or honey.)

CANNING (HOT PACK)

1. Place quart-sized canning jars in a large stockpot of boiling water. Keep them in hot water until ready to use.

2. In a separate pot, bring water to a boil. You'll need approximately 3 cups [708 ml] of boiling water per quart jar. Using an electric kettle can speed up this process.

3. Carefully remove the jars from the hot water and place them on a clean, heatproof surface.

4. Into each quart jar, add the cranberries and sugar. You can adjust the sugar amount to your taste.

5. Pour boiling water into each jar, leaving 1 inch (2.5 cm) of headspace.

6. Wipe the jar rim with a clean, damp towel or a vinegar-dampened towel to remove any residue.

7. Place the lid on top of the jar and secure with a band, screwing it on until finger light.

8. Place the filled jar back into the canning pot using a canning rack and repeat canning steps until all jars are filled and in the canner.

9. Ensure the jars are covered with at least 1 inch (2.5 cm) of water. Bring the water to a boil and, once boiling, start the timer: 25 minutes for quarts. Adjust processing time for altitude.

NO CRANBERRIES LEFT BEHIND!

* Patience rewarded. Allow your homemade cranberry juice to rest and meld its flavors for 4 to 6 weeks (yes, patience is a virtue, but the payoff is worth it!). This is an infused juice, so it's normal for the cranberries to float to the top of the jar while the sugars settle at the bottom.

* A little shake before sipping. Just before opening, give the jar a gentle shake to mix up the juice.

* Don't throw away the cranberries. When you strain off the juice to drink, remember that the used berries have more to offer. They make fantastic additions to baked goods like muffins, cookies, or pancakes. Or consider dehydrating them to create your own cran-raisins for sprinkling on granola or cereals, or simply enjoying as a wholesome snack.

Dandelion Jelly

Makes approximately 4 to 5 half-pint jars

Dandelion jelly is sometimes called "poor man's honey." That sells this preserve short: golden-hued, made from humble dandelion petals, this jelly captures the vibrant spirit of the outdoors and transforms it into a delightful spread that pairs beautifully with toast or tea biscuits, or as a sweet glaze for desserts.

What sets dandelion jelly apart from its traditional fruit-based counterparts is its unique flavor profile. While fruit jellies exhibit a familiar sweetness, dandelion jelly has a subtle, floral undertone. The bright and sunny notes of dandelion petals infuse this jelly with a delicate, honey-like taste, perfect for gifting.

This is my youngest son's favorite jelly. In fact, I routinely run out of it before the next crop of dandelions is ready to harvest, which leads to a little whining around my house when the last jar is gone.

---

4 cups (944 ml) water

4 cups (30 g) tightly packed dandelion petals (unsprayed)

½ cup (46 g) powdered pectin

2 tablespoons (30 ml) lemon juice

4 cups (800 g) granulated sugar

4 to 5 drops yellow food coloring (optional)

1 tablespoon (14 g) butter (optional)

STEP 1: MAKE DANDELION TEA

1. Bring the water to a boil.

2. Once the water is boiling, add the dandelion petals, then reduce the heat to low. Allow the petals to steep in the simmering water for 15 minutes.

3. After steeping, strain the petals through a fine-mesh sieve. The liquid you obtain is your dandelion tea. It takes 4 cups (944 ml) to make the jelly.

STEP 2: PREPARE DANDELION JELLY

1. Place canning jars in a canning pot filled with water. Bring to a simmer (180°F/82°C) to heat the jars.

2. In a separate large pot, combine 4 cups (944 ml) dandelion tea, pectin, and lemon juice. Bring this mixture to a boil.

3. Once it's boiling, add the sugar all at once, along with food coloring, if using. For those who prefer a smoother texture, you can add butter at this point to help soothe any foam that forms.

4. Stir the mixture constantly and bring it back to a boil, then allow it to boil hard for 2 minutes.

5. Complete spoon test (see page 49).

6. After the boiling time is complete, remove the pot from the heat and skim off any foam that has formed on the surface.

CANNING (HOT PACK)

1. Remove a hot jar from the canning pot using a jar lifter.

2. Place a canning funnel on top and ladle jelly into the jar, leaving ¼-inch (6-mm) headspace.

3. Wipe the jar rim with a clean, damp towel or a vinegar-dampened towel to remove any residue.

4. Place the lid on top of the jar and secure with a band, screwing it on until finger light.

5. Place the filled jars back into the canning pot using a canning rack. Ensure the jars are covered with at least 1 inch (2.5 cm) of water.

6. Bring the water to a boil and, once boiling, start the timer for 5 minutes for half pints or pints. Adjust processing time for altitude.

POMONA'S UNIVERSAL PECTIN AND FLOWER-PETAL JELLY

Pectin creates a gel with the help of natural fruit acids and sugars. This can limit your options when working with low-acid or low-sugar foods, like flower petals, which often lack the necessary components for gelling.

Pomona's Universal Pectin is my no-fail choice for pectin when making flower-petal jellies. It contains powdered pectin and calcium, essentially creating a two-part pectin system and giving you another option for your preserves. This makes it an ideal solution for creating jellies with unconventional ingredients, such as delicate flower petals. It also helps you control sweetness, texture, and flavor (see chapter 4 for more on pectin).

Lilac Jelly: Capturing the Essence of Spring

Makes 4 to 5 half pints. Recipe cannot be doubled.

Lilac jelly is floral and mildly citrusy, with subtle hints of honey and vanilla. It works well as a breakfast spread or a glaze for pastries and desserts.

Lilac blossoms are evanescent, so don't wait to make this recipe when you see the lilacs blooming in your neighborhood.

---

4 cups (944 ml) water

4 cups (56 g) tightly packed lilac petals (unsprayed)

1 (1.75 oz/49 g) package powdered pectin

¼ cup (60 ml) lemon juice

4 cups (800 g) granulated sugar

1 tablespoon (14 g) butter (optional)

STEP 1: MAKE LILAC TEA

1. Bring the water to a simmer, not quite boiling. Making the lilac tea with boiling water can make the tea bitter. Use just below boiling hot water.

2. Pack the lilac petals into two quart-size jars and pour the simmering water in the jars over the lilacs. Add the jar lids and allow the lilacs to steep overnight on the countertop. The tea liquid will be green or blue at this point.

3. After steeping, strain the petals by pressing them through a fine-mesh sieve. The liquid you obtain is your lilac tea. You will need 4 cups (944 ml) of this tea to make the jelly.

STEP 2: PREPARE LILAC JELLY

1. Place canning jars in a canning pot filled with water. Bring to a simmer (180°F/82°C) to heat the jars.

2. In a separate large pot, combine lilac tea with the pectin and lemon juice. Note that the lemon juice will change the tea from blue to pink. Bring this mixture to a boil.

3. Once boiling, add the sugar all at once. Stir the mixture constantly and bring it back to a boil, then allow it to boil hard for 2 minutes.

4. Complete spoon test (see page 49).

5. For those who prefer a smoother texture, add butter at this point to help soothe any foam that forms.

6. After boiling time, remove the pot from the heat and skim off any foam that has formed on the surface.

CANNING (HOT PACK)

1. Remove a hot jar from the canning pot using a jar lifter.

2. Place a canning funnel on top and ladle jelly into the jar, leaving ¼-inch (6-mm) headspace.

3. Wipe the jar rim with a clean, damp towel or a vinegar-dampened towel to remove any residue.

4. Place the lid on top of the jar and secure with a band, screwing it on until finger light.

5. Place the filled jars back into the canning pot using a canning rack. Ensure the jars are covered with at least 1 inch (2.5 cm) of water.

6. Bring the water to a boil and, once boiling, start the timer for 5 minutes for half pints or pints. Adjust processing time for altitude..

PETAL WISDOM: A LESSON IN PATIENCE

Flower petals offer delicate flavors, but they're notoriously low in pectin. This means that flower-petal jellies can take their own sweet time to set, usually 2 to 4 weeks. The key here is patience. While you may be tempted to sneak a peek at the setting point by tipping the jar, remember that this will disrupt the pectin's binding effect. If the jelly fails to set after 4 weeks, use the contents as syrup or reprocess by adding more pectin and recanning (see chapter 4).

Soda Pop Jelly

Makes about 4 half-pint jars. Recipe cannot be doubled.

I love recipes that make you think, "This is totally strange, but I have to try it!" Soda pop jelly is one of those: it captures the essence of your favorite soft drinks, like root beer, cream soda, or Dr. Pepper, but in spreadable form.

If you're looking for a one-of-a-kind gift for the soda pop lover in your life, soda pop jelly is sure to bring smiles and surprise. Craft a personalized gift basket with jars of different soda flavors, and you've got a thoughtful, homemade gift that's as unique as it is delicious.

4½ cups (1 L) your favorite soft drink

2 tablespoons (30 ml) lemon juice

1 (1.75 oz/49 g) package powdered pectin

1 tablespoon (14 g) butter (optional)

4½ cups (900 g) granulated sugar

This jelly may require up to two weeks to set fully. It's important to be patient during this process and avoid the temptation to tilt the jar to check for its setting point. This will disrupt the pectin's process of binding with the sugar.

1. Place canning jars in a canning pot filled with water. Bring to a simmer (180°F/82°C) to heat the jars.

2. In a medium saucepan, heat soft drink, lemon juice, and powdered pectin. Add butter, if using, to reduce foam.

3. Bring to a boil, whisking until pectin has dissolved, about 1 minute.

4. Add sugar all at once and return to a hard boil for 2 minutes. Stir continuously to keep jelly from boiling over the pot and scorching the pan. *Don't leave the stove during this step.*

CANNING (HOT PACK)

1. Remove a hot jar from the canning pot using a jar lifter.

2. Place a canning funnel on top and ladle jelly into the jar, leaving ¼-inch (6 mm) headspace.

3. Wipe the jar rim with a clean, damp towel or a vinegar-dampened towel to remove any residue.

4. Place the lid on top of the jar and secure with a band, screwing it on until finger light.

5. Place the filled jars back into the canning pot using a canning rack. Ensure the jars are covered with at least 1 inch (2.5 cm) of water.

6. Bring the water to a boil and, once boiling, start the timer for 15 minutes for half pints. Adjust processing time for altitude.

Hint of Mint

Bright and flavorful, hint of mint jelly combines the zingy freshness of lemons with the sweetness of honey and the aromatic essence of mint. This jelly is perfect for spreading on toast, drizzling over yogurt, or serving as a condiment with cheese and crackers.

¾ cup lemon juice, about 5 to 6 lemons

4 teaspoons (8 g) lemon zest

2½ cups (850 g) honey

1 (3-ounce/88-ml) package liquid pectin

4 tablespoons (24 g) fresh chopped mint

1. Place canning jars in a canning pot filled with water. Bring to a simmer (180°F/82°C) to heat the jars.

2. Pour the lemon juice through a wire-mesh strainer to remove any seeds or pulp.

3. In a 6-quart saucepan, combine the lemon zest, lemon juice, and honey, stirring well.

4. Bring the mixture to a rolling boil over high heat, stirring constantly.

5. Quickly stir in the liquid pectin.

6. Return the mixture to a rolling boil, and boil, stirring constantly, for 1 minute.

7. Perform the spoon test. Dip a cold metal spoon into the hot mixture: when the jelly sheets or drips off the spoon slowly rather than in a liquid stream, it's ready. Continue boiling until jelly passes the test.

8. Remove the saucepan from the heat and skim off any foam with a spoon, if necessary.

9. Add the mint to the jelly and stir to combine.

CANNING (HOT PACK)

1. Remove hot jars from the canning pot using a jar lifter.

2. Place a canning funnel on top of a jar.

3. Ladle hot jelly into hot jars, leaving ¼-inch (6 mm) headspace.

4. Wipe the jar rim with a clean, damp towel or vinegar-dampened towel to remove any residue.

5. Place lid on top of the jar and secure with a band, screwing it on until finger light.

6. Place the filled jars back into the canning pot. Ensure the jars are covered with at least 1 inch (2.5 cm) of water.

7. Bring the water to a boil and, once boiling, start the timer for 5 minutes for half pints. Adjust processing time for altitude.

No-Pectin Raspberry Jam

*Makes approximately
6 to 7 half pints or 3 pints.
Do not double or triple.*

This is a great jam recipe for beginners. Jams can be made without commercial pectin (for more on pectin, see pages 50–51), and many traditional recipes use only fruit and sugar to achieve the desired result.

In no-pectin recipes, we rely on fruits' natural pectin to thicken the jam. For raspberries, this is primarily in their seeds. If you don't like seeds in your raspberry jam, consider a pectin-added recipe to achieve the same result.

---

4 cups (500 g) raspberries

3 to 4 cups (600 to 800 g) granulated sugar, to taste

1 tablespoon (15 ml) lemon juice

1 tablespoon (14 g) butter (optional)

1. Place canning jars in a canning pot filled with water and bring it to a simmer (180°F/82°C) to heat the jars.

2. Place the raspberries in a large stockpot over medium heat and bring to a boil. Mash the berries using a potato masher or an immersion blender. Be careful not to overblend; berries should not be liquefied.

3. Cook for 4 minutes at full boil.

4. Add the sugar and lemon juice; stir well.

5. Bring back to a boil, stirring constantly. Add butter, if using, to reduce foam.

6. Continue boiling, stirring constantly for another 12 to 20 minutes. The time needed to cook down jam depends on the fruit's water content. Perform the spoon test to check for gel point (see page 49). Jam should change to a deep red color and be reduced by almost half.

CANNING (HOT PACK)

1. Remove hot jars from the canning pot using a jar lifter.

2. Place a canning funnel on top of a jar.

3. Ladle hot raspberry jam into hot jars, leaving ¼-inch (6 mm) headspace.

4. Wipe the jar rim with a clean, damp towel or vinegar-dampened towel to remove any residue.

5. Place lid on top of the jar and secure with a band, screwing it on until finger light.

6. Place the filled jars back into the canning pot. Ensure the jars are covered with at least 1 inch (2.5 cm) of water.

7. Bring the water to a boil and, once boiling, start the timer for 5 minutes for half pints or pints. Adjust processing time for altitude.

Peach Habanero Jam

Makes approximately 6 half pints. Do not double this recipe.

Pepper jellies and jams are excellent when served on crackers with cream cheese or cracker spreads. The velvety sweetness of ripe, juicy peaches mingling with the fiery intensity of habanero peppers is perfect for pairing with your baked goods. Try this peach habanero jam as an ice cream topping.

4 pounds (1.8 kg) peeled, chopped peaches

¼ cup (34 g) finely chopped habanero peppers

2 tablespoons (30 ml) lemon juice

1 (1.75 oz/49 g) package powdered pectin

5 cups (1 kg) granulated sugar

¼ teaspoon ground cinnamon

¼ teaspoon ground allspice

1 tablespoon (14 g) butter (optional)

PRODUCE PREPARATION

1. Place peaches and habaneros in a large stockpot over medium heat.

2. Mash peaches and peppers with a potato masher or an immersion blender. Consistency should be chunky so be careful not to overblend if using an immersion blender.

MAKING THE JAM

1. Place canning jars in a canning pot filled with water and bring it to a simmer (180°F/82°C) to heat the jars.

2. Over medium heat, add the lemon juice and pectin to the peaches and pepper mixture.

3. Bring the mixture to a full boil, stirring constantly. Jams will burn very quickly, so do not walk away from the pot and be sure to keep stirring to keep the pan from scorching.

4. Add the sugar and spices to the mixture all at once, stirring constantly until sugar is dissolved.

5. Keep the mixture at a boil for 5 minutes.

6. Jam will foam while cooking. To avoid this, you can add the butter at this point, which will help to soothe foaming.

CANNING (HOT PACK)

1. Remove hot jars from the canning pot using a jar lifter.

2. Place a canning funnel on top of a jar.

3. Skim and remove as much foam as you can, then ladle hot jam into hot jars, leaving ¼-inch (6 mm) headspace.

4. Wipe the jar rim with a clean, damp towel or vinegar-dampened towel to remove any residue.

5. Place the lid on top of the jar and secure with a band, screwing it on until finger light.

6. Place the filled jars back into the canning pot. Ensure the jars are covered with at least 1 inch (2.5 cm) of water.

7. Bring the water to a boil and, once boiling, start the timer: 5 minutes for half pints, 10 minutes for pints. Adjust processing time for altitude.

HOW MUCH HEAT: CANNING FOR YOUR TASTE BUDS

If this is your first time making a spicy jam, start with a small batch until you balance your preferred heat level. This jam tends to get sweeter over time, so give the jars 2 to 4 weeks to fully set and sweeten for the best end results. Adjust peppers (less or more) to your desired level of spice. Keep a canning journal to track changes you want to make from one canning season to the next.

Carrot Cake Jam

Makes approximately 8 half pints

This recipe brings all the warm, spiced goodness of carrot cake into a deliciously spreadable form. With the sweet aroma of cinnamon, the comforting presence of shredded carrots, and a touch of vanilla, this jam captures the essence of carrot cake—but you can slather it on toast, pair with cream cheese, or use as a filling for pastries.

1½ cups (165 g) grated carrots

1½ cups (188 g) peeled and chopped apples or pears

1 can (20 oz/567 g) crushed pineapple, undrained

6 tablespoons (90 ml) lemon juice

2 teaspoons (5 g) cinnamon

¼ teaspoon ground cloves

¼ teaspoon ground nutmeg

1 (1.75 oz/49 g) package powdered pectin

5 cups (1 kg) granulated sugar

1½ cups (225 g) brown sugar

1 cup (236 ml) flaked coconut (optional)

1 teaspoon vanilla extract

1. Place canning jars in a canning pot filled with water and bring it to a simmer (180°F/82°C) to heat the jars.

2. To a large stockpot, add carrots, apples or pears, crushed pineapple, lemon juice, and all spices.

3. Bring the mixture to a rolling boil. Reduce heat and simmer for 15 to 20 minutes until fruits are tender. Stir often to avoid scorching.

4. Stir in pectin and return to full boil.

5. Stir in sugars, coconut (if using), and vanilla extract. Return to full boil for 2 minutes, stirring constantly.

CANNING (HOT PACK)

1. Skim any foam off jam (my family eats the foam over toast or ice cream while I'm canning).

2. Remove a hot jar from the canning pot using a jar lifter.

3. Place a canning funnel on top and ladle jam into the jar, leaving ¼-inch (6 mm) headspace.

4. Wipe the jar rim with a clean, damp towel or a vinegar-dampened towel to remove any residue.

5. Place the lid on top of the jar and secure with a band, screwing it on until finger light.

6. Place the filled jar back into the canning pot using a canning rack and repeat canning steps until all jars are filled and in the canner.

7. Ensure the jars are covered with at least 1 inch (2.5 cm) of water.

8. Bring the water to a boil and, once boiling, start the timer for 10 minutes for half pints. Adjust processing time for altitude.

Tangy Tomato Jam

Makes approximately 5 half pints. Cannot be doubled.

Unlike typical sweet jams you might find on your morning toast, this savory tomato jam offers a more savory complexity thanks to combining ripe tomatoes with allspice, cinnamon, and cloves, plus lemon juice.

Spread it on a hearty sandwich, pair it with cheese and crackers for an appetizer, dollop it onto grilled meats, or use it as a glaze for roasted vegetables.

2½ pounds (1.1 kg) tomatoes (meaty tomatoes like Romas or Amish Paste work best)

½ teaspoon ground allspice

½ teaspoon ground cinnamon

¼ teaspoon ground cloves

¼ cup (60 ml) bottled lemon juice concentrate

1 (1.75 oz/49 g) package powdered pectin

4½ cups (900 g) granulated sugar

1. Wash tomatoes, and score an *X* on the bottom of each with a knife. Into boiling water, drop tomatoes in batches for 30 seconds. Remove tomatoes from boiling water and place into a bowl of ice water. The skins should slip off. Remove tomato skins. Save skins for dehydrated tomato powder in chapter 7.

2. Core and chop tomatoes and place them in a large stockpot. Bring tomatoes to a simmer on low, stirring constantly. Cover and simmer for 10 minutes, stirring occasionally.

3. Place canning jars in a canning pot filled with water and bring it to a simmer (180°F/82°C) to heat the jars.

4. Remove tomatoes from stove and measure 3 cups (708 ml) tomatoes into a saucepan.

5. Add spices, lemon juice, and pectin. Mix well.

6. Bring saucepan mixture to a boil over high heat.

7. Stir in sugar all at once and return saucepan to full rolling boil. Boil hard for 3 minutes, stirring constantly to prevent scorching.

8. Skim any foam off the top of the jam with a spoon.

CANNING (HOT PACK)

1. Remove hot jars from the canning pot using a jar lifter.

2. Place a canning funnel on top of a jar.

3. Ladle hot tomato jam into hot jars, leaving ¼-inch (6 mm) headspace.

4. Wipe the jar rim with a clean, damp towel or vinegar-dampened towel to remove any residue.

5. Place lid on top of the jar and secure with a band, screwing it on until finger light.

6. Place the filled jars back into the canning pot. Ensure the jars are covered with at least 1 inch (2.5 cm) of water.

7. Bring the water to a boil and, once boiling, start the timer for 5 minutes for half pints or pints. Adjust processing time for altitude.

Tutti Frutti

Makes approximately 6 to 7 half pints

Tutti frutti is Italian for "all the fruits," and that's what you get when you pop open a jar of this delicious jam.

2 pounds (910 g) pears, peeled, cored, and chopped (approximately 3 cups [375 g])

1 orange, peeled and thinly sliced

¾ cup (120 g) crushed pineapple (drained if using store-bought)

¼ cup (61 g) maraschino cherries, chopped

¼ cup (60 ml) lemon juice

1 (1.75 oz/49 g) package powdered pectin

5 cups (1 kg) granulated sugar

1. Using a food processor or blender, grind the pears, orange slices, and pineapple until you achieve a lump-free consistent texture.

2. Place canning jars in a canning pot filled with water and bring it to a simmer (180°F/82°C) to heat the jars.

3. In a large pot, combine the fruit mixture, maraschino cherries, lemon juice, and pectin. Stir until well combined.

4. Stir constantly over high heat, and bring the mixture to a full boil.

5. Gradually add the sugar, stirring continuously to ensure it dissolves completely. Bring the mixture back to a rolling boil.

6. Boil jam hard for 1 minute, stirring constantly. Remove from heat and skim off any foam.

7. Perform the spoon test (see page 49).

CANNING (HOT PACK)

1. Remove a hot jar from the canning pot using a jar lifter.

2. Place a canning funnel on top and ladle the tutti frutti mixture into the jar, leaving ¼-inch (6 mm) headspace.

3. Wipe the jar rim with a clean, damp towel or a vinegar-dampened towel to remove any residue.

4. Place the lid on top of the jar and secure with a band, screwing it on until finger light.

5. Place the filled jar back into the canning pot using a canning rack and repeat canning steps until all jars are filled and in the canner.

6. Ensure the jars are covered with at least 1 inch (2.5 cm) of water. Bring the water to a boil and, once boiling, start the timer for 5 minutes for half pints or pints. Adjust processing time for altitude.

Monkey Butter

Makes approximately 4 to 6 half pints. Recipe can be doubled or tripled.

Ripe bananas, shredded coconut, crushed pineapple, and lemon juice concentrate combine in this luscious spread that's like a trip to the tropics.

Savor monkey butter on your morning toast, pancakes, or waffles, or use it on desserts. It's also great on yogurt or oatmeal, as a filling for pastries, or drizzled over ice cream.

---

4 bananas

¼ cup (21 g) shredded coconut

1 can (20 oz/567 g) crushed pineapple, undrained

3 tablespoons (45 ml) lemon juice concentrate

3 cups (600 g) granulated sugar

1. Peel bananas and slice into ½-inch (1 cm) coin shapes.

2. Add bananas and remaining ingredients to a large stockpot.

3. Heat ingredients on medium for 10 minutes, stirring constantly to prevent scorching. Monkey butter should be the consistency of a chunky applesauce when finished.

CANNING (HOT PACK)

1. Place canning jars in a canning pot filled with water. Bring to a simmer (180°F/82°C) to heat the jars.

2. Remove a hot jar from the canning pot using a jar lifter.

3. Place a canning funnel on top and ladle hot monkey butter into the jar, leaving ½-inch (1.25-cm) headspace.

4. Use a bubble remover tool to remove air bubbles and adjust headspace if necessary.

5. Wipe the jar rim with a clean, damp towel or vinegar-dampened towel to remove any residue.

6. Place the lid on top of the jar and secure with a band, screwing it on until finger light.

7. Place the filled jars back into the canning pot using a canning rack. Ensure the jars are covered with at least 1 inch (2.5 cm) of water.

8. Bring the water to a boil and, once boiling, start the timer for 15 minutes for half pints. Adjust processing time for altitude.

Peach Mango Butter

Makes about 4 pints or 8 half pints. Recipe can be doubled or tripled.

Fruit butter is a sweet, spreadable fruit preserve made by cooking down ripe fruit to a smooth, velvety consistency. Unlike fruit jams or jellies, fruit butter contains no added pectin and has a creamy purée texture. Fruit butters are known for their intense fruit flavor, obtained from the slow-cooking process that concentrates the fruits' natural sugars and aromas.

If you've bought several flats of peaches, this recipe is an excellent way to convert them into butter you can enjoy for a long time. Be sure to double or triple this recipe if you have more peaches than you know what to do with.

Each jar of peach mango butter contains a blend of peaches alongside the essence of mango, brought together with a hint of citrus. Sweetness is added with sugar, and you have the option to elevate the flavor profile with a dash of cinnamon or cardamom.

---

3 pounds (1.4 kg) peaches, peeled, pitted, and quartered

1 pound (455 g) mango, cut and cored

½ cup (118 ml) water

1 lemon, juiced

3 cups (600 g) granulated sugar

1 teaspoon cinnamon or cardamom (optional)

1. To a large stockpot, add peaches, mango, water, and lemon juice.

2. Heat over medium heat for 10 minutes, or until fruits soften and release juices.

3. With an immersion blended or upright blender, purée fruit.

4. Return fruit purée to stockpot. Add sugar and cinnamon or cardamom (if using) to fruit purée. Return purée to simmer over medium heat until sugar is dissolved, stirring frequently.

5. Transfer peach mango butter to a slow cooker and heat with lid off on low, 8 to 10 hours, until fruit butter is thickened, stirring occasionally. You can also heat the peach butter on the stove for 1 to 2 hours, stirring constantly. The goal in this step is to cook off excess water, thickening the peach butter. The amount of time this takes depends on the water content of the peaches and the cooking method you choose.

6. Place canning jars in a canning pot filled with water and bring it to a simmer (180°F/82°C) to heat the jars.

CANNING (HOT PACK)

1. Remove a hot jar from the canning pot using a jar lifter.

2. Place a canning funnel on top and ladle hot fruit butter into the jar, leaving ¼-inch (6 mm) headspace.

3. Use a bubble remover tool to remove air bubbles and adjust headspace if necessary.

4. Wipe the jar rim with a clean, damp towel or a vinegar-dampened towel to remove any residue.

5. Place the lid on top of the jar and secure with a band, screwing it on until finger light.

6. Place the filled jar back into the canning pot using a canning rack and repeat until all jars are filled and in the canner.

7. Ensure the jars are covered with at least 1 inch (2.5 cm) of water. Bring the water to a boil and, once boiling, start the timer for 10 minutes for pints or half pints. Adjust processing time for altitude.

PEACHY KEEN PEACH SKIN USES

Don't toss those peach skins! They can be repurposed in creative ways. Here are some ways to make the most of these otherwise discarded parts of your peaches.

* **Peach-skin syrup.** Simmer peach skins with sugar and water to make a peach-flavored syrup.

* **Infused water.** Add peach skins to water for a subtle peach infusion.

* **Peach-skin tea.** Steep peach skins in hot water for a mild, fruity tea.

* **Smoothies.** Blend peach skins into fruit smoothies for added flavor and nutrients.

* **Fruit leather.** Make fruit leather by puréeing peach skins with other fruits.

* **Fruit infusions.** Combine peach skins with other fruits for refreshing beverages.

Pflaumenmus (Plum Butter)

Makes 4 to 5 pints or 8 to 10 half pints. Recipe can be doubled or tripled.

Pflaumenmus, or plum butter, is a rich fruit preserve that's great for spreading on toast, using as a pastry filling, or adding as a condiment. In our home we call plum butter "ham jam" because it works wonderfully as a ham glaze.

---

6 pounds (2.7 kg) plums, halved and pitted

4 cups (800 g) granulated sugar

1 teaspoon ground cinnamon

1 teaspoon ground allspice

½ teaspoon ground cloves

½ teaspoon ground anise (optional)

This recipe can be completed on the stove or in a slow cooker. You want to achieve a spreadable, buttery consistency, whichever cooking method you choose. I find the slow cooker to be less messy and labor intensive, so I have included instructions for that method here.

1. Place the plums, sugar, and spices in a slow cooker.

2. Cook on low for 8 to 10 hours, or until plums are soft and have released their juices. Stir periodically.

3. After plums are soft, use an immersion blend or upright blender (working in batches) to purée the plums into a smooth, buttery consistency.

4. Return plum butter to slow cooker and continue heating uncovered on low for 5 to 6 more hours until butter has thickened. Be sure to stir often during this time to keep sugar from burning as the plum purée starts to caramelize.

5. Check the taste, adding more sugar or spices as needed.

6. Place canning jars in a canning pot filled with water and bring it to a simmer (180°F/82°C) to heat the jars.

CANNING (HOT PACK)

1. Remove hot jars from the canning pot using a jar lifter.

2. Place a canning funnel on top of a jar.

3. Ladle hot plum butter into hot jars, leaving ¼-inch (6 mm) headspace.

4. Wipe the jar rim with a clean, damp towel or vinegar-dampened towel to remove any residue.

5. Place lid on top of the jar and secure with a band, screwing it on until finger light.

6. Place the filled jars back into the canning pot. Ensure the jars are covered with at least 1 inch (2.5 cm) of water.

7. Bring the water to a boil and, once boiling, start the timer: 10 minutes for pints or half pints. Adjust processing time for altitude.

Caramel Apple Butter

Makes 5 to 6 pints. Recipe can be doubled or tripled.

In the world of preserving traditions, apple butter holds a special place. For generations, it's been crafted with care in copper pots, simmered slowly, and stirred lovingly. I still remember the importance of adding copper pennies to prevent scorching as we cooked it down. These days, we don't use pennies, and most people don't even keep a traditional copper pot for cooking this recipe. These days, I rely on a slow cooker to cook down the apples. You can still make apple butter on a stove, but you'll need to stir constantly to keep the butter from scorching.

How long the cook-down takes depends on the water content of the apples used. While cooking down the apple butter, the goal is to allow the water to evaporate and the butter to thicken to a silky-smooth fruit butter.

---

8 pounds (3.6 kg) apples, peeled, cored, and quartered

4 cups (944 ml) water

3½ cups (700 g) granulated sugar

4 teaspoons (9 g) cinnamon

1 teaspoon ground cardamom

1. In a large saucepan, combine the apples and water. Cook the apples over medium heat, simmering until they are soft.

2. Purée the mixture in batches, using a food mill or high-speed blender.

3. Return the apple pulp to the saucepan and add the sugar and spices. Keep stirring until the sugar is dissolved.

4. Cook at a gentle boil over medium heat until the apple mixture is thick enough to mound on a spoon, stirring frequently to prevent sticking; this can take up to 2 hours. Alternatively, you can cook down apple butter in a slow cooker on low, 6 to 8 hours, stirring occasionally.

5. Remove from heat.

6. Place canning jars in a canning pot filled with water and bring it to a simmer (180°F/82°C) to heat the jars.

CANNING (HOT PACK)

1. Remove a hot jar from the canning pot using a jar lifter.

2. Place a canning funnel on top and ladle hot apple butter into the jar, leaving ¼-inch (6 mm) headspace.

3. Use a bubble remover tool to remove air bubbles and adjust headspace if necessary.

(continued)

4. Wipe the jar rim with a clean, damp towel or a vinegar-dampened towel to remove any residue.

5. Place the lid on top of the jar and secure with a band, screwing it on until finger light.

6. Place the filled jar back into the canning pot using a canning rack and repeat until all jars are filled and in the canner.

7. Ensure the jars are covered with at least 1 inch (2.5 cm) of water. Bring the water to a boil and, once boiling, start the timer for 15 minutes for pints or half pints. Adjust processing time for altitude.

DON'T TOSS, TRANSFORM

Before you throw away those leftover apple scraps, consider this: You can easily transform them into your very own apple cider vinegar. A little time, patience, and fermentation are all it takes. Check out the recipe on page 273.

Tomato Butter

*Makes approximately
8 to 10 half-pint jars*

Tomato butter balances the rich flavors of ripe tomatoes with a medley of warm spices.
This recipe transforms stewed tomatoes into a luscious spread that's perfect on breakfast toast or as a unique
twist to your culinary creations.

4 quarts (128 oz/3.6 g) stewed
tomatoes

7 cups (1 kg) brown sugar

1 tablespoon (7 g) ground cloves

1 tablespoon (7 g) cinnamon

1 teaspoon allspice

1. Using a blender, carefully blend the stewed tomatoes until you
achieve a smooth pulp.

2. In a large pot, combine the tomato pulp, brown sugar, cloves,
cinnamon, and allspice. Stir the mixture thoroughly to ensure
even distribution of the spices.

3. Place the pot over low heat and cook the mixture slowly until
it thickens. This process may take some time, so patience is
key. The tomato butter is ready when it reaches the desired
thickness: you should be able to coat a spoon with it, causing a
slow drip. On average, this takes about 1 hour or more.

4. Place canning jars in a canning pot filled with water and bring
it to a simmer (180°F/82°C) to heat the jars.

CANNING (HOT PACK)

1. Remove a hot jar from the canning pot using a jar lifter.

2. Place a canning funnel on top and ladle tomato butter into the
jar, leaving ¼-inch (6 mm) headspace.

3. Wipe the jar rim with a clean, damp towel or a vinegar-
dampened towel to remove any residue.

4. Place the lid on top of the jar and secure with a band, screwing
it on until finger light.

5. Place the filled jar back into the canning pot using a canning rack
and repeat canning steps until all jars are filled and in the canner.

6. Ensure the jars are covered with at least 1 inch (2.5 cm) of water.

7. Bring the water to a boil and, once boiling, start the timer for
10 minutes for half pints. Adjust processing time for altitude.

CHAPTER 6

Pressure Canning Recipes

*Elevating Traditions
with New Inspirations*

Early forms of pressure canning were used in the late nineteenth century. Back then, the primary goal was simple: extend the shelf life of perishable foods to ensure sustenance through long, harsh winters. But today, it's not just about preservation; it's also about transformation.

In this chapter, we'll look at some popular pressure canning recipes that I give a new twist. You can embrace the technique's rich heritage and pay homage to generations of home cooks while putting together meals that wow everyone in the present day. I seek to honor their wisdom, their meticulous techniques, and their unwavering dedication to quality. I do not seek to replace those traditions but rather to expand upon them.

Over the years I have drawn inspiration from global cuisines, pairing time-tested canning methods with exciting and diverse flavors. Imagine the robust flavors of a hearty Mexican salsa, the aromatic spices of Indian chutneys, or the mouthwatering tang of Korean beef—all lovingly preserved in your pressure canner.

So embrace your inner culinary explorer and make these recipes your own, adapting them according to your taste preferences and what seasonal produce is available. As you go, you'll do more than preserve the fruits of your labor: You'll capture the essence of your creativity and find new ways to stock your cantry with a treasure trove of flavors.

Unstuffed Cabbage Rolls

Makes about 5 quart jars. Recipe can be doubled or tripled.

Imagine you've rushed home from a long day at the office, and now your family is eagerly awaiting dinner. Instead of feeling despair, you reach for a little jar of culinary magic in your pantry—your homemade Unstuffed Cabbage Rolls, lovingly prepared and preserved for just such an occasion.

Simply reheat the contents of that jar, releasing the tantalizing aroma of simmered cabbage, tender meat (or plant-based substitute), and rich tomato sauce. As the fragrance fills your kitchen, you can take a deep breath, knowing that a satisfying dinner is almost ready.

But here's where the magic truly happens. Instead of the traditional plating of this classic dish, we've taken the convenience up a notch. Grab a ladle and pour that steaming goodness over a bed of perfectly cooked rice. You've transformed what you preserved into a complete, balanced meal that will leave your family craving more.

---

2 pounds (907 g) ground beef, cooked and strained

1 cup (160 g) chopped onions

3 tablespoons (30 g) minced garlic

1 cup (150 g) chopped green bell peppers

1 medium cabbage, cored and chopped

1 cup (130 g) thinly sliced carrots

½ pound (228 g) mushrooms, sliced

4 cups (720 g) chopped tomatoes with juice

2 cups (472 ml) tomato sauce

1 cup (236 ml) water

2 teaspoons (12 g) salt

2 teaspoons (4 g) black pepper

2 teaspoons (5 g) onion powder

3 teaspoons (6 g) Italian blend seasoning

1. Place canning jars in a canning pot filled with water and bring it to a simmer (180°F/82°C) to heat the jars.

2. In a large, heavy-bottomed pot, combine the ground beef, onions, garlic, green peppers, cabbage, carrots, and mushrooms.

3. Stir in the chopped tomatoes with their juice and the tomato sauce. Pour in the water to achieve the desired consistency.

4. Add the salt, black pepper, onion powder, and Italian blend seasoning. Stir the mixture thoroughly to evenly distribute the seasonings.

5. Bring the mixture to a boil over medium-high heat, then reduce the heat to low. Simmer the mixture for about 30 minutes, allowing the flavors to meld and the vegetables to soften.

CANNING (HOT PACK)

1. Remove a hot jar from the canning pot using a jar lifter.

2. Place a canning funnel on top and ladle hot food into the jar, leaving 1-inch (2.5 cm) headspace.

3. Debubble the jar, leaving 1-inch (2.5 cm) headspace. Add water or broth if needed to achieve the correct headspace.

4. Wipe the jar rim with a clean, damp towel or a vinegar-dampened towel to remove any residue.

5. Place the lid on top of the jar and secure with a band, screwing it on until finger light.

6. Return the filled jar to the canner and repeat canning steps until all jars are filled and in the canner.

7. Vent canner 10 minutes.

8. Add a 10# weight (or the appropriate weight for your altitude). Once the pressure is achieved, start timer: for pints, 75 minutes; for quarts, 90 minutes.

Comforting Chicken Pot Pie Filling

Makes approximately 7 quarts or 14 pints

There's something comforting about the aroma of a freshly baked chicken pot pie wafting through the kitchen. It's a dish that conjures up warm memories of family gatherings and cozy evenings.

Want to capture that same comfort and convenience in a jar? Let me introduce you to canned chicken pot pie filling, with tender chunks of chicken, an array of colorful vegetables, and a rich, creamy sauce. Get ready to transform these ingredients into a piping-hot pot pie, whenever you have a hankering for it.

---

10 whole chicken breasts

10 cups (2.4 L) water

3 tablespoons (54 g) Better Than Bouillon chicken base (optional)

2 cups (200 g) chopped celery

2 cups (320 g) chopped onions

¼ cup (28 g) butter

4 cups (520 g) fresh or frozen sliced carrots

2 cups (260 g) fresh or frozen corn

1 tablespoon (18 g) salt (optional)

1 tablespoon (6 g) black pepper

1 tablespoon (7 g) celery seeds

1 tablespoon (9 g) garlic powder

1 tablespoon (7 g) onion powder

1¼ cups (180 g) clear jel (if you don't have this, thicken sauce with cornstarch after opening the jar to reheat)

1. Place canning jars in a canning pot filled with water and bring it to a simmer (180°F/82°C) to heat the jars.

2. To a large pot, add chicken with enough water to cover 2 inches above the chicken (approximately 10 cups [2.4 L]), add Better Than Bouillon chicken base or similar base if desired, then boil chicken until cooked. Remove chicken from broth and cube or shred. Reserve broth.

3. Cook celery and onions in butter until translucent. Add remaining vegetables, spices, and 8 cups (1.9 L) of broth (reserving 2 cups [472 ml]). Bring to a boil, stirring frequently.

4. Add clear jel to boiling mixture and mix well, about 5 minutes. The pot pie filling will start to thicken.

5. Remove from heat. If mixture is too thick, add a little of the reserved broth until you get it to the desired consistency. Remember that sauces thicken when pressure-canned, so it will be fine if it's a little on the watery side.

CANNING (HOT PACK)

1. Remove a hot jar from the canning pot using a jar lifter.

2. Place a canning funnel on top and ladle hot food into the jar, leaving 1-inch (2.5 cm) headspace.

3. Debubble the jar, leaving 1-inch (2.5 cm) headspace. Add water or broth if needed to achieve the correct headspace.

4. Wipe the jar rim with a clean, damp towel or a vinegar-dampened towel to remove any residue.

5. Place the lid on top of the jar and secure with a band, screwing it on until finger light.

6. Place the filled jar back into the canner and repeat canning steps until all jars are filled and in the canner.

7. Vent canner 10 minutes.

8. Add 10# weight or the weight for your altitude. Once the pressure is achieved, start the timer: for pints, 75 minutes; for quarts, 90 minutes.

Ham Broth/Homestyle Ham and Navy Bean Soup

Makes approximately ½ gallon of ham broth and 1 quart of soup (see note)

As spring arrives, our household eagerly welcomes the return of ham to our dining table. With holiday sales making it the perfect time to stock up, there's no reason to waste any leftover ham bone or scraps after Easter.

To start crafting this comforting ham and navy bean soup, we'll prepare the ham bone broth. You can choose to either pressure-can it separately or use it as the soup base. If you're not making your own broth, substitute store-bought broth in the soup recipe.

HAM BONE BROTH

1 large ham (I use bone-in spiral-cut hams)

2 large chopped onions

½ bunch chopped celery, about 4 stalks

1 pound (454 g) peeled chopped carrots

1 teaspoon garlic powder

1 teaspoon onion powder

8 to 10 peppercorns

1 teaspoon salt

2 to 3 bay leaves

1 teaspoon liquid smoke (optional)

½ gallon (1.9 L) water

BONE BROTH INSTRUCTIONS

1. Trim the meat from the ham bone, setting the meat aside. Place ham bone and any leftover ham trimmings attached to the bone in a large pressure cooker/canner.

2. Add all the vegetables and spices to the cooker/canner.

3. Add the water, making sure it reaches the top of the ham approximately. *Note:* Do not fill the pressure cooker/canner more than two-thirds full.

4. Lock the pressure canner lid and heat on high until steam is coming out steadily from the vent pipe. Vent cooker/canner for 10 minutes.

5. After 10 minutes, add 15# weight.

6. After 15# pressure is achieved, turn down heat and maintain pressure for 90 minutes.

7. After 90 minutes, allow cooker/canner to depressurize naturally.

8. Strain and reserve broth. Shred any remaining ham meat and set aside.

HAM AND NAVY BEAN SOUP INGREDIENTS

NOTE: These quantities are for each quart jar. If you want to use pints, halve all ingredients in the jar.

1 cup (250 g) navy beans (dried, not presoaked)

½ cup (75 g) reserved shredded ham

1 stalk celery, chopped

¼ small onion, chopped

1 clove garlic, chopped

½ teaspoon garlic powder

½ teaspoon onion powder

½ teaspoon salt (optional)

½ teaspoon black pepper

1 bay leaf

½ to 2 cups (118 to 472 ml) ham broth

CANNING (COLD PACK)

1. Layer in each quart jar: dried navy beans, ham, celery, onions, garlic, and spices.

2. Place a canning funnel on top and ladle broth into the jars over soup ingredients, leaving a *generous* 1½–inch (4-cm) headspace.

3. Debubble the jars and add water or broth to jars if needed to achieve the correct headspace.

4. Wipe the jar rims with a clean, damp towel or a vinegar-dampened towel to remove any residue.

5. Place the lid on top of the jars and secure with a band, screwing it on until finger light.

6. Place the filled jars back into the canner.

7. Vent canner 10 minutes.

8. Add 10# weight or the weight for your altitude. Once the pressure is achieved, start the timer: for pints, 75 minutes; for quarts, 90 minutes.

FRUGAL COOKING: MONEY-SAVING TIPS FROM KITCHEN SCRAPS

For homemade bone broths, you can maximize savings by incorporating your vegetable scraps. Use celery tops, onion and garlic peels, carrot peelings, and any kitchen scraps that would typically be discarded. Start by collecting these veggie remnants in a gallon-sized zip-top bag and store them in your freezer. Once the bag is full, you'll have a ready supply of scraps to enhance your bone broths, ensuring you can put them to good use whenever animal bones are available. This practice minimizes waste and makes the most of your kitchen scraps.

New Year's Hoppin' John

Makes 4 to 5 quarts or 8 to 10 pints (see note)

Many families have special New Year's Day traditions, sometimes marked by time-honored traditions and superstitions about attracting luck and prosperity for the year ahead. For my family, eating Hoppin' John on the first day of January is integral to our celebration. The dish's ingredients hold profound symbolism.

Black-eyed peas are associated with coins and are thought to represent financial fortune. By eating them, we invite wealth into our lives. The peas also have a connection to resilience, as they thrive in adverse conditions, symbolizing the ability to weather life's storms.

The ham hock is a flavorful addition to Hoppin' John. It embodies progress and moving forward. Leafy collard greens or kale, often served on the side as a dish called Pot Likker, stand for dollar bills and are said to bring increased prosperity. We serve Hoppin' John poured over cornbread, which symbolizes gold.

On New Year's Day, it's customary to serve Hoppin' John, greens, and cornbread together, making a complete meal that captures all our hopes for the coming year: wealth, growth, richness, and prosperity. Canning Hoppin' John is a delicious addition to your cantry as well as a powerful symbol of optimism and positive expectations.

---

4 tablespoons (56 g) butter

1 large onion, diced

6 cloves garlic, minced

1 green bell pepper, diced

4 stalks celery, diced

1 pound (455 g) dried black-eyed peas, soaked overnight

1 whole ham hock or 2 cups (300 g) diced ham

1 pound (455 g) bacon, chopped

6 cups plus 2 cups (1.4 L plus 472 ml) chicken broth

Salt and pepper, to taste

4 bay leaves

2 tablespoons (30 ml) white vinegar

1. In a large stockpot, melt butter over medium heat. Add onions, garlic, green peppers, and celery. Cook for 4 to 5 minutes, or until soft.

2. Next day, strain peas and discard water.

3. To the stockpot, add the ham and chopped bacon. Add 6 cups (1.4 L) of chicken broth and drained peas. Add salt and pepper to taste and add bay leaves.

4. Bring to a boil, cover, and cook for 40 minutes, or until peas start to soften.

5. Remove from heat, stir in vinegar and additional 2 cups (472 ml) chicken broth: discard bay leaves and ham hock bone (if using).

6. Place canning jars in a canning pot filled with water and bring it to a simmer (180°F/82°C) to heat the jars.

CANNING (HOT PACK)

1. Remove a hot jar from the canning pot using a jar lifter.

2. Place a canning funnel on top and ladle Hoppin' John mixture into warmed jar, leaving a 1-inch (2.5 cm) headspace.

3. Add more water or broth to the jar if needed to achieve the correct 1-inch (2.5 cm) headspace.

4. Wipe the jar rim with a clean, damp towel or a vinegar-dampened towel to remove any residue.

5. Place the lid on top of the jar and secure with a band, screwing it on until finger light.

6. Place the filled jar into the canner and repeat canning steps until all jars are filled and in the canner.

7. Lock lid, turn heat to high, and vent canner 10 minutes.

8. Add 10# weight or the weight for your altitude. Once pressure is achieved, start the timer: for pints, 75 minutes; for quarts, 90 minutes.

NOTE: Jar estimation depends on the expansion of beans and size of ham hock. On average, this recipe yields 4 to 5 quarts or 8 to 10 pints. Have extra jars ready for canning and double or triple the recipe as needed.

Sloppy Joes

When it comes to sloppy joes, there's no comparison between the ones that come from store-bought, canned mix and homemade, canned sloppy joes.

With this recipe, you can savor the homestyle goodness of sloppy joes without the hassle of preparing a new batch each time. Simply pop open a jar, heat, and relish the ultimate comfort food experience.

INGREDIENTS	SINGLE BATCH: 3 pints or 1 quart and 1 pint	DOUBLE BATCH: 6 pints or 3 quarts	TRIPLE BATCH: 12 pints or 6 quarts	THE BIG 'UN BATCH: 15 pints or 7 quarts and 1 pint
Ground beef	2 pounds (908 g)	4 pounds (1.8 kg)	6 pounds (2.7 kg)	10 pounds (4.5 kg)
Chopped onion	1 cup (160 g)	2 cups (320 g)	3 cups (480 g)	5 cups (800 g)
Chopped green pepper	¼ cup (38 g)	½ cup (75 g)	¾ cup (113 g)	1¼ cups (188 g)
Chopped bell peppers (any color)	¼ cup (38 g)	½ cup (75 g)	¾ cup (113 g)	1¼ cups (188 g)
Chopped garlic	3 cloves	6 cloves	9 cloves	15 cloves
Worcestershire sauce	1 tablespoon (15 ml)	2 tablespoons (30 ml)	3 tablespoons (45 ml)	5 tablespoons (75 ml)
Ketchup	1½ cups (360 g)	3 cups (720 g)	4½ cups (1 kg)	7½ cups (1.8 kg)
Water	¼ cup (60 ml)	½ cup (120 ml)	¾ cup (180 ml)	1¼ cups (400 ml)
Apple cider vinegar	2 tablespoons (30 ml)	4 tablespoons (60 ml)	6 tablespoons (90 ml)	10 tablespoons (150 ml)
Mustard	2 teaspoons (8 g)	4 teaspoons (16 g)	6 teaspoons (24 g)	10 teaspoons (40 g)
Brown sugar	2 tablespoons (30 g)	4 tablespoons (60 g)	6 tablespoons (90 g)	10 tablespoons (150 g)
Salt	1 teaspoon	2 teaspoons (12 g)	3 teaspoons (18 g)	5 teaspoons (30 g)
Pepper	1 teaspoon	2 teaspoons (4 g)	3 teaspoons (6 g)	5 teaspoons (10 g)
Onion powder	2 teaspoons (5 g)	4 teaspoons (10 g)	6 teaspoons (15 g)	10 teaspoons (25 g)
Garlic powder	2 teaspoons (6 g)	4 teaspoons (12 g)	6 teaspoons (18 g)	10 teaspoons (30 g)
Oregano	2 teaspoons (4 g)	4 teaspoons (8 g)	6 teaspoons (12 g)	10 teaspoons (20 g)

1. Place canning jars in a canning pot filled with water and bring it to a simmer (180°F/82°C) to heat the jars.

2. Cook the beef until no longer pink, then drain. You can also rinse the beef under warm water to eliminate any remaining grease.

3. In a large bowl, mix all the remaining ingredients with the cooked beef thoroughly. If you find the mixture too dry, add a bit more water or ketchup until it reaches the desired consistency.

CANNING (HOT PACK)

1. Remove a hot jar from the canning pot using a jar lifter.

2. Place a canning funnel on top and ladle hot food into the jar, leaving 1-inch (2.5 cm) headspace.

3. Debubble the jar, leaving 1-inch (2.5 cm) headspace. Add water or ketchup if needed to achieve the correct headspace.

4. Wipe the jar rim with a clean, damp towel or a vinegar-dampened towel to remove any residue.

5. Place the lid on top of the jar and secure with a band, screwing it on until finger light.

6. Place the filled jar back into the canner and repeat canning steps until all jars are filled and in the canner.

7. Vent canner 10 minutes.

8. Add 10# weight or the weight for your altitude. Once the pressure is achieved, start the timer: for pints, 75 minutes; for quarts, 90 minutes.

PRESERVING WITH A PURPOSE: MORE WAYS THAN ONE

Don't limit your culinary creativity to just sloppy joe sandwiches! A large part of preserving with a purpose is finding ways to use your canned foods in as many ways as possible. Instead of giving your jars one use, look for new dishes you can try with what you've preserved. Your canned sloppy joes are the versatile base for many other mouthwatering recipes.

Here are some unique ways I use this recipe to mix things up on nights I need a quick meal.

* Sloppy joe–stuffed peppers
* Sloppy joe pizza
* Sloppy joe sliders
* Sloppy joe casserole
* Sloppy joe loaded nachos

Salisbury Steak in Mushroom Sauce

Makes 7 wide-mouth quart jars and about 42 patties

I grew up eating Salisbury steak in mushroom sauce, usually served over creamy mashed potatoes with a side salad. When I got older, a friend called this "poor man's steak," which I found a little offensive. This dish is a classic comfort food full of hearty flavors: served to a "poor man" or not, it's a staple canned meal in a jar in our home. Complemented with a rich mushroom sauce, Salisbury steaks are the centerpiece for a satisfying meal that can be enjoyed anytime, a truly convenient dinner for your busy life.

Canning this recipe in wide-mouth quarts makes it easy to serve up a tasty, home-cooked meal with minimal effort. The gravy is thickened upon opening, making it ready to enjoy in a few minutes.

8 pounds (3.6 kg) 90/10 ground beef

4 cups (440 g) breadcrumbs

4 cups (128 g) pork rinds, ground

2 eggs

1 (2 oz/56.7 g) package of onion soup mix

½ cup (28 g) dried onion flakes

1 tablespoon (9 g) garlic powder

1 tablespoon (18 g) salt

2 tablespoons (12 g) black pepper

2 tablespoons (6 g) Italian seasoning

FOR THE GRAVY

2 tablespoons (28 g) butter

1 pound (455 g) mushrooms, diced

7 teaspoons (56 g) beef base paste

MAKING THE SALISBURY STEAKS

1. Combine all Salisbury steak ingredients in a large mixing bowl and mix thoroughly.

2. Roll meat out on countertop to 1½ to 2 inches (4 to 5 cm) thick.

3. Using a wide-mouth screw ring, cut Salisbury steaks to size. This is like using a cookie cutter to cut cookies. The wide-mouth screw ring ensures your patties will fit into the jar properly. Press and shape meat into ring.

4. In a large skillet, fry patties until brown on both sides. Set in a warm oven as you work in batches.

5. Place canning jars in a canning pot filled with water. Bring to a simmer (180°F/82°C) to heat the jars.

PREPARING THE MUSHROOMS

1. Melt butter in a skillet over medium-high heat.

2. Add mushrooms to melted butter and stir for 3 to 5 minutes, or until mushrooms are soft.

CANNING (HOT PACK)

1. Remove a hot jar from the canning pot using a jar lifter.

2. Place 1 teaspoon of beef base in the bottom of the jar and stack the steaks (around five or six) inside.

3. Place a canning funnel on top and place a portion of cooked mushrooms into the jar, leaving 1-inch (2.5 cm) headspace. You may need to use a wooden skewer or knife to coax the mushrooms around the patties.

4. Add boiling water to the jar to achieve 1-inch (2.5 cm) headspace, which creates the sauce.

5. Debubble the jar, leaving 1-inch (2.5 cm) headspace. Add more boiling water if needed to achieve the correct headspace.

6. Wipe the jar rim with a clean, damp towel or a vinegar-dampened towel to remove any residue.

7. Place the lid on top of the jar and secure with a band, screwing it on until finger light.

8. Place the filled jar back into the canner and repeat canning steps until all jars are filled and in the canner.

9. Lock canner lid. Over high heat, vent canner 10 minutes.

10. Add 10# weight or the weight for your altitude. Once the pressure is achieved, reduce heat and start timer: 90 minutes for quarts.

FROM JAR TO GRAVY BOAT: THE MAGIC OF CANNING LIQUIDS

In canning recipes, the liquids are often thin to ensure even heating during the canning process. Many recipes create their own flavorful broths. Don't let those flavorful canning liquids go to waste! You can easily transform them into delicious gravies to enhance your meals.

When you open your canned recipe, strain and save the liquid. This liquid is often packed with natural flavors and can serve as an excellent base for gravy.

To make gravy, start by thickening the strained liquid. In a saucepan, create a roux by melting equal parts butter and flour. Cook it until it reaches a pale golden color. Add the strained canning liquid to the roux and stir well. You can also incorporate seasonings such as salt, pepper, herbs, or spices to enhance the flavor. Simmer until gravy thickens.

Meatball Madness: Choose Your Favorite

Makes 7 to 10 quarts or 14 to 20 pints, depending on meatball size

You are the meatball master! Whether you favor classic beef, adventurous bear, savory sausage, or any other ground meat, seasonings like garlic, onion, paprika, and Worcestershire sauce will make your meatballs burst with deliciousness.

But that's not all: these meatball madness recipes offer four unique sauce options, each bringing its own delightful twist to the table. Dive into rich beef broth, creamy Swedish sauce, tangy tomato juice, or zesty sweet-and-sour sauce. The choice is yours!

---

10 pounds (4.5 kg) ground meat of choice

½ cup (28 g) dried onion flakes

4 tablespoons (60 ml) Worcestershire sauce

3 teaspoons (54 g) beef bouillon powder

2 tablespoons (18 g) garlic powder

4 tablespoons (36 g) onion powder

2 teaspoons (5 g) paprika

2 teaspoons (13 g) kosher salt

2 teaspoons (4 g) black pepper

4 tablespoons (5 g) dried parsley

4 MEATBALL SAUCE OPTIONS
Beef Broth

18 to 20 cups (4.2 to 4.7 L) beef broth or stock

½ teaspoon paprika

2 teaspoons (6 g) garlic powder

1½ tablespoons (10 g) onion powder

1 teaspoon salt (optional)

1 tablespoon (15 ml) Worcestershire sauce

½ teaspoon black pepper

MEATBALL INSTRUCTIONS

1. Preheat oven to 375°F (190°C).

2. Mix all ingredients in a bowl.

3. Roll 1½ to 2-inch (4 to 5 cm) meatballs by hand and place on a parchment-lined baking sheet.

4. Bake meatballs for 20 minutes.

5. While meatballs are baking, prepare your canning equipment. Place canning jars in a canning pot filled with water and bring it to a simmer (180°F/82°C) to heat the jars.

6. Set cooked meatballs aside and make your chosen sauce.

SAUCE INSTRUCTIONS

1. In a large stockpot, combine all ingredients for your chosen sauce.

2. Bring ingredients to a boil, stirring until well mixed.

3. Cover with a lid, lower heat, and simmer sauce for 5 minutes.

4. Add meatballs to sauce and stir to coat.

5. Proceed to canning (hot pack).

Swedish Sauce

6 (10.5 oz/298 g) cans condensed cream of mushroom soup (not diluted)

9 tablespoons (135 g) plain yogurt

12 to 14 cups (2.8 to 3.3 L) beef broth

4 tablespoons (60 ml) fresh lemon juice

2 tablespoons (3 g) dried parsley

½ teaspoon ground nutmeg

1 teaspoon onion powder

1 teaspoon garlic powder

Dash of cinnamon, to taste

Tomato Juice

18 to 20 cups (4.2 to 4.7 L) tomato juice, store-bought or home canned

½ teaspoon paprika

2 teaspoons (6 g) garlic powder

1½ tablespoons (10 g) onion powder

2 tablespoons (3 g) dried parsley

Sweet-and-Sour Sauce

10 cups (2.4 L) pineapple juice

6¾ cups (960 g) light brown sugar

4 cups (944 ml) apple cider vinegar

1½ cups (360 g) ketchup

¾ cup (177 ml) low-sodium soy sauce

4½ tablespoons (36 g) grated fresh ginger or ¾ tablespoon (4 g) ground ginger

NOTE: You have the flexibility to adjust the sauce's thickness according to your preference after opening the jar and before serving. Warm the sauce, add your chosen thickening agent, and stir until it reaches the desired consistency.

CANNING (HOT PACK)

1. Remove a hot jar from the canning pot using a jar lifter.

2. Place a canning funnel on top and, using a slotted spoon, place a portion of meatballs into the jar.

3. Using a ladle, ladle hot sauce over meatballs leaving 1-inch (2.5 cm) headspace.

4. Debubble the jar, leaving 1-inch (2.5 cm) headspace. Add more sauce or water if needed to achieve the correct headspace.

5. Wipe the jar rim with a clean, damp towel or a vinegar-dampened towel to remove any residue.

6. Place the lid on top of the jar and secure with a band, screwing it on until finger light.

7. Place the filled jar back into the canner and repeat canning steps until all jars are filled and in the canner.

8. Vent canner 10 minutes.

9. Add 10# weight or the weight for your altitude. Once the pressure is achieved, start timer: for pints, 75 minutes; for quarts, 90 minutes.

Bourbon Chicken

Makes about 4 pint jars. This recipe can be doubled or tripled.

Surprise: This bourbon chicken recipe doesn't have any bourbon in it. This flavorful dish gets its name from New Orleans's famous Bourbon Street. It's simple to can, and as a cantry staple it's great for providing quick meals. The glaze is sweet and spicy, and so full of rich flavors it's sure to be one of your family's most requested meals.

Approximate yields

* Single recipe: 4 pints or 2 quarts
* Double recipe: 8 pints or 4 quarts
* Triple recipe: 12 pints or 6 quarts

INGREDIENTS

4 pounds (1.8 kg) boneless, skinless chicken breasts

2 cloves crushed garlic

2 teaspoons (3 g) crushed red pepper flakes (add more for spicier)

½ cup (118 ml) orange juice

4 tablespoons (60 g) ketchup

⅔ cup (150 g) brown sugar

2 tablespoons (30 ml) apple cider vinegar

⅔ cup (157 ml) soy sauce

1 cup (236 ml) water

SERVING SUGGESTIONS:

Using the lid, strain off the bourbon sauce in the jar into a saucepan over medium heat. Whisk 2 to 3 teaspoons (6 to 9 g) of cornstarch or clear jel to thicken the sauce into a glaze. If the sauce is too runny, keep adding cornstarch one teaspoon at a time until you get the thickness you want. Add chicken to the thickened sauce. Serve over rice garnished with green onions for a quick and easy meal your family is sure to request again.

1. Cut chicken breasts into 1-inch–by–1-inch (2.5 by 2.5 cm) square chunks. Set aside.

2. Add remaining ingredients to a saucepan and heat until sugar is dissolved.

3. Remove sauce from heat and add raw chicken. Stir until chicken is coated.

CANNING (COLD PACK)

1. Fill room-temperature jars with raw chicken and sauce, leaving 1-inch (2.5 cm) headspace.

2. Debubble jars with a wood utensil like a chopstick or wooden skewer. Add more sauce during debubbling until 1-inch (2.5 cm) headspace is achieved. Extra water or orange juice can be added to the jars until you get the proper headspace.

3. Wipe the jar rims with a clean, damp towel or a vinegar-dampened towel to remove any residue.

4. Place the lid on top of the jars and secure with a band, screwing it on until finger light.

5. Place the filled jars into the canner.

6. Lock lid and heat canner on high. Vent canner 10 minutes.

7. Add 10# weight or the weight for your altitude. Once the pressure is achieved, turn down heat and maintain pressure. Start timer: for pints, 75 minutes; for quarts, 90 minutes.

Corned Beef Hash

Makes 12 to 16 pint jars or 6 to 8 quart jars

Corned beef hash is a classic breakfast dish, though you can enjoy it any time of the day. This flavorful combination of corned beef, potatoes, and seasonings has a rich history. Originally, corned beef hash was a way to creatively use leftovers from the previous night's corned beef dinner. These ingredients would be diced, mixed, and fried to perfection.

Whether you're planning a lazy weekend breakfast, a busy morning on the go, or a campfire cookout, having canned corned beef hash in your pantry means you're ready for a tasty and convenient meal.

The number of jars you will need depends on how you prepare the meat (either cubed or ground), and whether you're making your recipe meat heavy or potato heavy. Have plenty of *wide-mouth jars* available before canning this recipe.

---

12 pounds (5.4 kg) corned beef (whole cut or ground)

5 pounds (2.3 kg) russet potatoes, peeled and cubed

3 large onions, diced

2 teaspoons (4 g) black pepper

2 teaspoons (36 g) salt

2 teaspoons (1 g) parsley

2 teaspoons (6 g) garlic powder

2 teaspoons (5 g) onion powder

1. If using a whole cut of meat, trim fat cap on corned beef by half the thickness. Slice and cube corned beef into 1-inch (2.5 cm) cubes. If you want ground meat, run cubed corned beef through meat grinder on medium grind. You can also use a food processor, working in small batches or leave corned beef in cubes.

2. Place potatoes in bowl of water while working in batches.

3. Drain potatoes from water. Add potatoes and onions to ground corned beef mixture.

4. Add all spices and mix thoroughly.

CANNING (RAW PACK)

1. The number of jars is estimated. Have a couple extra jars on hand and do your best to evenly distribute ingredients.

2. Pack approximately 1 pound (454 g) of raw corned beef hash to each wide-mouth pint jar, or 2 pounds (907 g) per wide-mouth quart jar, leaving 1-inch (2.5 cm) headspace.

3. Using the bottom of a 4-ounce jelly jar, pack down meat mixture to achieve 1-inch (2.5 cm) headspace and remove air pockets.

4. Wipe the jar rim with a clean, damp towel or a vinegar-dampened towel to remove any residue.

5. Place the lid on top of the jar and secure with a band, screwing it on until finger light.

6. Place the filled jar into the canner and repeat canning steps until all jars are filled and in the canner.

7. Lock lid and heat canner on high. Vent canner 10 minutes.

8. Add 10# weight or the weight for your altitude. Once the pressure is achieved, turn down heat and maintain pressure, then start timer: for pints, 75 minutes; for quarts, 90 minutes.

St. Patty's Day in a Jar

Makes approximately 6 quart jars

This is a great recipe for canning corned beef, with the added bonus of being convenient to reheat directly from the jar.

To make the most of your budget, I recommend purchasing corned beef during St. Patrick's Day sales and canning it to ensure a year-round supply on your cantry shelves. It's all about making those cantry dollars stretch!

6 cups (1.4 kg) cubed raw corned beef

6 cups (660 g) peeled and cubed potatoes

4 stalks of celery, sliced

3 cups (390 g) chopped/sliced carrots

3 cups (480 g) chopped onions

3 cups (270 g) chopped cabbage

8 to 10 cups (1.9 to 2.4 L) beef broth

3 teaspoons (54 g) salt (optional)

1. Place potatoes in bowl of water while working in batches.

2. Place canning jars in a canning pot filled with water and bring it to a simmer (180°F/82°C) to heat the jars.

3. In a large stockpot over medium heat, bring the beef broth to a gentle simmer.

4. Drain the water from the potatoes.

CANNING (HOT PACK)

1. Remove a hot jar from the canning pot using a jar lifter.

2. In each warmed quart jar, place a portion of corned beef, potatoes, celery, carrots, onions, and cabbage, in that order.

3. Place a canning funnel on top and ladle hot beef broth into the jar, leaving 1-inch (2.5 cm) headspace.

4. Debubble the jars, leaving 1-inch (2.5 cm) headspace. Add water or broth to jars if needed to achieve the correct headspace.

5. Wipe the jar rim with a clean, damp towel or a vinegar-dampened towel to remove any residue.

6. Place the lid on top of the jar and secure with a band, screwing it on until finger light.

7. Place the filled jar back into the canner and repeat canning steps until all jars are filled and in the canner.

8. Vent canner 10 minutes.

9. Add 10# weight or the weight for your altitude. Once the pressure is achieved, start timer: for pints, 75 minutes; for quarts, 90 minutes.

CREAM OF EVERYTHING SOUPS

There are any number of delicious "cream of" soups you can make from scratch. These versatile, creamy soups serve as the foundation for many recipes, and having them on hand in your cantry can be a real kitchen lifesaver. Once you taste these homemade cream soups, you won't want to go back to store-bought again.

When you're canning these soups, always avoid using vinegar to wipe the rims of the jars or in the canner. Since they are cream based, the vinegar can cause the soup to curdle.

My Amish friend shared a trick with me: Using flour and clear jel in the same recipe. The clear jel stabilizes the flour, keeps it from separating, and allows for even heating. Stabilizing the roux helps you to adjust the thickness without the worry of the flour breaking down (clumping) during canning. Since clear jel is more expensive than flour, using a little of it with your flour saves money in your canning budget.

Cream of Chicken Soup

Makes approximately 8 pints

2 cups (280 g) chicken, cubed and cooked

3 tablespoons (45 ml) olive oil

1 stick (112 g) butter

1 cup (125 g) flour

7 cups (1.7 L) chicken broth

1 (12 oz/354 ml) can evaporated milk

½ teaspoon thyme

½ teaspoon rosemary

¼ teaspoon black pepper

½ cup (72 g) clear jel plus ½ cup (118 ml) water

1. Cook cubed chicken in a frying pan with olive oil.

2. Melt butter in a stockpot and add flour, stirring to make a roux.

3. Add chicken broth, evaporated milk, cooked chicken, and spices. Bring to a gentle boil for 5 minutes.

4. In a small bowl, stir together the clear jel and water to make a slurry.

5. Add clear jel slurry to soup and return it to boil for 2 minutes. Soup should be thickened. If it is too thick, add a little water. If too thin, add a little clear jel.

6. Place canning jars in a canning pot filled with water and bring it to a simmer (180°F/82°C) to heat the jars.

CANNING (HOT PACK)

1. Remove a hot jar from the canning pot using a jar lifter.

2. Place a canning funnel on top and ladle soup into the jar, leaving a *generous* ¼-inch (6 mm) headspace.

3. Add more water or broth to the jar if needed to achieve the correct ¼-inch (6 mm) headspace.

4. Wipe the jar rim with a dampened towel to remove any residue.

5. Place the lid on top of the jar and secure with a band, screwing it on until finger light.

6. Place the filled jar into the canner and repeat canning steps until all jars are filled and in the canner.

7. Lock lid, turn heat to high, and vent canner 10 minutes.

8. Add 10# weight or the weight for your altitude. Once pressure is achieved, start timer: 75 minutes for pints.

Cream of Mushroom Soup

Makes approximately 10 pints

1 stick (112 g) butter

1 cup (125 g) flour

6 cups (1.4 L) beef broth

1 (12 oz/354 ml) can evaporated milk

2 cups (472 ml) water

1 pound (455 g) white mushrooms, minced

¼ teaspoon black pepper

1 tablespoon (1.3 g) dried parsley

1 tablespoon (7 g) dried onion flakes or powder

1 bay leaf

¼ cup (36 g) clear jel plus ¼ cup (60 ml) water

1. Melt butter in stockpot and add flour, stirring to make a roux.

2. Add beef broth, evaporated milk, water, mushrooms, and spices. Bring to a gentle boil for 5 minutes.

3. In a small bowl, stir together the clear jel and water to make a slurry.

4. Add clear jel slurry to soup and return it to boil for 2 minutes. Soup should be thickened. If it is too thick, add a little water. If too thin, add a little clear jel.

5. Remove bay leaf.

6. Place canning jars in a canning pot filled with water and bring it to a simmer (180°F/82°C) to heat the jars.

CANNING (HOT PACK)

1. Remove a hot jar from the canning pot using a jar lifter.

2. Place a canning funnel on top and ladle soup into the jar, leaving a *generous* ¼-inch (6 mm) headspace.

3. Add more water or broth to the jar if needed to achieve the correct ¼-inch (6 mm) headspace.

4. Wipe the jar rim with a dampened towel to remove any residue.

5. Place the lid on top of the jar and secure with a band, screwing it on until finger light.

6. Place the filled jar into the canner and repeat canning steps until all jars are filled and in the canner.

7. Lock lid, turn heat to high, and vent canner 10 minutes.

8. Add 10# weight or the weight for your altitude. Once pressure is achieved, start the timer: for pints, 75 minutes.

Cream of Celery Soup

Makes approximately 8 to 9 pints

1 stick (112 g) butter

½ cup (118 ml) vegetable oil

1 cup (125 g) flour

10 cups (2.4 L) chicken stock

1 (12 oz/354 ml) can evaporated milk

1 bunch of celery, chopped (approximately 4 cups [400 g])

1 teaspoon celery seeds

½ teaspoon ground mustard

¼ teaspoon black pepper

1 bay leaf

½ cup (72 g) clear jel plus ½ cup (118 ml) water

1. Melt butter in stockpot with oil and add flour, stirring to make a roux.

2. Add chicken broth, evaporated milk, celery, and spices. Bring to a gentle boil for 5 minutes, stirring until well mixed.

3. In a small bowl, stir together the clear jel and water to make a slurry.

4. Add clear jel slurry to soup and return it to boil for 2 minutes. Soup should be thickened. If it is too thick, add a little water. If too thin, add a little clear jel.

5. Remove bay leaf.

6. Place canning jars in a canning pot filled with water and bring it to a simmer (180°F/82°C) to heat the jars.

CANNING (HOT PACK)

1. Remove a hot jar from the canning pot using a jar lifter.

2. Place a canning funnel on top and ladle soup into the jar, leaving a 1-inch (2.5 cm) headspace.

3. Add more water or broth to the jar if needed to achieve the correct 1-inch (2.5 cm) headspace.

4. Wipe the jar rim with a dampened towel to remove any residue.

5. Place the lid on top of the jar and secure with a band, screwing it on until finger light.

6. Place the filled jar into the canner and repeat canning steps until all jars are filled and in the canner.

7. Lock lid, turn heat to high, and vent canner 10 minutes.

8. Add 10# weight or the weight for your altitude. Once pressure is achieved, start timer: 75 minutes for pints.

Old-Fashioned Beef Vegetable Soup

Makes approximately 7 quarts or 14 pints

In the corner of my grandmother's tiny kitchen, where the sunlight filtered through lace curtains, there was a large worn pot filled with old-fashioned beef and vegetable soup. Today that memory and the recipe itself are etched in the archives of my family history.

This recipe had been passed down from my great-grandmother to my grandmother and, eventually, to my mother. Each of them added her own unique touch, with a secret blend of seasonings known only to the women who had perfected them. This canning recipe is a distillation of all their wise additions. Now, whenever I stand in my own kitchen, reheating a jar of this Old-Fashioned Beef and Vegetable Soup, I am filled with a deep sense of nostalgia.

2 tablespoons (30 ml) olive oil

3 pounds (1.4 kg) stewing beef, cut into small cubes

10 cups (2.4 L) beef broth

4 large potatoes, peeled and cubed

4 small onions, chopped

4 stalks celery, chopped

4 large carrots, peeled and chopped

2 cups (300 g) peas, fresh or frozen

2 (28-oz/794 g) cans diced tomatoes

2 teaspoons (36 g) salt

2 tablespoons (26 g) sugar

2 teaspoons (4 g) black pepper

2 teaspoons (3 g) Italian seasoning

½ teaspoon dry thyme

½ teaspoon dry rosemary

1 teaspoon dry marjoram

1. Place canning jars in a canning pot filled with water and bring it to a simmer (180°F/82°C) to heat the jars.

2. In a large stockpot, heat olive oil and brown stew meat, locking in juices for canning.

3. Add all remaining ingredients and bring to a boil. Reduce heat and simmer for 10 minutes.

CANNING (HOT PACK)

1. Remove a hot jar from the canning pot using a jar lifter.

2. Place a canning funnel on top and, using a slotted spoon, fill the jar half full of the food solids (meat and vegetables).

3. Ladle the hot broth into the jar, leaving 1-inch (2.5 cm) headspace.

4. Debubble the jar, leaving 1-inch (2.5 cm) headspace. Add water or broth to the jar if needed to achieve the correct headspace.

5. Wipe the jar rim with a clean, damp towel or a vinegar-dampened towel to remove any residue.

6. Place the lid on top of the jar and secure with a band, screwing it on until finger light.

7. Place the filled jar back into the canner and repeat canning steps until all jars are filled and in the canner.

8. Vent canner 10 minutes.

9. Add 10# weight or the weight for your altitude. Once the pressure is achieved, start timer: for pints, 75 minutes; for quarts, 90 minutes.

Vegetarian Vegetable Soup

Makes about 4 quarts or 8 pints. This recipe can be doubled or tripled.

This recipe is a true celebration of the garden's bounty, and it's also an opportunity to embrace the "no waste" philosophy. Whether you're a vegetarian or just looking for a break from meat-based meals, this soup will delight you.

Use the vegetable scraps and trimmings you might typically discard to make the homemade vegetable broth. This elevates the overall flavor profile while adding an extra layer of sustainability to your *Preserving with a Purpose* journey.

Adjust and add ingredients to make this recipe your own. This could be including a bay leaf in each jar to ensure a gentle infusion of herbal notes or sprinkling salt and pepper to add a finishing touch.

---

2 tablespoons (30 ml) extra-virgin olive oil

1 medium onion, diced

1 medium sweet potato, peeled and diced

1 medium carrot, peeled and diced

Salt and pepper, to taste

¼ cup (60 ml) dry white wine

4 to 5 fresh tomatoes, cored and chopped, or 1 (14.5-oz/411 g) can diced tomatoes

4 garlic cloves, chopped

1 tablespoon (2.4 g) chopped fresh thyme

¼ teaspoon red pepper flakes

4 to 5 cups (944 ml to 1.2 L) vegetable broth

1 cup (180 g) cherry tomatoes, halved

1 cup (100 g) green beans

1 medium zucchini, peeled and diced

(continued)

1. Heat the oil in a large pot over medium heat. Add the onion, sweet potato, carrot, and salt and pepper to taste. Cook and stir for 10 minutes.

2. Pour wine over vegetables and let it simmer for about 30 seconds.

3. Add the fresh or canned tomatoes, garlic, thyme, red pepper flakes, and vegetable broth.

4. Bring the mixture to a boil. Cover the pot, reduce the heat to a gentle simmer, and cook for 20 minutes.

5. While the mixture is simmering, place canning jars in a canning pot filled with water and bring it to a simmer (180°F/82°C) to heat the jars.

6. Remove the pot from heat and add all remaining ingredients except bay leaves. Let soup sit for 10 minutes until kale begins to wilt. Stir to evenly distribute before canning.

CANNING (HOT PACK)

1. Remove a hot jar from the canning pot using a jar lifter.

2. Place a canning funnel on top and, using a slotted spoon, fill the jar approximately half full of the food solids (vegetables).

3. Add one bay leaf.

2 cups (480 g) cooked chickpeas or 1 (15-oz/439 g) can, drained and rinsed

2 tablespoons (30 ml) white wine vinegar

1½ cups (100 g) chopped kale

Bay leaves, 1 per jar

4. Ladle the hot broth into the jar, leaving 1-inch (2.5 cm) headspace.

5. Debubble the jar, leaving 1-inch (2.5 cm) headspace. Add water or broth to the jar if needed to achieve the correct headspace.

6. Wipe the jar rim with a clean, damp towel or a vinegar-dampened towel to remove any residue.

7. Place the lid on top of the jar and secure with a band, screwing it on until finger light.

8. Place the filled jar back into the canner and repeat canning steps until all jars are filled and in the canner.

9. Vent canner 10 minutes.

10. Add 10# weight or the weight for your altitude. Once the pressure is achieved, start the timer: for pints, 65 minutes; for quarts, 90 minutes.

White Bean Chicken Chili

Makes 5 to 6 pint jars. This recipe can be doubled or tripled.

This delicious white bean chicken chili offers a comforting, hearty meal that's perfect for any rainy day. Made with tender chunks of chicken, hearty white beans, and a flavorful blend of spices, it's sure to become a family favorite. Whether you're looking to warm up after a long day or want to impress guests with a flavorful meal, this white bean chicken chili is sure to hit the spot. It also pairs perfectly with cornbread.

1 large onion, chopped

6 stalks celery, chopped

4 cloves garlic, chopped

1 teaspoon butter

2 to 3 pounds (907 g to 1.4 kg) chicken, ground, cubed, or shredded

6 cups (1.4 L) chicken broth

1 (4-oz/113 g) can green chilis

3 cups (516 g) presoaked great northern beans

2 teaspoons (5 g) each: cumin powder, garlic powder, onion powder

1 teaspoon salt (optional)

1 teaspoon black pepper

1. Place canning jars in a canning pot filled with water and bring it to a simmer (180°F/82°C) to heat the jars.

2. In a stockpot, sauté onions, celery, and garlic in butter until translucent. Add chicken and cook until no longer pink.

3. Add the chicken broth, chilis, beans, and spices to the stockpot.

4. Bring soup to a boil, cover with a lid, turn down heat, and simmer for additional 5 minutes.

CANNING (HOT PACK)

1. Remove a hot jar from the canning pot using a jar lifter.

2. Place a canning funnel on top and ladle hot soup into the jar, leaving 1-inch (2.5-cm) headspace.

3. Debubble the jar, leaving 1-inch (2.5 cm) headspace. Add more soup liquid or water to jar if needed to achieve the correct headspace.

4. Wipe the jar rim with a clean, damp towel or a vinegar-dampened towel to remove any residue.

5. Place the lid on top of the jar and secure with a band, screwing it on until finger light.

6. Place the filled jar back into the canner and repeat canning steps until all jars are filled and in the canner.

7. Vent canner 10 minutes.

8. Add 10# weight or the weight for your altitude. Once the pressure is achieved, start timer: for pints, 75 minutes; for quarts, 90 minutes.

Chicken Tortilla Soup: Flavorful Fiesta in a Bowl

Make approximately 7 quarts or 14 pints

This chicken tortilla soup can help you turn a busy evening into a cozy fiesta. Customize with any toppings you like: tortilla strips, shredded cheese, diced avocado, sour cream or Greek yogurt, chopped fresh cilantro or parsley, sliced jalapeños, hot sauce, or lime wedges.

3 large boneless, skinless chicken breasts

2 cups (200 g) chopped celery

1½ cups (195 g) sliced carrots

1 large onion, chopped

3 cups (450 g) corn, frozen or canned

2 (15-oz/425 g) cans black beans, rinsed and drained

2 pints tomatoes and green chilis or 2 (14½-oz/425 g) cans RO*TEL

4 cups (720g) diced tomatoes with juice, fresh or canned

4 garlic cloves, minced

6 cups (1.4 L) water

6 cups (1.4 L) chicken broth

4 chicken bouillon cubes

1 teaspoon ground cumin

1 tablespoon (18 g) salt (optional)

1. Boil chicken in a covered pot of water until fully cooked and no longer pink. Once cooked, place chicken in a bowl and allow it to cool. Next, shred the chicken (I've found an electric hand mixer makes quick work of shredding chicken).

2. Set the shredded chicken aside.

3. Place canning jars in a canning pot filled with water and bring it to a simmer (180°F/82°C) to heat the jars.

4. In a large pot, combine all remaining ingredients except for the shredded chicken. Bring the mixture to a boil, cover the pot, and let it simmer for 3 minutes.

5. Add shredded chicken to the pot and lightly boil for 5 minutes.

CANNING (HOT PACK)

1. Remove a hot jar from the canning pot using a jar lifter.

2. Place a canning funnel on top and ladle hot soup into the jar, leaving 1-inch (2.5 cm) headspace.

3. Debubble the jar, leaving 1-inch (2.5 cm) headspace. Add more soup liquid or water to jar if needed to achieve the correct headspace.

4. Wipe the jar rim with a clean, damp towel or a vinegar-dampened towel to remove any residue.

5. Place the lid on top of the jar and secure with a band, screwing it on until finger light.

6. Place the filled jar back into the canner and repeat canning steps until all jars are filled and in the canner.

7. Vent canner 10 minutes.

8. Add 10# weight or the weight for your altitude. Once the pressure is achieved, start timer: for pints, 75 minutes; for quarts, 90 minutes.

THE WISDOM OF SMALL-BATCH CANNING: TASTE TESTING FOR CULINARY PERFECTION

When you choose to can a new recipe—or one that's new to you, the benefits of starting with small batches cannot be overstated. This will give you the freedom to experiment, adjust, and perfect your creations before committing yourself to canning a recipe. Work on building the right flavor balance and fine-tuning your seasonings and spice levels. If you don't like some aspect of the product, you can fix what's off with minimal impact.

I suggest marking the pages of this book with your canning notes. Put down how many jars you made, what challenges you encountered, and what spices you'd like to change for next time. Most important of all: Will there *be* a next time?

I hope this book serves as a living document sprinkled with your notes from year to year as your tastes evolve and your canning expertise grows.

Translating Success to Larger Batches

It all starts with a single jar.

Small-batch canning is your culinary laboratory, ensuring that the flavors and textures you desire are present in every jar. Once you've found the right balance of flavor on a small scale, multiply the ingredients and create larger batches.

Practicing small-batch canning offers a stepping stone to culinary excellence and food security, the delicious assurance that you'll have well-preserved meals ready when you need them.

Corn Chowder

Makes approximately 5 to 6 quarts or 10 to 12 pints

When you crave the fresh taste of summer, reach for this corn chowder in your cantry. You'll add luscious, heavy cream to the chowder after you open the jar, ensuring that each serving will be fresh and satisfying.

We love this grab-and-go jar packed in our lunches or as a warm-up meal around the bonfire during chilly fall camping trips. You can savor it on its own, pair it with a fresh garden salad, or dunk some crusty bread in it. For an extra layer of flavor, top off the chowder with crispy bacon bits, chives, or a sprinkle of paprika.

4 tablespoons (56 g) butter

2 medium onions, chopped

6 to 8 cloves garlic, minced

2 jalapeño peppers, diced (optional)

4 cups (600 g) diced mixed bell peppers

8 cups (1.2 kg) fresh or frozen corn kernels

4 large russet potatoes, cubed

2 medium tomatoes, chopped

6 cups (1.4 L) chicken or vegetable broth

½ teaspoon paprika

1 teaspoon garlic powder

1 teaspoon onion powder

¼ teaspoon cayenne pepper (optional)

Salt and pepper, to taste

¼ cup (36 g) clear jel plus ¼ cup (60 ml) water

1. In a large stockpot, melt butter over medium heat. Add onions, garlic, jalapeños, and bell peppers. Sauté for 1 to 2 minutes.

2. Add remaining ingredients except clear jel slurry; mix well.

3. Bring the soup to a boil, cover, reduce heat, and simmer uncovered for 15 to 20 minutes, or until potatoes have softened.

4. Remove one third of the soup into a bowl and, using an upright blender or immersion blender, blend until a smooth purée.

5. Return the purée to the stockpot and mix well.

6. In a small mixing bowl, mix clear jel and water to create a slurry.

7. Add slurry to soup and simmer another 5 minutes until soup thickens. If sauce is too thin for your liking, add more clear jel, 1 teaspoon (3 g) at a time, until desired consistency is achieved.

8. Place canning jars in a canning pot filled with water and bring it to a simmer (180°F/82°C) to heat the jars.

CANNING (HOT PACK)

1. Remove a hot jar from the canning pot using a jar lifter.

2. Place a canning funnel on top and ladle chowder to 1½-inch (4-cm) headspace.

3. Debubble the jar, leaving 1½-inch (4-cm) headspace. Add more water or broth to the jar if needed to achieve the correct headspace.

4. Wipe the jar rim with a clean, damp towel or a vinegar-dampened towel to remove any residue.

5. Place the lid on top of the jar and secure with a band, screwing it on until finger light.

6. Place the filled jar into the canner and repeat canning steps until all jars are filled and in the canner.

7. Lock lid, turn heat to high, and vent canner 10 minutes.

8. Add 10# weight or the weight for your altitude. Once the pressure is achieved, start timer: for pints, 75 minutes; for quarts, 90 minutes.

NOTE: If you want creamy corn chowder, add a splash of heavy cream when reheating jar contents.

REUSING CORNCOBS: THE STOCK EXCHANGE

You can substitute chicken or vegetable broth for the corn stock called for in this recipe. If you want to elevate the chowder's flavors and embrace a more sustainable kitchen, consider making your own corn stock. Corn stock is a flavorful liquid created by simmering corncobs in water—a fantastic way to use every part of the corn and reduce food waste in your kitchen.

To make corn stock, save your corncobs after removing the kernels for the chowder. Simmer the cobs in water for an hour. The result will be a rich and slightly sweet stock that adds a depth of flavor to your recipes while ensuring no part of the corn goes to waste.

Incorporating corn stock into your dishes enhances their taste and also aligns with sustainable kitchen practices by maximizing the use of ingredients and reducing unnecessary waste. It's a small but resourceful step toward making your canning journey more eco-friendly.

At-Home Cincinnati Chili

Makes 5 to 6 quart jars or 10 to 12 pint jars

Cincinnati, Ohio, is known for its unique style of chili, created in the first half of the twentieth century by Greek and Balkan immigrants to the city. Skyline Chili, a restaurant started in 1949, was one of the main originators of the distinctive blend of flavors that went into "Cincinnati chili." As I make it for my family, rich ingredients like unsweetened chocolate, cinnamon, and a complex mix of spices meld into a complex, distinctive chili that you'll love from the first spoonful.

Cincinnati chili can be served in a number of ways, including over spaghetti. This quirky preparation might sound unusual, but it's something that native Ohioans and many others crave. It's also delicious when used to top hot dogs or as a dip for corn chips. The best part is that you don't have to visit Cincinnati to savor this unique dish: you can craft your own version right at home.

---

12 cups (2.8 L) water

4 cups (1 kg) dried kidney beans

2½ pounds (1.4 kg) ground beef

2 (6-oz/170-g) cans tomato paste

1 ounce (28 g) unsweetened baking chocolate or 6 tablespoons (30 g) cocoa powder plus 2 tablespoons (30 ml) vegetable oil

½ cup (60 g) chili powder

2 teaspoons (5 g) cinnamon

2 teaspoons (6 g) garlic powder

2 teaspoons (5 g) cumin

½ teaspoon ground allspice

½ teaspoon ground cloves

½ teaspoon red pepper flakes

¼ teaspoon black pepper

1¼ teaspoons salt

1 teaspoon granulated sugar

4 tablespoons (60 ml) apple cider vinegar

1. Quick-soak beans by bringing the water to a boil over high heat in a large stockpot. Add the dried beans to the water and boil for 5 minutes uncovered. Add lid to the pot, turn off the heat, and allow the beans to sit undisturbed for 1 hour.

2. After 1 hour, drain beans, return to stockpot, and set aside.

3. In a skillet, brown the ground beef and drain fat.

4. To the beans, add ground beef and all remaining ingredients to create the chili.

5. Bring the chili to a simmer over medium heat for 30 minutes, stirring occasionally.

6. Place canning jars in a canning pot filled with water and bring it to a simmer (180°F/82°C) to heat the jars.

CANNING (HOT PACK)

1. Remove a hot jar from the canning pot using a jar lifter.

2. Place a canning funnel on top and ladle chili into the jar, leaving 1-inch (2.5 cm) headspace.

3. Debubble the jars, leaving 1-inch (2.5 cm) headspace. Add more water to the jar if needed to achieve the correct headspace.

4. Wipe the jar rim with a clean, damp towel or a vinegar-dampened towel to remove any residue.

5. Place the lid on top of the jar and secure with a band, screwing it on until finger light.

6. Place the filled jar into the canner and repeat canning steps until all jars are filled and in the canner.

7. Lock lid, turn heat to high, and vent canner 10 minutes.

8. Add 10# weight or the weight for your altitude. Once the pressure is achieved, reduce heat, and start timer: for pints, 75 minutes; for quarts, 90 minutes.

SERVING CINCINNATICHILI

Cincinnati is known for serving their chili in unusual ways. My personal favorites for the home-canned version are the 5-Way and the Cheese Coney, but here are several variations.

* **3 Layer.** A bowl of Cincinnati Chili served over a bed of cooked spaghetti and topped with a generous amount of finely shredded cheddar cheese.

* **4 Layer.** In addition to the ingredients for the 3 Layer, this version includes diced onions on top of the cheese.

* **5 Layer.** The 5 Layer includes all the components of the 4 Layer but adds a portion of red kidney beans.

* **Chili Cheese Dog.** This is a hot dog topped with Cincinnati chili, mustard, diced onions, and a mound of shredded cheddar cheese.

* **Chili Spaghetti.** A simpler version where the chili is served over spaghetti without the extra toppings.

Buttery Butternut Squash Soup

Makes approximately 6 pint jars; this recipe can be doubled or tripled

Nothing says sweater weather and cozy fall dishes like butternut squash. Indulge in the comforting embrace of a bowl of velvety butternut squash soup. With its rich, smooth texture and the unmistakable warmth of autumnal flavors, this soup is a delicious comfort food. Savor the essence of roasted butternut squash, blended with a touch of maple syrup and a hint of nutmeg. Each warm spoonful offers an antidote for chilly evenings.

2 large butternut squash, halved vertically with seeds removed

2 apples, peeled, cored, and chopped

1 cup (160 g) chopped onions

6 garlic cloves, minced

2 tablespoons (30 ml) olive oil

2 teaspoons (30 ml) maple syrup

½ teaspoon ground nutmeg

Salt and pepper, to taste

8 cups (1.9 L) chicken broth (vegetable broth can be substituted for vegetarian option)

½ stick (55 g) butter

1. Drizzle each half of the squash with enough olive oil to lightly coat the inside and then sprinkle with salt and pepper. Place on parchment paper–covered baking dish and cook for 50 minutes at 425°F (218°C). Set aside to cool.

2. In a large soup pot, add apples, onions, and garlic to 2 tablespoons (30 ml) olive oil over medium heat and cook until onions are translucent and apples are soft (about 5 to 7 minutes). Set aside to cool.

3. Place canning jars in a canning pot filled with water and bring it to a simmer (180°F/82°C) to heat the jars.

4. In an upright blender, add cooled scooped butternut squash and cooled onion/apple/garlic mixture. Discard the butternut squash skins. Only the squash's pulp goes in the blender.

5. Add maple syrup, nutmeg and salt and pepper to taste to the blender. Pour in 3 cups (711 ml) of broth and blend until creamy smooth.

6. Transfer blended veggies back into the pot and add remaining broth and butter. Whisk and bring to a simmer until soup is smooth and heated. Soup should be slightly runny; it will thicken during canning. If it is not runny, add more broth before canning.

CANNING (HOT PACK)

1. Retrieve hot jars from canner.

2. Place a canning funnel on top of a jar and fill a hot jar with hot soup, leaving 1-inch (2.5-cm) headspace. Do not overfill the jar or the lid will pop off and not seal.

3. Wipe rim with vinegar, and add lid and ring finger light. Repeat with remaining jars. Add jars to the pressure canner, lock the lid, and vent for 10 minutes.

4. Bring canner to 10# pressure (adjust for your elevation).

5. Process time: for pints, 75 minutes; for quarts, 90 minutes.

NOTE: It's normal for soup to separate after canning; stir after opening your jar to reheat.

SERVING SUGGESTION

For a creamy butternut squash soup, you can add various types of cream after opening your jar to reheat. Adjust the amount of cream to achieve the desired level of creaminess in the soup. Start with a smaller amount, taste, and add more as needed. Here are some options.

* **Heavy cream:** This is the classic choice for a rich and indulgent butternut squash soup. Heavy cream will make the soup incredibly creamy and luxurious.

* **Half-and-half.** For a lighter option than heavy cream, half-and-half contains equal parts whole milk and heavy cream, providing a balance between creaminess and a lighter texture.

* **Light cream.** With less fat than heavy cream, light cream will produce a soup that's creamy but not overly rich. It's a good choice if you're looking to reduce calorie content.

* **Coconut milk.** For a dairy-free or vegan option, coconut milk imparts a unique coconut flavor to the soup, adding a tropical twist to the traditional recipe.

* **Greek yogurt.** Greek yogurt can be used to add creaminess and a tangy flavor to the soup. It's a lighter alternative to traditional cream.

Tomato Garlic Soup

Makes approximately 6 to 8 pints or 3 to 4 quarts

Discover the exceptional taste of a homemade tomato soup, a canning recipe that surpasses any store-bought option. Ripe tomatoes, roasted peppers, celery, onions, and garlic come together to create a rich and robust blend that is perfect on its own or in your favorite recipes.

With approximately 12 to 13 pounds (5.4 to 5.9 kg) of cored tomatoes at its base, along with roasted vegetables and an array of carefully selected herbs and seasonings, this recipe is a cut above the rest. A touch of olive oil, fresh parsley, sugar, salt, pepper, and butter adds layers of flavor and balance.

For the ideal consistency, use clear jel to ensure that every spoonful is velvety perfection. Paired with grilled cheese sandwiches, it's a comforting meal to beat the chill of a fall day.

---

1 peck ripe tomatoes, cored (approximately 12 to 13 pounds [5.4 to 5.9 kg])

2 red bell peppers

3 bunches celery

10 small onions

3 heads garlic

2 tablespoons (30 ml) olive oil

5 sprigs fresh parsley

½ cup (100 g) granulated sugar

2 tablespoons (36 g) salt

1 teaspoon black pepper

½ cup (112 g) butter

¼ to ½ cup (36 to 72 g) clear jel

Lemon juice: 1 tablespoon (15 ml) per pint or 2 tablespoons (30 ml) per quart

1. Cook cored tomatoes in a large pot until soft and the juices have been released.

2. Sieve tomato juice or use a Foley mill to remove skins and seeds. Pour tomato juice back in the pot.

3. Chop red peppers, celery, onions, and garlic. Place on a sheet pan and drizzle with olive oil. Toss to coat and broil in oven for 5 to 6 minutes, or until lightly roasted and charred.

4. In a food processor, add cooled roasted vegetables and parsley. Grind into a pulp and add back to tomato juice in the pot.

5. Add sugar, salt, pepper, and butter. Bring everything to a slow and low boil for 30 minutes with the lid off the pot. Stir regularly.

6. Slowly add clear jel, stirring well until soup thickens to desired consistency.

7. Place canning jars in a canning pot filled with water. Bring to a simmer (180°F/82°C) to heat the jars.

NOTE: You can thicken your soup with a flour slurry instead of clear jel after opening the jar. If you choose to omit clear jel, your soup will be more like juice during the canning process. Make a note on the jar to add thickening agent (like flour) upon reheating.

CANNING (HOT PACK)

1. Remove a hot jar from the canning pot using a jar lifter.

2. Add 1 tablespoon (15 ml) lemon juice per pint jar or 2 tablespoons (30 ml) lemon juice per quart jar.

3. Place a canning funnel on top and ladle hot soup into the hot jar, leaving ½-inch (1.25-cm) headspace. Add water or broth to the jar if needed to achieve the correct headspace.

4. Wipe the jar rim with a clean, damp towel or a vinegar-dampened towel to remove any residue.

5. Place the lid on top of the jar and secure with a band, screwing it on until finger light.

6. Place the filled jar back into the canner and repeat canning steps until all jars are filled and in the canner.

7. Lock lid and heat canner on high, venting canner 10 minutes.

8. Add 10# weight or the weight for your altitude. Once the pressure is achieved, reduce heat and maintain pressure. Start timer: for pints, 60 minutes; for quarts, 75 minutes.

PRACTICAL ZERO WASTE FOR LEFTOVER TOMATO SKINS

Peeled tomato skins, often a by-product of canning tomato-based recipes, can be repurposed in various ways. These homemade infusions not only elevate your dishes but also make for wonderful, personalized gifts for your food-loving friends and family.

* Infused oils or vinegars. Place the tomato skins in a bottle or jar, add olive oil or vinegar, and let them infuse for a few weeks.

* Tomato-infused oil. Use this oil to drizzle over salads, pasta, or grilled vegetables. It's a fantastic addition to homemade salad dressings and dipping sauces for bread.

* Tomato-infused vinegar. This can be used to make tangy vinaigrettes, marinades, or pickling solutions. It adds a unique twist to your culinary creations.

Beef Taco Meat

Single batch makes approximately 1 pint jar

A jar of canned beef tacos on hand means you have something like a secret weapon at mealtime. Some of my favorite quick meals start with this handy recipe in a jar. Beef taco meat can be turned into a multitude of dishes.

You can create taco-inspired dishes with minimal effort: imagine the ease of whipping up a hearty taco salad on a busy weeknight, or maybe taco-stuffed bell peppers. Canning beef taco meat also makes for a mouthwatering addition to nachos, quesadillas, or a comforting taco soup for a chilly evening.

For every one pound of ground beef, you will need the ingredients below. Make as many pints or quarts as you have beef for. General approximations for ground beef are 1 pound (454 g) per pint jar or 2 pounds (907 g) per quart.

---

1 pound (454 g) ground beef

½ green bell pepper, diced

½ small onion, diced

2 tablespoons (14 g) onion powder

½ teaspoon garlic powder

1 tablespoon (7.5 g) chili powder

1 teaspoon dried oregano

1 teaspoon dried cumin

1 teaspoon salt (optional)

1. Place canning jars in a canning pot filled with water and bring it to a simmer (180°F/82°C) to heat the jars.

2. Brown the ground beef until slightly cooked, leaving some pink. The beef will finish cooking during the canning process.

3. Drain any excess fat.

4. In a large bowl, combine the vegetables and spices with the ground beef and mix well.

CANNING (COLD PACK)

1. Remove a hot jar from the canning pot using a jar lifter.

2. Place a canning funnel on top of a clean jar and ladle beef taco meat in, leaving 1-inch (2.5 cm) headspace.

3. Wipe the jar rim with a clean, damp towel or a vinegar-dampened towel to remove any residue.

4. Place the lid on top of the jar and secure with a band, screwing it on until finger light.

5. Place the filled jars back into the pressure canner.

6. Vent canner 10 minutes.

7. Add 10# weight or the weight for your altitude. Once the pressure is achieved, start timer: for pints, 75 minutes; for quarts, 90 minutes.

Seasonings per 1 pound (454 g) of ground beef

GROUND BEEF	1 POUND	2 POUNDS	3 POUNDS	10 POUNDS	20 POUNDS
Onion powder	2 tablespoons (14 g)	¼ cup (28 g)	¼ cup + 2 tablespoons (42 g)	1¼ cups (138 g)	2½ cups (276 g)
Garlic powder	½ teaspoon	1 teaspoon	1½ teaspoons (4.5 g)	1 tablespoon + 2 teaspoons (15 g)	2 tablespoons + 1 teaspoon (21 g)
Chili powder	1 tablespoon (7.5 g)	2 tablespoons (15 g)	3 tablespoons (22.5 g)	½ cup + 1 tablespoon (67.5 g)	1 cup + 2 tablespoons (135 g)
Dried oregano	1 teaspoon	2 teaspoons (3.6 g)	1 tablespoon (5.4 g)	3 tablespoons + 1 teaspoon (18 g)	6 tablespoons + 2 teaspoons (36 g)
Cumin	1 teaspoon	2 teaspoons (5 g)	1 tablespoon (7 g)	3 tablespoons + 1 teaspoon (24 g)	6 tablespoons + 2 teaspoons (48 g)
Salt	1 teaspoon	2 teaspoons (12 g)	1 tablespoon (18 g)	3 tablespoons + 1 teaspoon (60 g)	6 tablespoons + 2 teaspoons (120 g)

Burrito in a Jar

*Single recipe makes
1 quart jar*

There's a name for a hassle-free way to enjoy homemade burritos whenever you want them. That name is Burrito in a Jar.

The beans and rice in this recipe are added raw, but don't worry: everything cooks inside the jar during the canning process.

Let your imagination run wild when you open a jar of this tasty mix. Use it as a filling for tacos and enchiladas, or as a topping for nachos.

INGREDIENTS PER QUART JAR

½ cup (86 g) dried pinto beans, rinsed and dried

¼ cup (41 g) parboiled rice or brown rice, uncooked and rinsed

⅓ cup (50 g) chopped green bell peppers

⅓ cup (55 g) chopped onions

1 cup (200 g) ground beef, browned and drained

4 tablespoons (45 g) RO*TEL (tomatoes and green chilis)

1 tablespoon (7 g) taco seasoning

1½ cups (354 ml) beef broth

CANNING (COLD PACK)

1. Layer ingredients, except for beef broth, in order in a quart jar.

2. Place a canning funnel on top and ladle beef broth into the jar, leaving 1-inch (2.5 cm) headspace.

3. Debubble and add more water or broth to the jar if needed to achieve the correct 1-inch (2.5 cm) headspace.

4. Wipe the jar rim with a clean, damp towel or a vinegar-dampened towel to remove any residue.

5. Place the lid on top of the jar and secure with a band, screwing it on until finger light.

6. Place the filled jar into the canner and repeat canning steps until all jars are filled and in the canner.

7. Lock lid, turn heat to high, and vent canner 10 minutes.

8. Add 10# weight or the weight for your altitude. Once pressure is achieved, start timer: for quarts, 90 minutes.

TO RICE OR NOT TO RICE: PERFECTING BURRITO IN A JAR

After canning this recipe both with and without rice, I've found that parboiled or brown rice yields the best results; the rice helps maintain a smoother consistency.

Remember that including rice can make the contents in the jar a bit starchier or mushier. You can omit the rice if you find the product too thick, but make sure to compensate by adding extra beef to fill the jar space accordingly.

When making a new recipe for the first time, I suggest canning a small test batch first to ensure you enjoy the end product before canning in larger quantities. (See "The Wisdom of Small-Batch Canning" on page 183.)

Pork-and-Bean Chalupa

Makes approximately 6 quarts

This hearty dish combines the rich Tex-Mex flavors of tender pork, creamy beans, and zesty spices, ready for whenever you crave a quick and satisfying meal. Use this chalupa as a filling for tacos, spooned over crispy tostadas, or alongside fluffy rice and fresh salsa.

3 cups (750 g) dried pinto beans

9 cups (2.1 L) plus 6 cups (1.4 L) water

2 tablespoons (18 g) garlic powder

2 tablespoons (15 g) chili powder

2 teaspoons (5 g) cumin

2 tablespoons (8 g) oregano

1 teaspoon salt (optional)

4 pounds (1.8 kg) pork roast

3 (4-oz/113 g) cans diced green chili peppers

1 large onion, chopped and divided

1. Wash and strain dried beans and discard any debris. In a large bowl, soak the beans overnight in 9 cups (2.1 L) water. The next day, drain beans and set aside.

2. Mix 6 cups (1.4 L) water and all the spices in a saucepan. Bring to a simmer uncovered for 5 minutes. Remove from heat and cool.

3. Cube pork into 1-inch (2.5-cm) pieces.

CANNING (COLD PACK)

1. The number of jars estimated is 6 quarts (5.7 L). Have a couple of extra jars on hand and do your best to evenly distribute ingredients.

2. Place a canning funnel on top of each jar and layer ingredients in order: ½ cup (86 g) beans, 1 cup (175 g) cubed pork, ½ can (56 g) diced green chili peppers, 10 tablespoons (100 g) chopped onions.

3. Pour or ladle chalupa sauce over jar ingredients, leaving 1-inch (2.5-cm) headspace.

4. Debubble the jars, leaving 1-inch (2.5-cm) headspace. Add additional sauce liquid or water to jars if needed to achieve the correct headspace.

5. Wipe the jar rims with a clean, damp towel or a vinegar-dampened towel to remove any residue.

6. Place the lids on top of the jars and secure with a band, screwing it on until finger light.

7. Place the filled jars into the canner.

8. Vent canner 10 minutes.

9. Add 10# weight or the weight for your altitude. Once the pressure is achieved, start timer: for pints, 75 minutes; for quarts, 90 minutes.

Red Chili Pork Tamales

Makes approximately 25 tamales. This recipe can be doubled or tripled.

Making tamales can be a lot of work, but it's a labor of love, an art passed down through generations. The process is often turned into a joyous family event where large batches are cooked, filled, and wrapped.

This recipe for red chili pork tamales is designed to capture that spirit. Filled with savory pork and red chili sauce, these tamales are a wonderful treat to savor. If you have your own cherished tamale recipe, jump right to the canning instructions to enjoy your favorite variation on tamales year-round.

PULLED PORK FILLING

1½ pounds (681 g) pork shoulder or butt—if large-batch-canning tamales, use larger roast and increase spices

1 large onion, chopped

2 cloves garlic, chopped

2 bay leaves

½ teaspoon dried oregano

1 teaspoon cumin

1 teaspoon chili powder

1 teaspoon salt

1 teaspoon black pepper

RED CHILI SAUCE

4 dried chili pods

2 cups (472 ml) reserved pork broth (if using canned pork carnitas, use broth from jar)

1 teaspoon chili powder

1 teaspoon dried oregano

1 teaspoon onion powder

1 teaspoon cumin

½ teaspoon salt

3 cloves garlic

1 tablespoon (15 ml) vegetable oil

STEP 1: MAKING THE PULLED PORK FILLING

For a shortcut, you can use your canned pork carnitas from page 204.

COOKING PORK FILLING

1. Add all ingredients to a slow cooker, cover pork with water, and cook on low for 8 hours or overnight. Alternatively, you can pressure cook all ingredients in a pressure cooker 15 minutes per pound at 15# psi.

2. Drain broth, reserving 2 cups (472 ml) for red chili sauce. Discard bay leaves.

3. Shred pork and set aside.

STEP 2: MAKING THE RED CHILI SAUCE

1. Remove seeds and stems from chilis. In a saucepan with 2 cups (472 ml) of reserved broth, cook chilis uncovered for 20 minutes.

2. Add chilis to a blender, along with broth and remaining ingredients. Blend until smooth.

3. Add the sauce to the shredded pork, stir, and set aside.

4. Move on to making the dough.

(continued)

DOUGH

Dried corn husks, approximately 4 to 5 per quart jar

1 cup (200 g) lard

3 cups (708 ml) beef broth, divided

4 cups (504 g) masa harina flour

2 teaspoons (9 g) baking powder

½ teaspoon salt

1 teaspoon cumin

3 tablespoons (45 ml) beef broth per quart jar for canning

STEP 3: MAKING THE DOUGH AND ASSEMBLING THE TAMALES

1. Bring corn husks to a boil in a large stockpot. Boil husks for 10 minutes, cover pot with a lid, and turn off heat. Allow husks to soften for an additional 30 minutes while you make the dough.

2. In a large bowl, beat the lard and 2 tablespoons (30 ml) broth with an electric mixer for 3 to 5 minutes.

3. In a separate bowl, combine and mix masa harina flour, baking powder, salt, and cumin.

4. Pour dry ingredients into the lard mixture and beat well with an electric mixer.

5. Add the remaining beef broth a little at a time until a soft dough forms. As the dough thickens, beat on high for several minutes until dough consistency is similar to that of peanut butter and slightly sticky.

6. Assemble the tamales for canning. Retrieve a corn husk from the warm water and lay glossy side up. Add ¼ cup (160 g) of dough to wide end of corn husk.

7. Spread dough using the back of a spoon to ¼ inch (6 mm) thick from side to side on the wide end of the husk. Leave the bottom third (narrow end) of the husk dough-free. The bottom half is for folding.

8. Place 1 heaping tablespoon (14 g) of the pulled pork in red chili sauce down the center of the dough at the wide end of the corn husk.

9. Fold tamale into shape. Fold the right long side toward center of corn husk, then the left long side toward center, overlapping the right-side fold. Fold bottom third (dough-free area) up toward the top (wide area) of the corn husk (almost folded in half). Hold tamale up to quart jar to be sure it will fit before repeating on the rest of the batch. Adjust as needed.

STEP 4: CANNING THE TAMALES

1. Pack tamales (folded end down, open end up toward jar mouth) into wide-mouth quart jars, leaving 1-inch (2.5 cm) headspace. You should be able to get five medium-size tamales in each jar, more if you made smaller tamales.

2. Add 3 tablespoons (45 ml) broth to each quart jar. This will steam-cook tamales in the jar during canning.

3. Wipe rims with vinegar. Place the lids on top of the jars and secure with a band, screwing it on until finger light. Add filled jars to the pressure canner.

4. Heat canner on high and vent canner 10 minutes.

5. Add 10# weight or the weight for your altitude. Once pressure is achieved, reduce heat and maintain pressure, starting a timer for 90 minutes for quarts.

Fajitas in a Jar

Makes approximately 5 quarts

Canning chicken or beef fajitas preserves the robust flavors of Tex-Mex cuisine using a simple meal-in-a-jar approach. Enjoy the sizzling, savory goodness of fajitas without the fuss, whenever you want. Whether you're on a weekend getaway, a camping expedition, or just seeking a quick and delicious meal, your fajita jar is a culinary Swiss Army knife.

This method places the raw ingredients within the jar, offering a unique twist on the traditional fajita preparation.

---

6 cups (1.5 kg) dried pinto beans

2½ cups (375 g) colored sweet peppers, sliced into strips

5 medium tomatoes, chopped

1 (10 oz/283 g) can RO*TEL or 1 jar jalapeño tomatoes (see page 112)

5 to 7 large boneless, skinless chicken breasts, or 4 to 5 pounds (1.8 to 2.3 kg) flank or skirt steak

3 cups (480 g) diced onions

5 tablespoons (27 g) fajita spice blend

8 cups (1.9 L) chicken broth

5 teaspoons (75 ml) lime juice, per quart jar

HOMEMADE FAJITA SEASONING

Can be doubled depending on number of jars being canned; store-bought, premade fajita seasonings may also be used.

3 tablespoons (23 g) chili powder

1½ tablespoons (11 g) cumin

1 teaspoon salt

½ teaspoon black pepper

1 tablespoon (9 g) garlic powder

1 tablespoon (7 g) onion powder

INSTRUCTIONS (RAW PACK)

1. Line up five clean and dried wide-mouth quart jars on your countertop. Raw ingredients will be layered in the jar as you go.

2. Rinse and drain beans, and place in a bowl. Measure and add 1 cup (250 g) of pinto beans per quart jar.

3. Add ½ cup (75 g) peppers per quart jar on top of pinto beans. Using a spoon, gently press peppers down into the jar.

4. Add one fifth of the chopped tomatoes to each quart jar on top of peppers.

5. Add 1 to 2 tablespoons (11 to 22 g) RO*TEL to each quart jar on top of chopped tomatoes.

6. Cut chicken breast or beef steak into 1-inch (2.5 cm) strips. Layer 1 chicken breast/beef steak per quart jar on top of RO*TEL. *Sizes of chicken breast vary widely; pack jars as meat heavy or meat light, according to your preference.* Using a spoon, gently press chicken/beef down into the jar.

7. Layer approximately ½ cup (80 g) diced onions in each quart jar. Using a spoon, gently press onions down into the jar.

8. Add 1 tablespoon (5 g) homemade or store-bought fajita spice mix.

9. Pour chicken broth into each quart jar, leaving 1-inch (2.5 cm) headspace. Using a debubbling tool or wooden spoon handle, tamp the chicken broth down around the food, filling any air pockets around food in the jars.

1 tablespoon (7 g) paprika

1 teaspoon ground mustard

1 tablespoon (15 g) brown sugar

½ teaspoon red pepper flakes
(optional)

HAVE TORTILLAS WILL TRAVEL

* **Campfire delight.** Heat the contents of your jar over a campfire for a delicious outdoor meal.

* **Roadside feast.** Take your fajita jar on road trips: all you need is a portable stove to heat up your meal for a savory feast on the go.

* **Quick and easy meal.** At home or in the office, these jars make for a speedy, delectable lunch or dinner option.

10. Add 1 teaspoon of lime juice to each jar.

11. Debubble and add more broth to adjust headspace to 1 inch (2.5 cm).

CANNING (RAW PACK)

1. Wipe the jar rims with a clean, damp towel or a vinegar-dampened towel to remove any residue.

2. Place the lids on top of the jars and secure with a band, screwing it on until finger light.

3. Place the filled jars into the canner. Lock lid and heat canner on high heat.

4. Vent canner 10 minutes.

5. Add 10# weight or the weight for your altitude. Once the pressure is achieved, start timer: for pints, 75 minutes; for quarts, 90 minutes.

Red Enchilada Sauce

If you love Mexican cuisine, then you know how important a good enchilada sauce is for making an exciting dish. Fortunately, canning your own enchilada sauce at home is easier than you might think. Whether you're including it in your enchiladas, using it as a dip, or drizzling it over tacos, this enchilada sauce will be essential in your kitchen.

3 tablespoons (23 g) ground chili powder

3 teaspoons (7 g) ground cumin

1½ teaspoons (5 g) garlic powder

¾ teaspoon dried oregano

¾ teaspoon salt, to taste

¼ teaspoon cinnamon

8 tablespoons (72 g) clear jel plus 8 tablespoons (120 ml) water

9 tablespoons (135 ml) olive oil

6 tablespoons (96 g) tomato paste

6 cups (1.4 L) chicken or vegetable broth

4 teaspoons (60 ml) apple cider vinegar

½ teaspoon black pepper

1. Combine chili powder, cumin, garlic powder, oregano, salt, and cinnamon in a bowl and set aside.

2. In a small bowl, mix clear jel and water to create a slurry and set aside.

3. Warm the oil in a saucepan over medium heat. Add the spices, then whisk constantly for 1 minute, or until mixture darkens in color.

4. To the spice mixture in the saucepan, add tomato paste. Whisk until smooth.

5. Slowly add chicken or vegetable broth to saucepan and whisk again until smooth.

6. Add clear jel slurry and bring the mixture to a simmer.

7. Reduce heat and cook 5 to 7 minutes, or until sauce has thickened. If the sauce doesn't reach the desired consistency, add additional tablespoons of clear jel, one at a time, until your sauce has thickened adequately.

8. Place canning jars in a canning pot filled with water. Bring to a simmer (180°F/82°C) to heat the jars.

9. Remove enchilada sauce from heat and stir in vinegar and black pepper. Taste and adjust seasonings as needed.

CANNING (HOT PACK)

1. Remove a hot jar from the canning pot using a jar lifter.

2. Place funnel on top of jar and ladle hot enchilada sauce into hot jar, leaving ½-inch (1.25 cm) headspace.

3. Wipe rim with vinegar, add lids, and secure with a band, screwing it on until finger light. Repeat filling each jar and add all filled jars to the pressure canner.

4. Lock lid and heat canner on high, venting canner 10 minutes.

5. Add 10# weight or the weight for your altitude. Once pressure is achieved, turn down heat, maintain pressure, and start timer: 50 minutes for pints.

SAGE ADVICE

Spices and herbs used in recipes intensify when they're pressure canned. It's always best to go lighter on spices before canning and to add more as needed after opening the jar. Knowing this detail is the difference between a cook's brain and a canner's brain. Predicting how the "end product" of a recipe will turn out when canned vs. cooked comes with experience. *One herb that doesn't can well is sage.* It becomes incredibly bitter under pressure and can ruin the whole recipe. If a recipe calls for sage, omit this ingredient before canning and only add the herb once the jar is opened to reheat.

I learned this lesson the hard way: I once ruined 50 pounds (22.7 kg) of sausage because I didn't know it had been preseasoned with sage before I canned it. To my dismay, even the dog wouldn't eat the sausage.

Pork Carnitas

Single recipe makes 1 pint jar

Irresistibly juicy and tender, canned pork carnitas offer a delightful culinary shortcut that saves money by using budget-friendly cuts like shoulder or butt. You get the desired rich, slow-cooked taste, with only a little over an hour's preparation. No one will believe you haven't spent all day cooking.

INGREDIENTS PER PINT JAR

½ pound (227 g) pork (shoulder, butt, loin), cubed into 1-inch (2.5-cm) pieces

½ teaspoon cumin

½ teaspoon dried oregano

½ teaspoon salt

1 bay leaf

¼ teaspoon onion powder

¼ teaspoon garlic powder

½ teaspoon orange juice concentrate

½ teaspoon lime juice concentrate

CANNING (COLD PACK)

1. Pack raw cubed pork into a clean jar, leaving 1-inch (2.5 cm) headspace.

2. Place a canning funnel on top of a jar and add remaining ingredients on top of cubed pork.

3. Wipe the jar rim with a clean, damp towel or a vinegar-dampened towel to remove any residue.

4. Place the lid on top of the jar and secure with a band, screwing it on until finger light.

5. Place the filled jars into the pressure canner.

6. Vent canner 10 minutes.

7. Add 10# weight or the weight for your altitude. Once the pressure is achieved, start timer: for pints, 75 minutes; for quarts, 90 minutes.

UNLOCKING VERSATILITY WITH THE ONE WEEK, ONE MONTH, ONE YEAR METHOD

My One Week, One Month, One Year Method gives you a versatile way to plan your meals, especially when those enticing pork sales at the grocery store come around. Applying this method to all the recipes in this chapter is a great way to build your purposeful pantry.

Below are my calculations for the number of jars required to feed my family of four for a whole year. We usually have 1 quart jar of pork carnitas per week—whether it's on tortillas, in nachos or casseroles, or as sliders.

* One quart requires one pound of pork.

* One quart per week multiplied by 52 weeks equals a total of 52 pounds of pork needed for the year.

Asian Orange Chicken

Makes approximately 6 to 8 pints or 3 to 4 quarts; can be doubled or tripled

This is one of my lazy night favorites. Pop a jar and reheat the contents over rice for a meal that will be ready in minutes. You can also add bell peppers, onions, or any vegetables you enjoy to make this one a complete meal.

3 tablespoons (18 g) minced ginger

4 minced garlic cloves

3 tablespoons (45 ml) rice wine vinegar

3 cups (708 ml) orange juice

6 tablespoons (90 ml) water

¾ cup (180 ml) white vinegar

6 tablespoons (90 ml) soy sauce

1½ teaspoons (23 ml) sesame oil

¾ cup (150 g) granulated sugar

½ teaspoon black pepper

2 teaspoons (2 g) crushed red pepper

Juice and zest of 1 orange

½ cup (72 g) clear jel

6 pounds (2.7 kg) chicken, cut into 1-inch (2.5 cm) cubes

1. Place canning jars in a canning pot filled with water. Bring to a simmer (180°F/82°C) to heat the jars.

2. In a large saucepan, combine all of the ingredients but the chicken and the clear jel and gently bring them to a light boil.

3. To thicken the sauce, ladle approximately 1 cup (236 ml) of the sauce mixture into a separate bowl. Then whisk in the clear jel to create a slurry.

4. Add this slurry mixture back into the saucepan and stir thoroughly. You should notice the sauce gradually thickening. Feel free to incorporate a little more clear jel as necessary until you achieve your preferred consistency.

5. Remove sauce from heat once desired consistency is achieved.

CANNING (HOT PACK)

1. Remove a hot jar from the canning pot using a jar lifter.

2. Pack raw chicken cubes into the jar, leaving 1-inch (2.5 cm) headspace. Ladle orange sauce into the jar.

3. Debubble jar with a non-metal utensil, making sure the orange sauce is throughout the jar evenly. Add extra orange sauce, orange juice, or water to top off the jars to achieve 1-inch (2.5 cm) headspace.

4. Wipe rim with vinegar, add lid, and secure with a band, screwing it on until finger light. Add filled jars to the pressure canner.

5. Vent canner 10 minutes.

6. Add 10# weight or the weight for your altitude. Once pressure is achieved, start timer: pints, 75 minutes; quarts, 90 minutes.

Sweet-and-Sour Chicken

Makes approximately 6 to 8 pints or 3 to 4 quarts; can be doubled or tripled

This sweet-and-sour chicken recipe offers an excursion into Asian American cuisine, complete with vibrant colors, contrasting flavors, and a hint of nostalgia. Get ready for easy—and delicious—gatherings, family dinners, and fast weeknight meals.

5 pounds (2.3 kg) boneless, skinless chicken breasts

2 onions

2 large green bell peppers

2 large red bell peppers

4 (20-oz/567 g) cans pineapple chunks

¾ cup (170 g) brown sugar

1¼ cups (296 ml) white vinegar

6 tablespoons (90 ml) soy sauce

4 tablespoons (60 g) ketchup

1 teaspoon powdered ginger

1. Place canning jars in a canning pot filled with water. Bring to a simmer (180°F/82°C) to heat the jars.

2. Cut chicken into 1-inch (2.5 cm), bite-sized pieces and set aside.

3. Chop onions and peppers and set aside.

4. Strain cans of pineapple, and reserve juice in separate bowl.

5. Heat brown sugar, vinegar, soy sauce, ketchup, ginger, and 3 cups (708 ml) reserved pineapple juice to create the sweet-and-sour sauce. Bring to a light boil, stirring often until sugar is dissolved.

CANNING (HOT PACK)

1. Remove a hot jar from the canning pot using a jar lifter.

2. In each jar, layer raw ingredients in this order, leaving 1-inch (2.5 cm) headspace:

   Chicken
   Onions and peppers
   Pineapple

3. Ladle hot sweet-and-sour sauce into jars, leaving 1-inch (2.5 cm) headspace.

4. Debubble jars with a non-metal utensil, making sure the sweet-and-sour sauce fills the jars evenly. Add extra sauce, pineapple juice, or water to top off the jars to achieve 1-inch (2.5 cm) headspace.

5. Wipe rims with vinegar, add lids, and secure with a band, screwing it on until finger light. Add filled jars to the pressure canner.

6. Vent canner 10 minutes.

7. Add 10# weight or the weight for your altitude. Once the pressure is achieved, start timer: for pints, 75 minutes; for quarts, 90 minutes.

COOKING FROM THE CANTRY

When it comes to purposeful food preservation, always keep in mind the potential for creating a wide range of dishes from a single jar. This will help you maximize the utility of your preserved meals and opens the door to a wide range of flexible menu options.

For example, let's look at several of the possible meals you can create with this sweet-and-sour chicken recipe as the base.

* **Quick weeknight dinner.** Heat and serve canned sweet-and-sour chicken over steamed rice.

* **Stir-fry base.** Stir-fry your favorite vegetables, then add the canned sweet-and-sour chicken for an instant sauce and protein.

* **Party fare.** Impress your guests by incorporating canned sweet-and-sour chicken into party dishes. Use it as a filling for mini tacos or lettuce wraps.

* **Pizza topping.** Spread over pizza dough with cheese and bake for a sweet-and-sour chicken pizza.

* **Meatball glaze.** Use extra sauce to pour over cooked meatballs in a slow cooker for a sweet and tangy meatball dish.

* **Noodle bowl.** Create noodle bowls by combining canned sweet-and-sour chicken with cooked noodles and fresh vegetables.

* **Pasta sauce.** Toss with cooked pasta for a unique pasta creation.

Asian-Inspired Beef

Makes approximately 5 pints

Adding global flavors to your canning repertoire is an excellent way to infuse your cantry with exciting and diverse options for meal planning. The bold Asian flavors of soy sauce, brown sugar, ginger, garlic, and other seasonings blended with beef will make you think twice about ordering takeout.

Whether you use it in stir-fries, mix it with steamed veggies, use it as a filling for dumplings, or add it to jazz up your fried rice, this jar will never disappoint.

Feel free to use any cuts of beef with this recipe for even more variety on your shelves.

3¾ pounds (1.7 kg) ground beef

2¼ cups (532 ml) soy sauce

1½ cups (265 g) brown sugar

1½ cups (240 g) diced onions

1½ teaspoons (8 g) ginger powder

½ tablespoon chopped garlic

1½ teaspoons (2 g) red pepper flakes

3 tablespoons (45 ml) sesame oil

NOTE: To serve, you may top with a sprinkle of sesame seeds.

1. In a skillet, brown the ground beef (the meat should still be slightly pink) and drain fat.

2. Add remaining ingredients to a bowl and add ground beef, mixing well.

3. Place canning jars in a canning pot filled with water and bring it to a simmer (180°F/82°C) to heat the jars.

CANNING (HOT PACK)

1. Retrieve hot jars from canner.

2. Place a canning funnel on top of a jar and ladle hot Asian beef into jars, leaving 1-inch (2.5 cm) headspace.

3. Use a bubble remover tool to remove air bubbles. Add more sauce or water to correct headspace if needed.

4. Wipe the jar rims with a clean, damp towel or a vinegar-dampened towel to remove any residue.

5. Place the lids on top of the jars and secure with a band, screwing it on until finger light.

6. Place the filled jars into the canner. Lock lid and heat canner on high heat.

7. Vent canner 10 minutes.

8. Add 10# weight or the weight for your altitude. Once the pressure is achieved, start timer: for pints, 75 minutes.

Bold and Spicy Szechuan Chicken

Makes approximately 8 pints or 4 quarts

Elevate your cantry with the fiery flavors of Szechuan chicken. This mouthwatering recipe combines the bold and aromatic elements of Szechuan peppercorns, garlic, ginger, and chili paste into a savory sauce that will add an irresistible kick to your meals.

You can customize the level of heat by adjusting the amount of peppercorns and chili paste. Serve this chicken over rice or noodles, stuff it in tortillas for an Asian twist on lunches, or incorporate it into stir-fries, soups, and more.

---

4 to 8 teaspoons (16 to 32 g) Szechuan peppercorns or substitute standard black peppercorns to taste, according to the desired heat level

⅓ cup (48 g) clear jel plus ⅓ cup (79 ml) water

2 cups (472 ml) soy sauce

1½ cups (510 g) honey

½ cup (118 ml) sesame oil

½ cup (118 ml) rice wine vinegar

½ cup (118 ml) Chinese cooking wine (Shaoxing or mirin)

24 garlic cloves, approximately ½ cup (68 g), finely minced

⅓ cup (32 g) finely minced fresh ginger

½ cup (120 g) garlic chili paste or substitute 8 teaspoons (29 g) chili flakes

4 teaspoons (9 g) Chinese five-spice powder

8 pounds (3.6 kg) boneless, skinless chicken breasts, cubed: approximately 1 pound (454 g) per pint jar

1. In a hot, dry skillet, toast Szechuan or black peppercorns for 1 to 2 minutes, or until they are fragrant.

2. Remove from heat and crush peppercorns with a mortar and pestle or grind lightly in a coffee grinder or food processor.

3. In a small bowl, combine clear jel and water to make a slurry. Set aside.

4. In a medium saucepan, whisk soy sauce, honey, sesame oil, rice wine vinegar, Shaoxing or mirin, garlic, ginger, garlic chili paste, and Chinese five-spice powder. Bring to a simmer over medium heat for 5 to 7 minutes, or until honey is dissolved and sauce is smooth.

5. Add clear jel slurry. Whisk until smooth and continue heating until thickened. If sauce is too thin, add more clear jel, 1 teaspoon at a time, until desired thickness is achieved.

NOTE: Sauce will thin when canned with chicken, as the chicken releases its natural broth into the Szechuan sauce.

CANNING (RAW PACK)

1. The number of jars estimated is 8 pints or 4 quarts. Have a couple of extra jars on hand and do your best to evenly distribute ingredients.

2. Pack approximately 1 pound (454 g) of raw cubed chicken into each pint jar or 2 pounds (907 g) per quart jar, leaving 1-inch (2.5 cm) headspace.

3. Place a canning funnel on top of each jar and ladle sauce over chicken, leaving 1-inch (2.5 cm) headspace.

4. To ensure the sauce evenly settles around the chicken cubes in the jar, gently debubble the jar using a wooden skewer or the handle of a wooden spoon. Maintain 1-inch (2.5 cm) headspace while doing so. If necessary, add more sauce or water to the jar to achieve the correct headspace.

5. Wipe the jar rim with a clean, damp towel or a vinegar-dampened towel to remove any residue.

6. Place the lid on top of the jar and secure with a band, screwing it on until finger light.

7. Place the filled jar into the canner and repeat canning steps until all jars are filled and in the canner.

8. Lock lid and heat canner on high. Vent canner 10 minutes.

9. Add 10# weight or the weight for your altitude. Once the pressure is achieved, turn down heat and maintain pressure. Start timer: for pints, 75 minutes; for quarts, 90 minutes.

Savory Beef or Venison Stroganoff

Makes approximately 8 pints or 4 quarts; recipe can be doubled or tripled

Beef stroganoff likely originated in nineteenth-century Russia. The dish traditionally features tender pieces of beef in a sour cream and mustard sauce, served over egg noodles or rice.

Our recipe takes the classic concept and makes it canning friendly: tender chunks of beef or venison are accented with garlic, mushrooms, and a medley of herbs combined in a savory broth. The result is a satisfying stroganoff base. When strained off and reheated, the broth can be easily transformed with sour cream or yogurt to make the signature creamy stroganoff sauce. Be sure to mark your cantry jars "add sour cream" to complete this meal-in-a-jar dish.

Substituting venison for beef can really make this recipe pop, whether you're a traditionalist or an adventurous foodie.

---

2 tablespoons (30 ml) olive oil

4 pounds (1.8 kg) beef stew meat (round or chuck roast) or venison, cut into 2-inch (5 cm) cubes

4 cloves garlic, chopped

2 onions, chopped

2 cups (224 g) mushrooms, sliced

2 teaspoons (4 g) black pepper

4 teaspoons (72 g) salt (or non-bitter, non-clouding salt substitute)

4 teaspoons (6 g) dried thyme

4 teaspoons (1.2 g) dried parsley

½ cup (130 g) tomato paste

½ cup (118 ml) Worcestershire sauce

2 tablespoons (22 g) prepared mustard

4 to 6 cups (944 g to 1.4 L) beef broth

1. In a large skillet, heat olive oil and lightly sear meat on all sides. This locks in the flavors: meat should not be cooked, only seared. Place seared meat in a large bowl.

2. Place garlic, onions, and mushrooms in the bowl and stir to combine.

3. Add all spices and herbs, tomato paste, Worcestershire sauce, and mustard. Mix well to combine.

CANNING (RAW PACK)

1. Place a canning funnel on top of a jar and pack with meat and vegetable mixture to 1-inch (2.5 cm) headspace. Use clean hands or a spoon to firmly tamp contents down into the jars.

2. Add beef broth to the jars, leaving 1-inch (2.5 cm) headspace.

3. Debubble the jars, leaving 1-inch (2.5 cm) headspace. Add more broth or water to jars if needed to achieve the correct headspace.

4. Wipe the jar rims with a clean, damp towel or a vinegar-dampened towel to remove any residue.

5. Place the lids on top of the jars and secure with a band, screwing it on until finger light.

6. Place the filled jars into the canner. Lock lid and heat canner on high heat.

7. Vent canner 10 minutes.

8. Add 10# weight or the weight for your altitude. Once the pressure is achieved, reduce heat, maintain pressure, and start timer: for pints, 75 minutes; for quarts, 90 minutes.

A MEATY EXCHANGE

When it comes to canning recipes like beef stroganoff, you can add variety by using different meats. Most proteins (though not fish or shellfish) tend to have nearly identical processing times when canned. Exchanging meat choices helps you stretch your budget if you find meat on sale or have game from a hunting expedition. Swap out the meat of your choice based on what you have on hand.

For instance, for this beef stroganoff recipe, you can exchange venison, pork, or even poultry for beef, and the processing times will be the same.

One caveat: *Pay attention to the canning times and temperature charts for your creations.*

Mediterranean Dolmas

Makes approximately 10 to 12 wide-mouth pints

Dolmas, also known as stuffed grape leaves, are a beloved side dish in eastern Mediterranean cuisine. Somewhat reminiscent of stuffed cabbage rolls, dolmas go by many names and can be produced with a variety of recipes, reflecting the diversity of flavors and techniques found in the countries where they're enjoyed. Some include lamb, others are simply vegetarian, replacing meat with aromatic rice.

The choice is yours: this recipe is a canvas on which to paint with the flavors you love.

(For reference, my family of four eats around twenty-four pint jars of dolmas per year.)

1½ to 2 cups (293 to 390 g) rice

60 to 65 small grape leaves

3 cups (708 ml) water

1 onion, finely chopped

12 ounces (336 g) lean ground beef or lamb (omit meat and double rice for vegetarian option)

1 teaspoon black pepper

1 teaspoon salt

1 teaspoon ground allspice

½ teaspoon ground cumin

½ cup (32 g) chopped fresh dill

½ cup (48 g) chopped fresh mint

½ cup (32 g) chopped fresh parsley

4 cups (944 ml) chicken broth (substitute vegetable broth for vegetarian option)

Juice of 2 lemons

1. Soak rice in cold water for 15 minutes and then drain.

2. Blanch grape leaves, in batches, by boiling in water for 1 minute and then transferring to a bowl with ice cold water.

3. In a saucepan, boil the water. Add the drained rice and return to boil. Cover and remove from heat. Allow rice to parboil for 10 minutes. Rice will finish cooking during the canning process. Drain rice.

4. Add parboiled rice, onion, raw beef, and all the spices and herbs to a large mixing bowl and mix well to incorporate. This is your dolma filling.

5. To a large bowl, add chicken broth and the lemon juice. I use a pitcher for this to make transferring to the jars easier.

6. To stuff the grape leaves, work on one leaf at a time. Place one grape leaf with the rough/textured side facing you on a cutting board.

7. Add 1 heaping teaspoon of the filling to the center of the leaf. Fold the sides of the leaf over the filling and roll like a cigar or spring roll.

8. Repeat with the remaining grape leaves or until all stuffing is used.

CANNING (RAW PACK)

1. Arrange rolled dolmas standing upright in wide-mouth pint jars. Hold one dolma in place to pack the next one, filling in a circle around the inside of the jar. Add one dolma in the middle to fill the center space.

2. Repeat until all jars are full.

3. Ladle or pour from a pitcher the broth and lemon juice mixture over the dolmas, leaving 1-inch (2.5 cm) headspace.

4. Debubble the jars. Add more broth or water to jars to achieve the correct 1-inch (2.5 cm) headspace.

5. Wipe rims with vinegar, add lids, and secure with a band, screwing it on until finger light. Add filled jars to the pressure canner.

6. Heat canner on high and vent canner 10 minutes.

7. Add 10# weight or the weight for your altitude. Once pressure is achieved, reduce heat, maintain pressure, and start timer: for pints, 75 minutes; for quarts, 90 minutes.

TIMING IS EVERYTHING

Grape leaves, the star ingredient in dolmas and other Mediterranean delights, are a true seasonal delicacy. To capture their tenderness and flavor, it's essential to harvest them at the right time.

The window for gathering grape leaves is relatively short, typically in late spring and early summer, around May and June. Waiting too long may result in tougher, less desirable leaves.

If you find yourself with an abundance of grape leaves, pickled grape leaves retain their lovely texture and can be a convenient addition to your pantry. When the grape leaves are pickled, you'll have the freedom to create dolmas and other dishes whenever you desire.

Butter Chicken Curry

Makes approximately 6 to 8 pints or 3 to 4 quarts (see note)

Butter chicken curry is enjoyed from Delhi to New York to London. While it's a dish that continues to evolve, at its core the recipe features chicken marinated in yogurt and spices, enveloped in a luscious sauce composed of butter, onions, ginger, and tomatoes.

This recipe steps outside the box, proving that canning isn't just for fruits and vegetables: it's also a fantastic way to preserve the rich, aromatic global dishes like butter chicken.

While the ingredient list may seem extensive, don't be discouraged. Many of the components are aromatic spices that are repeated in the marinade and the sauce.

Once you've canned your butter chicken curry, you'll find it opens the door to many unique culinary possibilities. Use it as a base for traditional butter chicken dishes or explore your creativity by inventing new ones. Serve over rice and soak up the buttery sauce with naan.

MARINADE

⅓ cup (77 g) Greek yogurt

6 cloves garlic, ground to paste

2-inch (5 cm) piece fresh ginger, ground to paste

¾ teaspoon salt

2 teaspoons (3 g) garam masala

2 teaspoons (4 g) ground coriander

1 teaspoon ground turmeric

2 teaspoons (5 g) paprika

½ teaspoon ground cayenne (optional heat if desired)

3½ to 4 pounds (1.6 to 1.8 kg) boneless chicken thighs, cut into 2-inch (5-cm) cubes; or skinless, boneless chicken breasts (will end up like shredded chicken in the jar)

MARINATE THE CHICKEN

1. Combine all marinade ingredients in a bowl and mix well with chicken to incorporate. Cover bowl and refrigerate 4 hours or overnight.

BAKE THE CHICKEN

1. Turn oven to broil on high.

2. Add ½ cup (118 ml) water to a deep-dish pan. Place a grated cooking rack (like a cookie cooling rack) over the pan.

3. Place the marinated chicken on the rack and broil on high for 3 to 5 minutes, or until chicken starts to brown. Flip chicken over and broil another 3 to 5 minutes, or until brown on the opposite side.

4. Remove the chicken from oven and set aside. Reserve the chicken drippings from the bottom of the pan; this will be added to the sauce in the next steps.

MAKE THE SAUCE

1. Prepare canning equipment. Place canning jars in a canning pot filled with water. Bring to a simmer (180°F/82°C) to heat the jars.

SAUCE

2 (14½-oz/411 g) cans stewed tomatoes, with juices

½ cup (118 ml) water

6 tablespoons (85 g) butter

1 onion, chopped

2 inches (5 cm) fresh ginger, chopped

5 cloves garlic, chopped

4 teaspoons (6 g) garam masala

2 tablespoons (14 g) paprika

½ teaspoon ground cayenne (optional heat if desired)

½ teaspoon ground cloves

½ teaspoon ground cardamom

½ teaspoon salt

2 tablespoons (30 g) brown sugar, packed

½ to 1 cup (118 to 236 ml) water, as needed to thin sauce

NOTE: Yields are approximate depending on what cut of chicken or how much sauce you pack into the jars. Have extra jars on hand in case you make more than planned.

2. In a blender, blend stewed tomatoes with juices, water, and chicken drippings from the deep-dish pan. Set aside.

3. In a large stockpot or Dutch oven, melt butter and add onions, ginger, garlic, and all the spices. Stir 3 to 4 minutes over medium heat until spices are fragrant.

4. Add sugar and blended tomatoes to spices. Heat to a simmer over medium heat 8 to 10 minutes, or until sugar is dissolved. Add ½ to 1 cup (118 to 236 ml) water to thin sauce as needed.

5. Remove from heat and gently stir in chicken until evenly coated.

CANNING (HOT PACK)

1. Remove a hot jar from the canning pot using a jar lifter.

2. Place a canning funnel on top and ladle hot food into the hot jar, leaving 1-inch (2.5 cm) headspace.

3. Debubble the jar, leaving 1-inch (2.5 cm) headspace. Add water or broth to jars if needed to achieve the correct headspace.

4. Wipe the jar rim with a clean, damp towel or a vinegar-dampened towel to remove any residue.

5. Place the lid on top of the jar and secure with a band, screwing it on until finger light.

6. Place the filled jar back into the canner and repeat canning steps until all jars are filled and in the canner.

7. Lock lid and heat canner on high, venting canner 10 minutes.

8. Add 10# weight or the weight for your altitude. Once the pressure is achieved, start timer: for pints, 75 minutes; for quarts, 90 minutes.

CANNING TRADITIONAL DISHES

＊ The end products of canning traditional recipes may be different than what you are accustomed to: meat may be softer, sauces thicker or thinner, and spices may be more intense. Small-batch-canning new recipes allows you to adjust spices to make your product perfect for you and as close as possible to the traditional dish you love.

＊ Thicken sauces after opening the jar. Your sauces should be thin for canning; they can be thickened later before serving.

＊ Add heavy cream or coconut milk after opening the jar during reheating to create the creamy sauce you want for dishes like Butter Chicken Curry.

Spiced Lentil Soup

Makes approximately 6 to 7 quarts or 12 to 14 pints

This canned lentil soup features warm Indian spices, a meal ready in minutes to warm your soul even on the busiest days. Crafted with a blend of red or yellow lentils, a medley of aromatic spices, and a touch of citrus brightness, this soup is all about balance and depth of flavor.

Use chicken broth, or vegetable stock for a vegetarian option. Customize your soup with garnishes like a dollop of Greek yogurt or sour cream, a sprinkle of fresh cilantro, parsley, or chives, or a drizzle of extra-virgin olive oil. These additions enhance the flavor while adding visual appeal.

2⅔ cups (512 g) dried red or yellow lentils

12 cups (2.8 L) chicken broth; for vegetarian option, vegetable stock

4 (28-oz/794 g) cans fire-roasted tomatoes

2 teaspoons (4 g) turmeric

2 teaspoons (5 g) cumin

½ teaspoon cayenne pepper

½ teaspoon cardamom

5 bay leaves

6 tablespoons (85 g) butter

4 garlic cloves, finely chopped

4 teaspoons (15 g) mustard seeds

Salt and pepper, to taste

1 to 2 lemons, juiced

1. Rinse and drain the lentils, removing any debris. Add to large stockpot.

2. Add the chicken or vegetable stock, tomatoes, turmeric, cumin, cayenne, cardamom, and bay leaves. Bring soup to a boil.

3. Reduce heat to a simmer, cover pot, and simmer until lentils are soft, approximately 30 minutes.

4. Place canning jars in a canning pot filled with water and bring it to a simmer (180°F/82°C) to heat the jars.

5. When lentils are soft, remove bay leaves.

6. In a small frying pan, melt butter. Sauté garlic and mustard seeds lightly and add mixture to the soup.

7. Add salt and pepper to taste and the lemon juice to taste.

CANNING (HOT PACK)

1. Remove a hot jar from the canning pot using a jar lifter.

2. Place a canning funnel on top and ladle hot soup to a generous 1½-inch (4-cm) headspace. This recipe likes to expand in the jars, making headspace especially important to ensure a proper seal.

3. Debubble the jar, leaving 1-inch (2.5 cm) headspace. Add more sauce liquid or water to jar if needed to achieve the correct headspace.

(continued)

4. Wipe the jar rim with a clean, damp towel or a vinegar-dampened towel to remove any residue.

5. Place the lid on top of the jar and secure with a band, screwing it on until finger light.

6. Place the filled jar back into the canner and repeat canning steps until all jars are filled and in the canner.

7. Vent canner 10 minutes.

8. Add 10# weight or the weight for your altitude. Once the pressure is achieved, start timer: for pints, 75 minutes; for quarts, 90 minutes.

NOTE: Before serving, open a jar and dump the contents into a bowl. Using an immersion blender or a potato masher, blend or mash the lentils in the lentil soup to a chunky consistency. You can also add coconut milk when reheating to transform this into a creamy lentil soup. Heat and serve.

NOURISHING ON A BUDGET: LENTILS FOR FOOD SECURITY

In times when food budgets are tight, it's vital to find cost-effective, nourishing options to feed your family. Dried lentils are often overlooked, but they can appear on your culinary horizon as a hero in the world of affordable, nutrient-dense foods.

Here's why lentils should be a staple in your pantry.

* **Affordability.** A pound of dried lentils typically costs about a dollar, but it can yield around 8 to 9 hearty ½-cup (40-g) servings when cooked. That's roughly 13 cents per serving.

* **Protein powerhouses.** Lentils may be small, but they pack a protein punch. A mere ½-cup (40-g) serving of cooked lentils delivers approximately 12 grams of protein, making them an ideal choice as a cost-effective, protein-rich food source. When meat prices are too high, lentils offer a great protein alternative that can save your budget.

Zuppa Toscana

Makes approximately 8 pints or 4 quarts

Zuppa Toscana is a rich Italian soup that's perfect for a cozy night in. It's made with creamy potatoes, spicy Italian sausage, and tender kale, all simmered together in a flavorful broth.

3 pounds (1.4 kg) ground mild or spicy pork sausage

1 pound (454 g) bacon (cut into 1-inch [2.5 cm] pieces)

2 onions, diced

4 cloves garlic, minced

4 large potatoes, peeled and cubed into 1-inch (2.5 cm) pieces

1 bunch of kale or 3 cups (90 g) spinach, rough chopped

1 teaspoon each: salt, pepper, oregano

3 quarts (2.8 L) chicken broth

VEGETARIAN OPTIONS

* Omit meats.
* Add extra potatoes and kale.
* Add red pepper flakes for heat.
* Substitute veggie broth for chicken broth.

1. In a frying pan, sauté pork sausage and bacon. Drain fat.

2. Add all vegetables, spices, and chicken broth to a large pot or bowl. This recipe is for cold pack, meaning no cooking before canning is required.

CANNING (COLD PACK)

1. Ladle soup evenly between jars, leaving 1-inch (2.5 cm) headspace. Add water or broth to jars if needed to achieve the correct headspace.

2. Wipe rims with vinegar, add lids, and secure with a band, screwing it on until finger light. Add filled jars to the pressure canner.

3. Vent 10 minutes.

4. Add 10# weight or the weight for your altitude. Once pressure is achieved, start timer: for pints, 75 minutes; for quarts, 90 minutes.

DAIRY CREAMS AND PRESSURE CANNING

Cream adds a rich, velvety texture and flavor to soups. Be mindful of the downsides of using heavy creams when pressure canning, as it can curdle or separate without a stabilizer like clear jel (see "Cream of Everything Soups" on page 172 for more details). For this reason, it's best to leave out heavy cream when canning Zuppa Toscana, adding it later, after opening the jar. When you reheat this soup, add ¼ cup (60 ml) heavy cream for each pint jar or ½ cup (112 ml) for each quart jar.

CANNING MEATS

Plain canned meat, preserved without extra ingredients, offers a powerful option for building meal plans around. Each jar becomes a blank canvas for your culinary dish creations.

Unfortunately, it can be one of the ugliest jars on your shelves. We lovingly call canned chicken "ugly chicken" in our home. Do not be fooled by the unattractive appearance of canned meat, though: the taste and tenderness of what's in these jars will blow your mind.

Benefits of Canning Meat

❋ Easy for beginners. It's as simple as cutting the raw meat, packing it in jars, then pressure-canning.

❋ Food security. Meat portions can be easily calculated per person, per meal, then multiplied when planning your One Week, One Month, One Year blueprint.

❋ Convenience. No more forgetting to take the meat out of the freezer the night before. Fully cooked meat in a jar means that cooking a homemade meal takes mere minutes.

❋ No refrigeration, no freezer, no problem. Canned meat frees up space in your refrigerator and freezer. If you've ever had a freezer break or experienced an extended power outage, you know how quickly you can lose hundreds of dollars' worth of food. Canning meat also avoids the risk of food loss and freezer burn.

❋ Taste. Canned meats hit your palate differently than fresh or frozen meat, offering a deep, rich flavor profile. The qualities of tender, juicy canned meat are hard to replicate in traditional cooking. Think of it as pressure cooking, in a jar.

Ingredients Per Jar

Here are some examples to help you decide how many jars you'll need when canning meat. These are rough estimates, and the actual volume can vary based on factors such as the meat's density and how finely it's ground or chopped. It is good practice to have additional canning jars and lids ready before you start canning meat.

1 pint= 2 cups (473 ml)

1 quart= 4 cups (946 ml)

❋ 1 pound (454 g) of ground beef/pork = approximately 2 cups (400 g)

❋ 1 pound (454 g) of ground chicken or turkey = approximately 2 1/4 to 4 cups (394 to 700 g)

❋ 1 pound (454 g) of boneless, skinless chicken breast = approximately 2 1/2 cups (350 g)

* 1 pound (454 g) of boneless beef, pork, or lamb chunks = approximately 2½ cups (350 g)

* Salt (optional): ½ teaspoon per pint, 1 teaspoon per quart

* Packing liquid of your choice: water, meat broths, vegetable broths, or tomato juice

Instructions for Raw-Pack Canned Meat

1. Choose your meat from the chart on page 225.

2. Prep your meat: cut, cube, slice, chop, grind, form into patties or links.

Canning

1. Fill jars tightly with meat, leaving 1-inch (2.5 cm) headspace.

2. If using, add salt to the jar: ½ teaspoon for pints, 1 teaspoon for quarts.

3. Wipe the jar rims with a clean, damp towel or a vinegar-dampened towel to remove any residue.

4. Place the lids on top of the jars and secure with a band, screwing it on until finger light.

5. Place the filled jars into the canner. Lock lid and heat canner on high heat.

6. Vent canner 10 minutes.

7. Add 10# weight or the weight for your altitude. Once the pressure is achieved, start timer using canning meat chart on page 225.

Instructions for Hot-Pack Canned Meat

1. Choose your meat from the chart on page 225.

2. Prep your meat: cut, cube, slice, chop, grind, then form into patties or links.

3. Place canning jars in a canning pot filled with water and bring it to a simmer (180°F/82°C) to heat the jars.

4. Sear whole meats to lock in flavors by heating a large pan and browning all sides of the meat. Parcook ground meats by heating in a large skillet until partially done but not cooked all the way through. Drain off any fats.

Canning

1. Remove a hot jar from the canning pot using a jar lifter.

2. Place a canning funnel on top and using a large spoon, pack meat into the jar, leaving 1-inch (2.5 cm) headspace.

3. Ladle hot packing liquid of your choice: water, meat broth, vegetable broth, or tomato juice.

4. Debubble the jar, leaving 1-inch (2.5 cm) headspace. Add more water or broth to jar if needed to achieve the correct 1-inch (2.5 cm) headspace.

5. Wipe the jar rim with a clean, damp towel or a vinegar-dampened towel to remove any residue.

6. Place the lid on top of the jar and secure with a band, screwing it on until finger light.

7. Place the filled jar into the canner and repeat canning steps until all jars are filled and in the canner.

8. Lock lid, turn heat to high, and vent canner 10 minutes.

9. Add 10# weight or the weight for your altitude. Once the pressure is achieved, start timer using meat canning chart at right.

Canning Meat Chart

MEAT	CUT	COOK	PACK	TIME/PRESSURE (PINTS AND HALF PINTS)	TIME/PRESSURE (QUARTS)
Bear	Ground	Parcook	Hot	75 minutes/10psi	90 minutes/10psi
Bear	Strip, cube, chunk	Seared	Hot	75 minutes/10psi	90 minutes/10psi
Beef	Ground	Parcook	Hot	75 minutes/10psi	90 minutes/10psi
Beef	Strip, cube, chunk	Seared	Hot	75 minutes/10psi	90 minutes/10psi
Chicken (Bone-In)	Pieces	None	Raw or hot	65 minutes/10psi	75 minutes/10psi
Chicken (Boneless)	Strip, cube, chunk	None	Raw or hot	75 minutes/10psi	90 minutes/10psi
Elk	Ground	Parcook	Hot	75 minutes/10psi	90 minutes/10psi
Elk	Strip, cube, chunk	Seared	Hot	75 minutes/10psi	90 minutes/10psi
Lamb	Ground	Parcook	Hot	75 minutes/10psi	90 minutes/10psi
Lamb	Strip, cube, chunk	Seared	Raw or hot	75 minutes/10psi	90 minutes/10psi
Moose	Ground	Parcook	Hot	75 minutes/10psi	90 minutes/10psi
Moose	Strip, cube, chunk	Sauté	Raw or hot	75 minutes/10psi	90 minutes/10psi
Pork	Ground	Parcook	Hot	75 minutes/10psi	90 minutes/10psi
Pork	Strip, cube, chunk	Seared	Raw or hot	75 minutes/10psi	90 minutes/10psi
Rabbit (Bone-In)	Pieces	None	Raw or hot	65 minutes/10psi	75 minutes/10psi
Rabbit (Boneless)	Strip, cube, chunk	None	Raw or hot	75 minutes/10psi	90 minutes/10psi
Sausage	Ground	Parcook	Hot	75 minutes/10psi	90 minutes/10psi
Sausage	Links, patties	Seared	Raw or hot	75 minutes/10psi	90 minutes/10psi
Turkey (Bone-In)	Pieces	None	Raw or hot	65 minutes/10psi	75 minutes/10psi
Turkey (Boneless)	Strip, cube, chunk	None	Raw or hot	75 minutes/10psi	90 minutes/10psi
Veal	Ground	Parcook	Hot	75 minutes/10psi	90 minutes/10psi
Veal	Strip, cube, chunk	Seared	Raw or hot	75 minutes/10psi	90 minutes/10psi
Venison	Ground	Parcook	Hot	75 minutes/10psi	90 minutes/10psi
Venison	Strip, cube, chunk	Seared	Raw or hot	75 minutes/10psi	90 minutes/10psi

NOTE: *Pressures are shown for 1,000 feet (304 m) elevation or less. Adjust as needed using altitude chart on page 36.*

Spiced Ham, Canned Ham-Style

Makes approximately 6 pint jars or 12 half-pint jars

At our house, we sometimes call this spiced ham "Mock Spam," in homage to the flavors of yesteryear, particularly the delightful taste of my childhood. Creating spiced ham requires a meat grinder to get the perfect texture and consistency. We use Morton Tender Quick, a specialized curing mix that adds a unique flavor and helps set the texture.

To serve, cut the spiced ham into thin slices and pan-fry for a classic breakfast experience, or use it as a filling for sandwiches. You can also dice it into salads. For an exciting twist, explore the ham's potential in Asian-inspired recipes, such as pairing it with soy sauce, rice, and a perfectly fried egg.

---

5 pounds (2.3 kg) pork shoulder

1 pound (454 g) ham steak

2 tablespoons + 1 teaspoon (33 g) Morton Tender Quick

3 tablespoons (39 g) granulated sugar

3 tablespoons (24 g) cornstarch

1 tablespoon (19 g) kosher salt

1 cup (236 ml) cold water

1. Cut pork and ham into cubed pieces that will fit into your meat grinder. Do not remove the excess fats, as they are needed for this recipe and help create the binding gel.

2. Place cut meats in the freezer for 1 to 2 hours, or until they are semi-frozen; semi-frozen meat will cut and grind much easier.

3. Grind pork and ham steak through a meat grinder with a medium grinder plate.

4. Grind the meat mixture a second time using the fine grinder plate. The second grind is the key to a tender meat mixture: if the meat feels coarse, it will be grainy after canning.

5. Mix Morton Tender Quick, sugar, cornstarch, kosher salt, and cold water together until everything dissolves into a slurry.

6. Pour the slurry mixture over the meat mixture and mix well with gloved hands.

CANNING (RAW PACK)

1. Pack meat mixture tightly into wide-mouth pint jars. The quickest way to do this is by piping the mixture into the jar with a piping bag. Use the bottom of a half-pint jar to press meat mixture down in the jar, removing any air pockets.

2. Using the handle of a wooden spoon, poke a hole through the meat mixture down the middle of the jar. This will allow for more even heating.

3. Wipe the jar rim with a clean, damp towel or a vinegar-dampened towel to remove any residue.

4. Place the lid on top of the jar and secure with a band, screwing it on until finger light.

5. Place jars into pressure canner and lock lid. Heat the canner on high and vent canner 10 minutes.

6. Add 10# weight or the weight for your altitude. Once the pressure is achieved, start timer: 75 minutes for half pints or pints.

Canned Bacon

Approximately 1 pound (454 g) of raw bacon strips per pint jar

Canned bacon has been a part of my cantry for as long as I can remember, and I can confidently say that it's been a game-changer in my kitchen. The history of canned bacon stretches back more than a century.

During World War I and World War II, canned bacon became a critical part of soldiers' rations due to its long shelf life and transportability. After the wars, canned bacon gained popularity among home cooks for its convenience. More recently, canned bacon—often called military bacon—has become popular again in the emergency preparedness communities because it offers a reliable source of protein during times of crisis or natural disasters, or as part of a survival kit.

While canned bacon has been a long-standing tradition for many, keep in mind food preservation practices and recommendations may evolve over time. It's a good idea to stay informed about the latest information by checking in with your local food safety agency.

1. Parcook bacon on a griddle or fry pan. This method releases a lot of its grease, a factor that will be important during canning. This ensures that you get a better bacon end product instead of a jar full of grease.

2. Set parcooked bacon on paper towel–lined plate as you work in batches preparing bacon.

3. Cut 2 pieces of parchment paper approximately 24 inches (61 cm) long. Do not use wax paper, as it is not made to withstand the temperatures of canning and will melt.

4. Cut one of the 2 pieces of parchment paper in half horizontally.

5. Lay 12 to 15 strips of bacon on the full 24-inch (61 cm) sheet of parchment paper.

6. Lay one half of the cut parchment paper on top of the bacon.

7. Place your forearm under the length of the parchment paper and flip the bacon in half on itself. This creates layers (parchment paper—bacon, parchment paper—bacon) that will keep the bacon from sticking to itself during canning.

8. Cigar-roll parchment-wrapped bacon into a tight spiral. Cut or tuck the ends of parchment paper if there is excess.

9. Stuff bacon roll into pint jars. Smash and pack bacon roll tightly, leaving a 1-inch (2.5 cm) headspace.

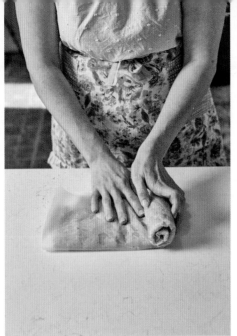

STEP 7 **STEP 8** **STEP 9**

CANNING (COLD PACK)

1. Wipe rims with vinegar, add lids, and secure with a band, screwing it on until finger light. Add filled jars to the pressure canner.

2. Lock lid, heat canner on high, and vent canner 10 minutes.

3. Add 10# weight or the weight for your altitude. Once pressure is achieved, turn down heat to maintain pressure and start timer: for pints, 75 minutes.

REUSE, REDUCE, RECYCLE: LIQUID GOLD AND FIRE STARTER

In the spirit of a "waste not, want not" approach in your kitchen, go to page 268 to learn how to clean and reuse that bacon grease we call "liquid gold."

Before you toss that used parchment paper from your bacon jar, consider this eco-friendly hack. After enjoying your jar of bacon, you'll have parchment paper with smears of flavorful grease. Instead of discarding it, place the greased parchment paper in a resealable plastic bag and pop it in the freezer. This simple trick allows you to repurpose the paper as a convenient and effective fire starter for future use.

FISH

Canned salmon is one of my favorite fish to can. Whether you've reeled in a fresh catch or found a great deal on fish at your local market, canning allows you to enjoy the flavors of the sea year-round.

When I grew up on Lake Michigan, every July the steelheads and coho salmon ran to deeper waters and so did I, chasing them!

Whether you're a seasoned canner or a newcomer to the world of home preservation, this process can be a stellar addition to your pantry.

Canning Fish

1. Begin by removing the head, tail, fins, and scales.

2. Thoroughly wash the fish, ensuring all traces of blood are removed.

3. Optionally, split the fish lengthwise according to your preference.

4. Cut the cleaned fish into 3- to 4-inch (8 to 10 cm) strip lengths.

5. When filling jars, place the fish with the skin side next to the glass, leaving a 1-inch (2.5 cm) headspace.

6. If desired, you can add 1 teaspoon of salt per pint or ½ teaspoon per half pint. For low-fat fish like cod or halibut, you can add 1 to 2 tablespoons (15 to 30 ml) olive oil to keep the fish from drying out.

7. Note that no additional liquids should be added to the jars. For smoked fish, add 10 minutes to the processing times.

Canning

1. Wipe rims with vinegar, add lids, and secure with a band, screwing it on until finger light. Add filled jars to the pressure canner.

2. Lock lid, heat canner on high, and vent canner 10 minutes.

3. Add 10# weight or the weight for your altitude. Once pressure is achieved, turn down heat to maintain pressure and start timer: for pints and half pints, 100 minutes.

Examples of fish for your cantry: cod, flatfish, salmon, mackerel, steelhead, trout

CRYSTALS IN CANNED FISH: SAFE AND DISSOLVABLE

When canning salmon, you may occasionally come across glass-like crystals. There's no method to prevent the formation of these crystals, but they aren't a concern. These tiny crystalline structures typically dissolve when the salmon is heated, and they pose no harm to your health. You can rest assured that your canned salmon will be safe to eat, and any crystals you encounter will vanish with a little heat.

BEANS: TINY BUT MIGHTY

When you look at shelves lined with jars of ready-to-eat meals, you can take comfort in knowing that you have the basis for feeding your family, come rain or shine. When lean times roll around, these jars will be there to keep you going.

Beans are a key ingredient in any canner's stockpile: canning beans in large batches not only saves time but also ensures that you have a reliable source of nourishment at your fingertips.

They're little nutritional powerhouses, packed with protein, fiber, and essential nutrients. Having them readily available ensures you're not just eating well but eating smart, even when resources are limited.

Tex-Mex Ranch Beans

Single batch makes 1 pint jar

There's no ranch dressing in ranch beans! These beans, a mainstay in Tex-Mex cooking, hold a special place on dinner tables across the Southwest. Featuring protein-rich pinto beans infused with a blend of zesty spices, this recipe is also convenient because it requires very little prep work. Just stack each ingredient in the jar and you're ready for canning.

Ranch beans serve as a delightful side dish or a key ingredient in Tex-Mex classics like burritos, enchiladas, and chili. The beans are a fantastic source of essential nutrients, making them a wholesome choice for a well-rounded meal.

The ingredient measurements given here are for each pint jar (if using quart jars, double the ingredients).

½ cup (125 g) dried pinto beans, washed, no presoak needed

½ teaspoon of each: salt, paprika, chili powder, cumin, onion powder, garlic powder, and oregano

1 teaspoon of diced green chilis

Enough water for each jar

CANNING (COLD PACK)

1. In clean pint jars, add pinto beans, spices, and green chilis.

2. Add enough water to each jar to a 1-inch (2.5 cm) headspace.

3. Debubble jars with a non-metal utensil and add extra water to top off the jars to achieve 1-inch (2.5 cm) headspace.

4. Wipe rims with vinegar, add lids, and secure with a band, screwing it on until finger light. Add filled jars to the pressure canner.

5. Vent canner 10 minutes.

6. Add 10# weight or the weight for your altitude. Once pressure is achieved, start timer: for pints, 75 minutes; for quarts, 90 minutes.

Savory British Tomato Beans

Makes approximately 8 pints or 4 quarts

British-style baked beans have been a beloved staple for generations. You can enjoy the authentic essence of these beans by crafting them in your own home and having them ready to heat and eat from your cantry.

With a blend of tomato, Worcestershire sauce, and seasonings, these beans are not just a side dish: they can be the star of your meal. In the UK, beans on toast are a popular choice and a favorite for a quick, protein-packed breakfast. Serve them atop a warm, buttered slice of toast with or without a slice of melted cheese. They're also a fantastic accompaniment to a full English breakfast and, of course, they make an excellent side dish for any meal.

4 cups (860 g) dried white navy beans (haricot)

4 cups (944 ml) chicken broth, or vegetable broth for a vegetarian option

2 cups (472 ml) water

4 teaspoons (60 ml) Worcestershire sauce

¾ cup (180 g) ketchup

6 tablespoons (96 g) tomato paste

6 tablespoons (90 g) brown sugar

2 tablespoons (30 ml) apple cider vinegar

1 teaspoon garlic powder

1 teaspoon onion powder

1 teaspoon black pepper

2 teaspoons (12 g) salt

1. Soak the beans in water overnight (8 to 10 hours). Unlike some other bean canning recipes, I recommend presoaking the beans here: being high in acid, tomato-based liquids do not absorb into the hard shells of dried beans. By presoaking the beans, you ensure they won't remain hard after canning.

2. Strain water from beans and set aside.

3. In a large bowl, mix the remaining ingredients well to create the sauce.

CANNING (COLD PACK)

1. Add ½ cup (91 g) presoaked beans to each pint jar, 1 cup (182 g) to each quart jar. Do not use more beans per jar than stated, as the beans will expand during canning, absorbing the liquid and filling the jars.

2. Place a canning funnel on top and ladle tomato sauce to a generous 1½-inch (4-cm) headspace. The beans in this recipe will expand in the jars, making headspace especially important to ensure a proper seal.

3. Debubble the jar, leaving 1½-inch (4-cm) headspace. Add more broth or water to the jar if needed to achieve the correct headspace.

4. Wipe the jar rim with a clean, damp towel or a vinegar-dampened towel to remove any residue.

5. Place the lid on top of the jar and secure with a band, screwing it on until finger light.

6. Place the filled jar into the canner and repeat canning steps until all jars are filled and in the canner.

7. Vent canner 10 minutes.

8. Add 10# weight or the weight for your altitude. Once the pressure is achieved, start timer: for pints, 75 minutes; for quarts, 90 minutes.

Colonial-Style Boston Baked Beans

Makes 6 to 8 pints or 3 to 4 quarts

Boston baked beans are as much a part of Boston's history as the Red Sox and the city's historic cobblestone streets. They have a unique character that combines the hearty essence of slow-cooked navy beans with a rich infusion of smoky flavors and sweet molasses.

Boston baked beans trace their roots back to the early days of colonial New England, where they were slow-cooked in brick ovens, their flavor deepening as they absorbed the essence of salt pork, molasses, and spices. Over time, the dish evolved, being adapted to modern tastes while maintaining the core flavors that Bostonians love. The result is a dish that's both satisfying and indulgent.

This recipe takes four hours to cook, but through canning the beans will be waiting on your shelves, ready for you to enjoy at a moment's notice.

Whether you plan to serve them as a standalone side dish, a topping for hot dogs, or a flavor-packed accompaniment to your favorite barbecue, these beans will evoke the rich culinary heritage of Boston.

---

4 cups (860 g) dried navy beans

½ pound (227 g) salt pork or bacon, cut into ½-inch (1.3-cm) pieces

3 large onions, diced

⅔ cup (150 g) brown sugar, packed

⅔ cup (227 g) molasses

3 teaspoons (9 g) ground mustard

2 teaspoons (36 g) salt

4 cups (944 ml) water

For vegetarian option: Omit pork and add extra teaspoon of salt.

1. In a large bowl, soak the dried beans in water, 8 to 10 hours or overnight

2. Drain beans and bring to a boil in a large stockpot filled with new water. Cover pot, reduce heat, and cook beans 45 minutes, or until skins begin to split.

3. Drain beans and set aside.

4. In a large stockpot (4 quarts or larger), heat remaining ingredients until sugars are completely dissolved. The barbecue sauce will be thin at this point.

5. Add beans to barbecue sauce mixture and preheat oven to 300°F (149°C).

6. In a 4-quart Dutch oven with a snug-fitting lid, add barbecue beans. Cook approximately 4 hours.

7. Check the beans every hour. As needed, add water to maintain a soupy consistency, as the beans absorb the barbecue sauce. Typically, this requires 4 to 6 cups (944 ml to 1.4 L) of water.

8. Place canning jars in a canning pot filled with water and bring it to a simmer (180°F/82°C) to heat the jars.

CANNING (HOT PACK)

1. Remove a hot jar from the canning pot using a jar lifter.

2. Place a canning funnel on top and ladle hot barbecue bean mixture into warmed jar, leaving a 1-inch (2.5 cm) headspace.

3. Add more water or broth to the jar if needed to achieve the correct 1-inch (2.5 cm) headspace.

4. Wipe the jar rim with a clean, damp towel or a vinegar-dampened towel to remove any residue.

5. Place the lid on top of the jar and secure with a band, screwing it on until finger light.

6. Place the filled jar into the canner and repeat canning steps until all jars are filled and in the canner.

7. Lock lid, turn heat to high, and vent canner 10 minutes.

8. Add 10# weight or the weight for your altitude. Once the pressure is achieved, start timer: for pints, 75 minutes; for quarts, 90 minutes.

Hearty Pork and Beans

Pork and beans is a classic dish that works as a simple weeknight dinner, a great meal for camping trips, or for sustenance during an emergency. It's a perfect side dish, or it can be the star of the show when poured over cornbread or rice. It also works for creating stews, casseroles, or a quick chili. Simply open a jar and let your creativity run wild.

2 pounds (908 g) dried navy or great northern beans, approximately 5 cups (1.1 kg) dried beans

¼ cup (60 g) brown sugar

¾ teaspoon prepared yellow mustard

2 tablespoons (40 g) molasses or honey

2 (15-oz/425 g) cans tomato sauce

3 cups (708 ml) water

1½ teaspoons (27 g) salt (optional)

2 onions, chopped

8 pieces bacon, salt pork, or fatback (omit for vegetarian option)

1. Quick-soak beans: add cleaned and sorted dried beans to a large stockpot and fully cover them with water. Bring to a boil, stirring occasionally to ensure even heating. Boil for 5 to 10 minutes, then remove from heat. Cover with a lid and let them soak undisturbed for 1 hour.

2. To a saucepan, add brown sugar, yellow mustard, molasses or honey, tomato sauce, water, and salt (if using). Bring to a boil, stirring until sugars are dissolved, and remove from heat.

3. Rinse beans in colander prior to filling jars.

CANNING

To make this recipe in quart jars, double the ingredients in each jar.

1. In each pint jar, add 1 cup (182 g) presoaked beans.

2. Distribute onions evenly among pint jars.

3. Add 1 piece of pork of choice to each pint jar.

4. Add 1 cup (236 ml) sauce to each pint jar.

5. Debubble the jars. Add additional water to jars to achieve the correct 1-inch (2.5 cm) headspace.

6. Wipe rims with vinegar, add lids, and secure with a band, screwing it on until finger light. Add filled jars to the pressure canner.

7. Heat canner on high and vent canner 10 minutes.

8. Add 10# weight or the weight for your altitude. Once pressure is achieved, reduce heat and maintain pressure. Start timer: for pints, 75 minutes; for quarts, 90 minutes.

BEAN BOOZLED

Canning beans dried or presoaked: What to choose for canning?

Soaking the beans before canning results in beans that have already absorbed liquid, offering a softer, plumper texture after canning. Canning dried beans can achieve the same result, depending on the bean type and the liquid it's canned in. Whichever you choose, your beans will be cooked during the canning process, but the texture results may be different.

When deciding which method to use, remember that tomato-based (high-acid) sauces may not effectively break down the bean shells and absorb into the beans adequately during the canning process. This can lead to beans that remain firm rather than softening as desired. Because of this, when canning beans with tomato-based sauces, you may need to take extra care to achieve the desired texture.

The choice between canning dried beans and canning presoaked beans ultimately depends on your preferences and how you plan to use the beans in your recipes. Note that either method will not affect safety or shelf stability.

Boston Brown Bread

Makes 5 wide-mouth pint jars. Recipe can be doubled or tripled.

Boston brown bread, that humble, dark-hued loaf, dates back to early New England, and it's still served at that region's Saturday night suppers. Its rich, slightly sweet taste hides a secret: its remarkable shelf stability. Once properly canned, this bread can grace your pantry shelves for up to ten years, ready to serve you a taste of history whenever you please.

Traditionally steamed in cans, Boston brown bread offers a unique, harmonious blend of whole wheat and cornmeal, molasses for sweetness, and a slight tang from buttermilk. It's often served alongside dishes like baked beans, franks, and cuts of meat. For a true New England experience, try this bread smothered in Boston baked beans (see recipe page 236).

---

1 cup (125 g) white flour

1 cup (125 g) graham flour

1 cup (128 g) rye flour

1 cup (140 g) cornmeal

1 teaspoon salt

1 teaspoon ground allspice

1 teaspoon baking powder

1 teaspoon baking soda

2 eggs, whisked

2 teaspoons (10 ml) vanilla extract

2 cups (472 ml) buttermilk

1 cup (340 g) molasses

1. Mix all flours and dry ingredients in a bowl.

2. In a separate bowl, whisk eggs, vanilla, and buttermilk.

3. Add dry ingredients to wet ingredients in a stand mixer and mix until smooth. Alternatively, use a hand mixer.

4. Add the molasses to the bread mixture and mix until consistency is similar to that of cake batter.

CANNING

1. Spray clean wide-mouth pint jars with non-stick cooking spray.

2. Using a funnel, pour bread mixture into the jars to the halfway point. Do *not* overfill jars or they will not seal. The bread will rise and cook in the jar.

3. Wipe rims with vinegar, add lids, and secure with a band, screwing it on until finger light. Add filled jars to the pressure canner.

4. Fill canner with enough water for it to come up to the bottom of the rings of the jar. This effectively creates a bain-marie inside the canner, preventing it from running dry during the bread's long processing time. (Note that this is a deviation from normal canning instructions.)

5. Heat pressure canner on high and vent canner 10 minutes.

6. Add 10# weight or the weight for your altitude. Once pressure is achieved, reduce heat and maintain pressure, starting a timer for 2 hours.

7. Depressurize pressure canner naturally when timer is up.

GRAHAM FLOUR AND BOSTON BROWN BREAD

Graham flour is a type of whole-wheat flour made from the entire wheat kernel, including the bran, germ, and endosperm. It is coarsely ground, which gives it a rough texture compared to regular wheat flour.

The use of graham flour is often associated with the creation of graham crackers and graham bread, which were developed in the nineteenth century by Sylvester Graham, a notable figure in the early health food movement.

If you need to substitute graham flour because it's unavailable, substitute with whole-wheat flour. Since graham flour is coarsely ground whole-wheat flour, using the more common whole-wheat flour will provide a similar nutty flavor and nutritional profile.

Keep in mind that whole-wheat flour has a finer texture compared to graham flour, so your end product may be slightly different in texture, but it will still work well in this recipe. The substitution ratio is generally one-to-one, but you can experiment with the texture and flavor to achieve the desired result in your specific recipe.

Traditional Canned Butter

Single recipes makes 6 pint jars. Can be doubled or tripled.

What goes with bread? Butter, of course!

Imagine preserving butter in a jar for long-term storage: That's what we do in our home. Canned butter has been a regular staple on our cantry shelves for decades. Canned butter is akin to clarified butter or ghee. By removing the milk solids, you are left with a rich-flavored, shelf-stable butter.

---

3 pounds (1.4 kg) unsalted butter

3 pounds (1.4 kg) salted butter

Start this recipe early in the day, as some of the steps take a few hours.

1. Soften the butter at room temperature overnight.

2. In the morning, add softened butter to large stockpot and melt until liquid. This takes some time: a full rolling boil isn't necessary, but butter should be hot enough to skim the foam off the top.

   TIPS: *I like to add half my butter to the pot, melt it down, then add the second half stick by stick until it's all melted. Another option is to use the microwave and work in batches until butter is melted, then transfer to a pot.*

3. Place jars on cookie sheets and put in a room-temperature oven. Heat jars and your oven at the same time. Do not put cold jars into a preheated oven, as this will stress the glass. Set oven to 250°F (121°C) with the jars inside and heat both oven and jars at the same time. Once the oven reaches temperature, start a timer for 20 minutes.

4. Warm pressure canner and canner water. All equipment and materials should be warm/hot at the same time: hot jars, hot butter, hot canner.

5. Keep stirring butter while jars are heating and skim milk foam off the top of the melted butter. I reserve this foam for popcorn or baking.

6. Once you have removed most of the milk foam, take the hot jars out of the oven.

7. Ladle hot butter into hot jars, leaving 1-inch (2.5 cm) headspace.

8. Wipe rims well with vinegar, add lids, and secure with a band, screwing it on until finger light. This step is crucial, as butter is oily and can prevent adequate lid seals.

9. Add jars to canner, lock lid, and vent for 10 minutes.

10. Add 10# weight or the weight for your altitude. Once the pressure is achieved, start timer: for pints, 75 minutes.

11. When done, remove jars and allow to cool. After the jars have sealed and cooled enough to handle, give the jars a light swirl or shake every 20 to 30 minutes for the next few hours. Continue shaking periodically until the jars are completely cooled. This will mix any residual milk solids that fall to the bottom of the jar as the mixture cools, keeping all the contents liquid.

NOTES: It's common for any residual milk solids to sink to the bottom during cooling. This will not affect your process: you can stir the jar after opening it or leave the milk solid layer on the bottom of the jar.

This recipe has an approximate shelf life of five years, although we use so much of this butter that our jars never make it that long.

Buttery Crunchy Kernel Corn

Single recipe makes either 1 quart jar or 1 pint jar (see "How Many Jars?")

As the seasons change and fresh produce becomes abundant, I seize the opportunity to buy corn in bulk from local farmers' markets and a nearby farm. I've developed a canning process that keeps our pantry stocked all year.

How Many Jars?

On average, a quart jar will hold 4½ pounds (2 kg) of sweet corn and a pint jar will hold 2¼ pounds (1 kg) of corn. Adjust the recipe for the amount of corn you will be canning.

Approximate yields:

* 35 pounds (15.9 kg) (in husk) of sweet corn = 8 quarts

* 31½ pounds (14.3 kg) (in husk) of sweet corn = 7 quarts

* 20 pounds (9 kg) (in husk) of sweet corn = 9 pints

INGREDIENTS PER QUART JAR

4 cups (600 g) kernel corn

1 tablespoon (14 g) butter (optional)

1 teaspoon salt (optional)

INGREDIENTS PER PINT JAR

2 cups (300 g) kernel corn

1 teaspoon butter (optional)

½ teaspoon salt (optional)

1. Shuck corn husk away from corncob. Peel away any extra corn silk from cobs. Save husks and silk for recipes in chapter 7.

2. Cut corn from cob at about three-fourths the depth of kernel. To do this easily, I set a Bundt pan right-side up on a table, then I place the shucked corncob in the center hole of the Bundt pan. Slice the kernels away, as close to the cob as possible, allowing the kernels to be captured in the Bundt pan bowl.

3. Save corncobs for corncob jelly on page 260.

CANNING (RAW PACK)

1. Fill a jar tightly with raw corn kernels, leaving 1-inch (2.5 cm) headspace.

2. Add butter and salt to the jar, if desired.

3. Add fresh boiling water, leaving 1-inch (2.5 cm) headspace.

4. Debubble the jar, leaving 1-inch (2.5 cm) headspace. Add more water to the jar if needed to achieve the correct headspace.

5. Wipe the jar rim with a clean, damp towel or a vinegar-dampened towel to remove any residue.

6. Place the lid on top of the jar and secure with a band, screwing it on until finger light.

7. Place the filled jar into the canner and repeat canning steps until all jars are filled and in the canner.

8. Vent canner 10 minutes.

9. Add 10# weight or the weight for your altitude. Once the pressure is achieved, start timer: for pints, 55 minutes; for quarts, 85 minutes.

UNLOCKING THE FULL POTENTIAL OF CORN

When you're canning corn, it's easy to focus solely on the kernels. But don't forget the many other parts of the vegetable that afford opportunities for creative, sustainable kitchen practices. By saving everything the corn has to offer, you can unlock its full potential and reduce waste in your kitchen.

Look forward to special recipes using corn in the next part of this book. Here are some highlights:

* **Corncob jelly.** Turn those leftover corncobs into delicious jelly. This sweet concoction can add a delightful twist to your breakfast spreads and desserts, all while reducing kitchen waste.

* **Corn silk tea.** Corn silk can be used to brew a soothing tea, known to have diuretic properties—an excellent way to make the most of this often-overlooked part of the corn plant.

* **Corn husk for tamale wraps.** Tamale wraps are traditionally made with corn husks. These natural wrappers infuse your tamales with a subtle, earthy flavor, elevating your culinary creations to new heights.

Green Beans with a Bacon Twist

Single recipe makes either 1 quart jar or 1 pint jar (see "How Many Jars?")

If you're new to growing your food, bush green beans are an excellent starter crop to try. Canning this recipe allows you to capture green beans at the peak freshness of this beloved vegetable; you can also add a delightful twist to the classic by including bacon. The combination of tender green beans and smoky bacon creates a side dish that's sure to become a family favorite.

One of the advantages of canning your own green beans is the opportunity to source them in bulk directly from local farmers or farmers' markets. Buying in bulk during the harvest season not only ensures the freshest produce but often comes at a lower cost than store-bought alternatives in the off-season. Plus, you're supporting your local agricultural community and reducing your carbon footprint in the process.

How Many Jars?

On average, a quart jar will hold 2 pounds (908 g) of green beans while a pint jar will hold 1 pound (454 g). Adjust the recipe for the amount of green beans you will be canning.

Approximate yields:

* 30 pounds (13.6 kg) green beans = 15 quarts

* 14 pounds (6.4 kg) green beans = 7 quarts

* 9 pounds (4.1 kg) ground beans = 9 pints

INGREDIENTS PER QUART JAR

2 pounds (908 g) snapped green beans

2 cooked bacon strips, cut into ½-inch (1.25-cm) pieces

1 teaspoon salt (optional)

CANNING (RAW PACK)

1. Fill jars tightly with raw beans, leaving 1-inch (2.5 cm) headspace.

2. Add cooked bacon strip pieces to the jars.

3. If using, add salt to the jars.

4. Add boiling water to the jars, leaving 1-inch (2.5 cm) headspace.

5. Debubble the jars, leaving 1-inch (2.5 cm) headspace. Add more water to jars if needed to achieve the correct headspace.

6. Wipe the jar rims with a clean, damp towel or a vinegar-dampened towel to remove any residue.

7. Place the lids on top of the jars and secure with a band, screwing it on until finger light.

8. Place the filled jars into the canner. Lock lid and heat canner on high heat.

9. Vent canner 10 minutes.

10. Add 10# weight or the weight for your altitude. Once the pressure is achieved, start timer: for pints, 20 minutes; for quarts, 25 minutes.

INGREDIENTS PER PINT JAR

1 pound (454 g) snapped green beans

1 cooked bacon strip, cut into ½-inch (1.25-cm) pieces

½ teaspoon salt (optional)

Wash green beans. Snap beans in halves or thirds and remove any strings from string beans.

NOTE: With its scant amount of bacon, this recipe does not require "meat" times to process. If you want to be absolutely sure, process for meat times: 75 minutes for pints, 90 minutes for quarts, or omit the bacon altogether. This recipe is written according to my own practice for my shelves.

Canning French Fries

Approximately 7 quarts or 14 pints. Adjust quantity by using estimates below.

Store-bought, frozen French fries are convenient, but they never quite match the taste of fresh-cut fries. With this recipe, you'll can your own French fries and enjoy the best of both worlds. Preserve your potatoes with a purpose!

These canned fries deliver a delightful crunch on the outside and a tender, fluffy interior. In fact, they might just outshine the fresh-cut fries you've made before.

The best part? You'll always have a stash ready to go whenever you want. Just grab a jar, rinse and drain the fries, dry them off, and pop them in the air fryer at 350°F (175°C) for 3 to 5 minutes.

Approximate yields:

* 1 quart = 2½ to 3 pounds (1.1 to 1.4 kg)

* 7 quarts = 20 pounds (9 kg)

* 9 pints = 13 pounds (5.9 kg)

* 18 to 22 quarts = 50 pounds (22.7 kg)

INGREDIENTS

20 pounds (9 kg) russet potatoes, peeled and cut into French-fry shapes

1 teaspoon citric acid (optional, to prevent darkening)

1 gallon (3.8 L) water

7 teaspoons (126 g) salt (optional)

1. Place the potatoes in a bowl or bucket of cold water.

2. After 15 minutes, drain the water and cover in fresh cold water.

3. Repeat step 2 three more times to remove some of the starch from the potatoes, which will keep them from gluing together in the jar during canning.

4. Add 1 teaspoon citric acid, if desired, to 1 gallon of water for filling jars.

CANNING (RAW PACK)

1. Tightly stack and pack potatoes upright into wide-mouth pint or quart jars.

2. Add the salt, if desired: ½ teaspoon to each pint jar or 1 teaspoon to each quart jar.

3. Cover potatoes with plain water or citric acid water, if using, to a 1-inch (2.5 cm) headspace.

4. Debubble the jars, leaving 1-inch (2.5 cm) headspace. Add more water to jars if needed to achieve the correct headspace.

5. Wipe the jar rims with a clean, damp towel or a vinegar-dampened towel to remove any residue.

6. Place the lids on top of the jars and secure with a band, screwing it on until finger light.

7. Place jars into pressure canner and lock lid. Heat the canner on high and vent the canner for 10 minutes.

8. Add 10# weight or the weight for your altitude. Once the pressure is achieved, reduce heat and maintain pressure. Start timer: 35 minutes for pints, 40 minutes for quarts.

MAKE THE MOST OF POTATO WATER

The starchy liquid left from soaking your potatoes can be repurposed in various ways. In other words, don't let that potato water go down the drain. You can refrigerate your potato water or use it right away. Get creative and use it to enhance your dishes and reduce food waste in the process.

* **Soup base.** Potato water can be used as a base for soups and stews.

* **Bread making and baking.** Substitute some or all the water in your bread recipes with potato water. It can improve the texture and taste of baked goods like muffins, pancakes, or waffles.

* **Cooking vegetables.** Use potato water to boil other vegetables, like carrots, beans, or peas.

* **Cooking rice or pasta.** When preparing rice or pasta, replace some of the cooking water with potato water. It imparts a mild potato flavor to the grains or noodles.

* **Fertilizer.** If you're into gardening, potato water can be used as a natural plant fertilizer.

Harvest Treasure Soup Starter

Makes approximately 6 quarts. Recipe can be doubled or tripled.

The soup starter is your golden ticket to preserving the bountiful harvest of the season. You can leave out any vegetables you don't have or adjust the quantities to suit your preference, making it truly your own creation.

With your homemade soup starter, you have the beginnings of any number of meal preparations. From hearty vegetable soups to savory stews, this starter lays the foundation for meals you can customize with your favorite ingredients. By batch-preparing vegetables and canning them for your shelves, dinner can be ready in minutes instead of hours.

Here are a few ideas to spark your dinner creativity.

* Classic vegetable soup. Add seasonings and reheat.

* Hearty potato soup. Combine your soup starter with a splash of cream, some crispy bacon bits, and grated cheese for a rich and creamy potato soup.

* Chicken and rice soup. Throw in some cooked chicken, rice, and a touch of lemon for a comforting chicken and rice soup.

* Beef stew. Add chunks of tender beef, some savory herbs, and a touch of red wine for a robust beef stew.

* Lentil soup. Simmer your soup starter with lentils, cumin, and a dash of lemon for a nutritious, flavor-packed lentil soup.

* Minestrone. Elevate your soup starter with pasta, beans, and an aromatic blend of Italian herbs for a scrumptious minestrone.

---

9 cups (1.8 kg) peeled and cubed potatoes (approximately 4 pounds)

6 cups (780 g) peeled and sliced carrots

3 cups (480 g) diced onions

3 cups (300 g) chopped celery

6 teaspoons (108 g) salt (optional)

8 to 10 cups (1.9 to 2.4 L) water or chicken broth

CANNING

1. The number of jars estimated is 6 quarts. Have a couple extra jars on hand and do your best to distribute ingredients evenly.

2. Place a canning funnel on top of each quart jar and layer ingredients in order. Tamp down ingredients as you layer.

   ½ cup (55 g) potatoes

   1 cup (130 g) carrots

   ½ cup (80 g) onions

   ½ cup (50 g) celery

   1 teaspoon salt (optional)

3. Pour water or chicken broth over jar ingredients, leaving 1-inch (2.5 cm) headspace.

4. Debubble the jars, leaving 1-inch (2.5 cm) headspace. Add more water or broth to jars if needed to achieve the correct headspace.

5. Wipe the jar rims with a clean, damp towel or a vinegar-dampened towel to remove any residue.

6. Place the lids on top of the jars and secure with a band, screwing it on until finger light.

7. Place all the filled jars into the canner.

8. Heat canner over high heat and vent canner 10 minutes.

9. Add 10# weight or the weight for your altitude. Once the pressure is achieved, turn down heat and start timer: for pints, 60 minutes; for quarts, 75 minutes.

SUSTAINABLE COOKING AT ITS BEST

In the spirit of sustainable cooking, don't let the celery tops from this recipe go to waste. Instead, put them to good use by transforming them into celery vinegar, a zesty addition to your kitchen arsenal (see recipe on page 275).

Celery vinegar adds a refreshing twist to dressings, marinades, and more. It's a small step toward a more sustainable kitchen and a delicious way to make the most of every ingredient.

Autumn Acorn Squash

With its slightly sweet and nutty flavor, acorn squash is a delightful addition to your pantry. While these winter squashes store well in a cool, dark basement, canning offers a quick and convenient way to enjoy them without the prep work.

Canned acorn squash, with a touch of cinnamon, nutmeg, brown sugar, and maple syrup, is like capturing the essence of autumn in a jar.

Here are some delicious ways to enjoy your canned acorn squash.

* Side dish. Reheat the canned squash and drizzle with a little extra maple syrup before serving.

* Squash casserole. Mix your canned acorn squash with other vegetables, like carrots or sweet potatoes, and bake them with brown sugar and nutmeg topping for a delightful casserole.

* Squash pancakes, waffles, or muffins. Blend the canned squash into your pancake or waffle batter for a nutritious twist on breakfast, or add to your favorite muffin recipe.

* Squash dessert. Turn your canned acorn squash into a dessert. Mix it with eggs, sugar, and spices to make a squash pie filling. Pour it into a piecrust and bake for a delectable squash pie.

* Squash smoothie. Combine canned squash with yogurt, a ripe banana, a pinch of cinnamon, and a drizzle of honey for a creamy and nutritious smoothie.

Approximate yields:

* 1 acorn squash = approximately 2 quarts

INGREDIENTS

3 acorn squash

2 teaspoons (5 g) ground cinnamon

1 teaspoon nutmeg

12 tablespoons (180 g) brown sugar, divided

12 tablespoons (180 ml) maple syrup, divided

3 teaspoons (54 g) salt, divided (optional)

Water

1. For stability, slice ¼ inch (6 mm) off the stem end and base of the squash. Stand it up on a cut end and chop it in half, from top to bottom. Remove seeds and any fibrous strings by scooping the insides with a metal spoon.

2. Using a vegetable peeler, peel the skins of the acorn squash. Hold the squash with a kitchen towel for stability.

3. Cut squash into 1- to 2-inch (2.5- to 5-cm) cubes and place in a bowl.

4. Toss squash with cinnamon and nutmeg, stirring to coat evenly.

CANNING (RAW PACK)

1. Place a canning funnel on top and pack squash into wide-mouth quart jars to 1-inch (2.5-cm) headspace. Lightly tap jar on countertop to settle squash and make room for adding more.

2. To each quart jar, add 2 tablespoons (30 g) brown sugar, 2 tablespoons (30 g) maple syrup, and ½ teaspoon salt (if using).

3. Add enough water to the jars to cover squash, leaving a 1-inch (2.5 cm) headspace.

4. Debubble the jars, leaving 1-inch (2.5 cm) headspace. Add more water to jars if needed to achieve the correct headspace.

5. Wipe the jar rims with a clean, damp towel or a vinegar-dampened towel to remove any residue.

6. Place the lids on top of the jars and secure with a band, screwing it on until finger light.

7. Place jars into pressure canner and lock lid. Heat the canner on high and vent the canner for 10 minutes.

8. Add 10# weight or the weight for your altitude. Once the pressure is achieved, reduce heat and maintain pressure. Start timer: for pints, 55 minutes; for quarts, 90 minutes.

NOTE: Recipe yield depends on size and weight of acorn squash. Have extra jars available when canning.

Maple-Glazed Carrots

Yield varies; see ingredients list for details

There are few things more colorful on your shelves than carrots. Whether you're looking to preserve the vibrant flavors of the season or add a unique twist to your cantry, this recipe for maple-sweetened carrots is a must-try.

Carrots can be a delicious blank canvas for your weekly meal planning. You can preserve a bushel of carrots in 18 to 24 quart jars, each holding the promise of future freshness. As a versatile pantry staple, carrots are always good for enhancing your side dishes, soups, stews, or family dinners.

Carrots. A bushel of carrots weighs approximately 50 pounds (22.7 kg) and will average 18 to 24 quart jars or 2½ pounds (1.4 kg) per quart. Here are the averages per pounds of carrots needed per jar.

* 7 quart jars = 17 to 18 pounds (7.7 to 8.2 kg)

* 9 pints = 11 pounds (5 kg)

Maple syrup: 1 tablespoon (15 ml) per pint or 2 tablespoons (30 ml) per quart

Salt (optional): ½ teaspoon per pint or 1 teaspoon per quart

1. Scrub and wash carrots well. Peel carrots using a vegetable peeler and place in a bowl of cold water to keep fresh as you work in batches.

2. Slice into coins, dice, or cut into matchsticks. Whatever shape you prefer.

CANNING (RAW PACK)

1. To the bottom of each jar, add maple syrup.

2. Fill jars tightly with raw cut carrots, leaving 1-inch (2.5 cm) headspace. Carrots will shrink during canning, so pack them in. Tapping the jar on the table helps.

3. If using, add salt to the jars.

4. Add water to the jars, leaving 1-inch (2.5 cm) headspace.

5. Debubble the jars, leaving 1-inch (2.5 cm) headspace. Add more water to jars if needed to achieve the correct headspace.

6. Wipe the jar rims with a clean, damp towel or a vinegar-dampened towel to remove any residue.

7. Place the lids on top of the jars and secure with a band, screwing it on until finger light.

8. Place the filled jars into the canner. Lock lid and heat canner on high heat.

9. Vent canner 10 minutes.

10. Add 10# weight or the weight for your altitude. Once the pressure is achieved, start timer: for pints, 25 minutes; for quarts, 30 minutes.

CARROT PEEL CHIPS: TRANSFORMING PEELS INTO A HEALTHY SNACK

Did you know that carrot peels boast a surprising nutritional edge over the vegetable's inner flesh? Research conducted by Tufts University reveals that carrot peels contain approximately one-third more fiber than the inner carrot itself. What's more, these vibrant peels also pack a higher concentration of essential nutrients, including vitamin C and B3, compared to the inner carrot flesh. Instead of discarding them, consider turning these nutritious peels into a crunchy treat. Carrot peel chips offer a creative way to reduce food waste and are also a healthy snack. See page 271 for a carrot peel chips recipe.

CHAPTER 7

Budget Pantry Planning Using Depression-Era Wisdom

Keeping a Thrifty Kitchen

As we progress through an era of seemingly constant innovation, it's important to acknowledge where we come from. This is especially true for our foodways: how our forebears made the most of available resources, stretched every dollar to feed their families, and crafted the food they prepared with love and ingenuity. These practices, many born out of necessity during the Great Depression, are with us even today.

My two grandmothers weathered the storm of the Great Depression, and my childhood was shaped by their tales of resilience. It is an honor to bring you the lessons of collecting, preserving, and sharing nutritious foods that I learned from them, along with the insights I have built on the foundations they laid for me.

In this chapter, we'll explore treasured recipes from the kitchens of yesteryear. These impressive examples of thrift and practicality honor the wisdom of our ancestors while guiding us to embrace a sustainable, budget-friendly approach to modern living. By adopting these time-honored methods, we'll discover the art of mindful consumption, learn to save money and resources, and create a home that thrives on the principles of simplicity and resilience.

Something from Nothing: Food Scrap Recipes and Uses

In this section, we'll explore methods for transforming food scraps into meals, snacks, and more by employing a "make something from nothing" philosophy. Here, every onion peel, carrot top, or stale bread crust can be reforged as an opportunity to experiment and enhance flavor. In a world where every dollar is important, I'll share how I make my resources stretch as far as possible.

And it's not just about saving money for its own sake. These recipes can help reduce waste while at the same time adding a touch of magic to your meals.

Apple Scrap Jelly

Makes approximately
5 to 6 half pints. Do not
double or triple recipe.

Wasting food is so common in our time, no one pays attention to the little scraps and end pieces that go into the trash. Our first example of salvaging useful food from what others might throw away comes to us in the form of lowly apple scraps, left behind after slicing, dicing, and canning your apple recipes.

6 quarts (2.8 kg) apple peels and cores

4 to 5 quarts (3.8 to 4.7 L) water, for boiling

1½ (1.75 oz/49 g) boxes powdered pectin (2.6 oz total)

3 cups (600 g) granulated sugar

4 tablespoons (60 ml) lemon juice

EQUIPMENT

Jelly strainer or nut milk bag

1. In a large stockpot, boil apple peels, cores, and water for about 30 minutes, or until the apple scraps are soft and mushy.

2. With a colander over a bowl, drain the apple scraps. Let sit 10 to 15 minutes, allowing apple juice to drain naturally; do not press.

3. Transfer the apple scraps to a jelly strainer or nut milk bag and hang for 1 to 2 hours over the bowl to drain the remaining juice; do not press (this makes jelly cloudy).

4. Place canning jars in a canning pot filled with water. Bring to a simmer (180°F/82°C) to heat the jars.

5. In a medium stockpot, add 4 cups (944 ml) strained apple scrap juice and stir in pectin.

6. Bring to a boil for 1 minute.

7. Add the sugar and lemon juice, and stir to dissolve. Bring jelly mixture to a boil, stirring constantly for 10 minutes.

8. Test gel point (see page 49).

9. Once gel point is achieved, remove pot from the heat and skim off any foam that has formed on the surface.

CANNING (HOT PACK)

1. Remove a hot jar from the canning pot using a jar lifter.

2. Place a canning funnel on top and ladle jelly into the jar, leaving ¼-inch (6 mm) headspace.

3. Wipe the jar rim with a clean, damp towel or a vinegar-dampened towel to remove any residue.

4. Place the lid on top of the jar and secure with a band, screwing it on until finger light.

5. Place the filled jars back into the canning pot using a canning rack. Ensure the jars are covered with at least 1 inch (2.5 cm) of water.

6. Bring the water to a boil and, once boiling, start the timer for 5 minutes for half pints. Adjust processing time for altitude as needed.

OVERCOMING JELLY SETBACKS

We looked at some problems you can face with jams and jellies—and how to overcome them— in chapter 4. Here are a few more tips to handle issues with your jelly.

Sometimes your jelly will simply refuse to cooperate. Apple scrap jelly requires a more advanced canning technique, and it can take anywhere from 4 to 6 weeks to fully set, so don't be discouraged if your jelly won't set up on the first try.

If it refuses to gel after 6 weeks, that's where you should consider using it as fruit syrup. Drizzle it on pancakes, use it as a flavor enhancer for cocktails, or include it as a sweet surprise on desserts.

Honey Corncob Jelly

Makes approximately 5 half-pint jars

The sweet taste of corn on the cob, captured in a jelly. Where traditional jelly production can require weeks of patience as the gel sets, Pomona's Universal Pectin can speed up the process for this recipe.

---

12 to 15 corncobs, kernels removed

1 teaspoon calcium powder (Calcium powder is included with Pomona's Universal Pectin.)

½ cup (118 ml) water

½ cup (118 ml) lemon juice

1 box Pomona's Universal Pectin (follow package instruction sheet)

2 cups (680 g) honey

1. Place corncobs in a large stockpot and cover with water; bring to a boil for 1 hour.

2. Remove the corncobs and strain the corncob water with a mesh strainer to remove any bits of corn, reserving 3½ cups (826 ml) corncob water to make the jelly.

3. Add the calcium powder to the ½ cup (118 ml) water and stir until dissolved.

4. In a saucepan, combine 3½ cups (826 ml) corncob water and the lemon juice.

5. Add 1 teaspoon of calcium water to saucepan of corncob water and bring mixture to a boil over high heat.

6. In a bowl combine 4 teaspoons (12 g) of Pomona's Universal Pectin with the honey. Stir until mixed.

7. Add honey and pectin mixture to saucepan and return to boiling, stirring to dissolve honey.

8. Place canning jars in a canning pot filled with water. Bring to a simmer (180°F/82°C) to heat the jars.

9. Skim foam off the top of the jelly.

CANNING (HOT PACK)

1. Remove a hot jar from the canning pot using a jar lifter.

2. Place a canning funnel on top and ladle jelly into the jar, leaving ¼-inch (6 mm) headspace.

3. Wipe the jar rim with a clean, damp towel or a vinegar-dampened towel to remove any residue.

4. Place the lid on top of the jar and secure with a band, screwing it on until finger light.

5. Place the filled jars back into the canning pot using a canning rack. Ensure the jars are covered with at least 1 inch (2.5 cm) of water.

6. Bring the water to a boil and, once boiling, start the timer for 10 minutes for half pints. Adjust processing time for altitude as needed.

THIRD TIME'S THE CHARM

Have you ever thought about giving your corncobs a third chance to shine? You've already taken advantage of the corn harvest, canned the kernels, and turned the cobs into delightful jelly. What's left can still be put to work as kindling or fire-starter fuel.

Using your corncobs as fire starters is a practical and eco-conscious approach to reduce waste and stay warm.

* Cut the corncobs into manageable sections, about 4 to 6 inches (10 to 15 cm) in length.

* Place the corncob sections in a well-ventilated, dry area, such as a garage or covered porch. Allow them to air-dry for several weeks.

* Once your corncobs are thoroughly dried, store them in a dry place until needed. Dried corncobs make excellent kindling and fire starters for your fireplace, campfire, or wood-burning stove.

Repurposing Eggshells: Creative and Sustainable Ideas

Eggshells, often viewed as kitchen waste, can be repurposed in various creative, sustainable ways. Rather than tossing them into the trash, consider giving eggshells a second life.

* Garden fertilizer. Crush clean eggshells into small pieces and sprinkle them in your garden to enrich the soil with calcium. This material can also act as a barrier to deter snails, slugs, and other garden pests.

* Seed starters. Fill halved eggshells with potting soil, plant seeds, and, once the seedlings are ready to transplant, place the whole eggshell into the ground. The shell will decompose, adding nutrients to the soil.

* Homemade toothpaste. Bake and grind eggshells into a fine powder, then mix with coconut oil and a touch of peppermint oil for a natural toothpaste. It's gentle on your teeth and friendly on your budget.

* Beauty scrub. Eggshells ground with a mortar and pestle or in a coffee bean grinder make an excellent exfoliating scrub for your skin. Mix finely crushed eggshells with your regular facial cleanser for a gentle and natural exfoliation.

* Chicken calcium supplements. Bake eggshells on a cookie sheet for 3 minutes in a 350°F (175°C) oven. Crush shells and place them in a separate dish or scatter them on the ground in your chicken coop or run. Chickens will peck at the eggshells to consume them for extra calcium.

From Corn Husks to Tamales

Crafting your own corn husks for tamales is a sustainable choice that reduces kitchen waste, especially if you're already canning corn recipes. In a world that increasingly values eco-friendly practices, repurposing corn husks aligns perfectly with the principles of reducing, reusing, and recycling in the kitchen.

1. Remove the silk. Carefully remove the silk (the fine threads) from the corn husks. A soft brush can help with this process.

2. Soak the husks. Place the husks in a large bowl of warm water to soak for at least 30 minutes.

3. Trim and cut. After soaking, carefully trim the husks into uniform sizes and cut away any damaged or torn portions.

4. Dry the husks. Lay the trimmed husks out to dry. The traditional method is to do this outdoors on a patio or another suitable space where the sun and air can help with the drying process. Make sure the husks are laid flat and not overlapping. The amount of time this takes varies depending on ambient temperatures and humidity.

5. Store for future use. Once the husks are thoroughly dried, keep them in an airtight container or a sealed plastic bag to prevent moisture from rehydrating them.

6. Rehydrate before use. When you're ready to make tamales, rehydrate the dried corn husks by soaking them in warm water for at least 30 minutes.

The kitchens of yesteryear (and the resourceful people inside them) were masterful at creating waste-not want-not recipes. In this next section, we'll explore recipes made from everyday food scraps.

Corn Silk Tea

Makes approximately 4 cups (944 ml)

Corn silk tea is made from the silky threads on ears of corn. It's renowned for its potential health benefits and gentle, earthy flavor.

1 cup (96 g) corn silk

4 cups (944 ml) water

Honey or lemon (optional, for added flavor)

Fresh mint leaves (optional, for garnish)

1. Gather the corn silk from pesticide-free corncobs. Make sure it's free of any debris and gently rinse under cool water.

2. In a pot, bring the water to a boil.

3. Add the dried corn silk to the water.

4. Reduce the heat to a gentle simmer and let it steep for about 10 to 15 minutes. The longer you steep, the stronger the flavor.

5. After steeping, strain the tea to remove the corn silk. If desired, add a drizzle of honey or a squeeze of lemon to enhance the flavor. For a touch of freshness, consider garnishing your corn silk tea with a few fresh mint leaves.

Dehydrating Tomato Scraps into Tomato Peel Powder

In the world of food preservation and sustainability, peel powder is often overlooked. Typically discarded as waste, tomato peels can now be easily dehydrated and turned into a vibrant, flavorful powder that can enhance your meals.

1. After peeling the tomatoes, spread the skins on a baking sheet.

2. Allow them to air-dry or place them in an oven set to its lowest temperature (around 150°F/65°C) until completely dried or in a food dehydrator for 8 to 10 hours.

3. Once dry, grind the tomato skins into a fine powder using a blender or coffee grinder.

4. Store the tomato powder in an airtight container.

USES FOR TOMATO POWDER

* **Seasoning.** Sprinkle over roasted vegetables, popcorn, or homemade potato chips.

* **Soup and sauce enhancer.** Add a spoonful to soups, stews, and sauces to boost their tomato flavor without adding extra liquid.

* **Pizza and pasta.** Dust tomato powder on pizza crusts or pasta dishes.

* **Bloody Mary mix.** Incorporate tomato powder into your Bloody Mary mix for a robust tomato profile.

* **Marinades.** Use as an ingredient in marinades for meats and tofu to infuse with a savory tomato essence.

* **Dips and dressings.** Add a pinch of tomato powder to dips, salad dressings, and mayonnaise for a subtle tomato twist.

* **Rice and grain dishes.** Mix tomato powder into rice, couscous, or quinoa for a delightful flavor boost.

Upcycling Tomato Pulp for a Mock Lawry's-Style Seasoning

Makes approximately ½ cup (130 g)

Creating a homemade Lawry's-style seasoning with tomato pulp can be a delightful way to infuse your dishes with unique, savory flavors while giving your tomato pulp new life and reducing kitchen waste. Adjust the cayenne pepper to suit your preferred level of spiciness and explore how this flavorful blend can elevate your recipes.

¼ cup (63 ml) tomato pulp

2 tablespoons (37 g) kosher salt

2 tablespoons (14 g) onion powder

1 tablespoon (9 g) garlic powder

1 tablespoon (7 g) paprika

½ teaspoon black pepper

½ teaspoon dried thyme

½ teaspoon dried oregano

¼ teaspoon cayenne pepper (adjust for heat preference)

1. In a bowl, mix the tomato pulp with the kosher salt. Stir until the mixture is well combined.

2. Add the onion powder, garlic powder, paprika, black pepper, dried thyme, dried oregano, and cayenne pepper to the tomato and salt mixture.

3. Stir all the ingredients together until they are well incorporated, creating a consistent seasoning blend.

STORAGE

* **Fridge.** Store in your refrigerator for up to 4 weeks.

* **Freezer.** Press seasoning into ice cube trays and freeze overnight. Pop frozen seasoning cubes into a zip-top bag and store in the freezer for up to 12 months.

Water-Glassing Eggs with Pickling Lime

Makes 12 to 15 eggs

Water-glassing eggs with pickling lime is a classic method for preserving farm-fresh eggs. Water glassing involves submerging fresh eggs in a pickling lime solution. The result is a powerful technique that allows you to store fresh eggs for extended periods without refrigeration. Explore the art of water glassing, merging traditional wisdom with modern-day practicality.

1 ounce (28 g) pickling lime

1 quart (946 ml) filtered water

12 to 15 clean, unwashed fresh eggs. Eggs must be free of chicken excrement and dirt, with the bloom still fully intact. *Do not use store-bought eggs.*

EQUIPMENT

Kitchen scale

Half-gallon canning jar or container with a lid

1. In a clean half-gallon jar, gently place the eggs into the jar with the pointed side facing downward.

2. Combine the pickling lime and filtered water in a quart jar.

3. Vigorously whisk the lime into the water until thoroughly mixed.

4. Pour the pickling lime mixture into the half-gallon jar over the eggs.

5. Seal the jar with an airtight lid to prevent water evaporation and oxygen exposure.

6. Store your water-glassed eggs in a cool, dark location for up to a year.

LESSONS I'VE LEARNED ABOUT EGG GLASSING

* Egg glassing is most effective in containers no larger than a half-gallon jar. My attempts with gallon buckets have proved cumbersome, since they get heavy and are prone to damaging eggs when stacked.

* Although water-glassed eggs can be preserved for up to a year, their consistency changes over time. They become runnier, which affects their suitability for certain preparations like over-easy fried eggs.

* Egg glassing excels in preserving eggs during molting or reduced egg production, particularly in winter. This technique offers a reliable solution for sustaining your supply through periods of lower egg laying.

* Notably, eggs stored in a water-glass solution gradually acquire a subtle pickling lime flavor, depending on how long they are immersed in the solution.

Homemade Vegetable Stock

A 1-gallon zip-top bag will yield approximately ½ gallon vegetable stock.

This homemade vegetable stock is great for soups, stews, and risottos.

Vegetable scraps (carrot peels, onion skins, celery leaves, etc.)

Herbs (parsley, thyme, bay leaves)

Water

1. Collect vegetable scraps in a container or zip-top bag and freeze until you have enough to make a batch of stock.

2. In a large pot, add the scraps, herbs, and enough water to cover them.

3. Simmer for an hour or more and strain the liquid.

BACON GREASE: LIQUID GOLD

There's a secret treasure hidden in that sizzling pan of bacon: bacon grease.

From flavoring vegetables and searing meats to enhancing the flakiness of biscuits or seasoning your cast-iron pans, the uses for bacon grease are limited only by your imagination. By preserving this liquid gold, you're not just recycling a cooking by-product, you're investing in a delicious future.

1. After cooking bacon, allow the grease to cool slightly but not solidify. It should still be in liquid form.

2. Using a fine-mesh strainer or cheesecloth, strain the bacon grease into a clean, heatproof container. This will remove any bacon bits and impurities from the grease.

3. Let the strained grease cool to room temperature.

4. Seal the container with an airtight lid to prevent the introduction of any contaminants.

5. Store the container in a cool, dark place or in the refrigerator. It can also be frozen for long-term storage. This will keep the bacon grease fresh and ready for use in future recipes.

Candied Watermelon Rinds

Makes approximately 4 cups (600 g)

Candied watermelon rinds are a fun treat and a perfect way to use the often-discarded rind. This classic recipe combines the sweet and slightly tangy flavor of watermelon rinds with a rich, sugary syrup, resulting in a unique and delicious confection. Not only is this a delightful snack on its own, but it can also be used in dessert recipes as garnish or as an addition to your favorite tea.

---

4 cups (600 g) watermelon rind

4 cups (800 g) of granulated sugar

1 cup (236 ml) water

1 lemon, thinly sliced (optional, for added flavor)

1 tablespoon (15 ml) of vanilla extract (optional)

Extra granulated sugar for coating (about 1 cup/200 g)

NOTE: You can adjust the flavor of the syrup by adding spices like cinnamon or cloves or experimenting with different extracts for a personalized touch.

1. Start by peeling the tough green outer skin from the watermelon rind, leaving behind the white flesh. Cut the rind into small, bite-sized pieces, removing any remaining pink fruit.

2. Place the watermelon rind pieces in a large pot and cover with water. Bring the water to a boil, then reduce the heat to a simmer. Cook the rinds until they become slightly translucent and tender. This usually takes about 10 to 15 minutes. Drain the rinds and set them aside.

3. In the same pot, combine the granulated sugar, 1 cup (236 ml) water, and lemon slices (if using). Bring the mixture to a boil, stirring until the sugar dissolves completely.

4. Add the boiled watermelon rind pieces to the syrup mixture. If desired, add the vanilla extract for extra flavor. Reduce the heat to a gentle simmer.

5. Simmer the rinds in the syrup for about 45 minutes to 1 hour, or until they become translucent and slightly glossy. Stir occasionally to ensure even coating.

6. Using a slotted spoon, remove the candied rinds from the syrup and place them on a wire rack to cool and dry for a few hours. They should become slightly tacky to the touch.

7. Roll the cooled candied watermelon rinds in granulated sugar to coat them evenly. This step adds extra sweetness and prevents sticking.

8. Store your candied watermelon rinds in an airtight container at room temperature.

Candied Lemon Peels

Makes approximately 1 cup (119 g)

In this recipe, we transform lemon peels into candied treats—a delightful fusion of simplicity and sweetness, capturing the essence of citrus while repurposing lemon rinds to minimize waste.

---

3 lemons

10 cups (2.4 L) cold water, or as needed

2 cups (400 g) granulated sugar, or as needed

1. Cut lemons into slices about ¼-inch (6 mm) thick and remove the fruit pulp. Cut the rings in half so the peels are in long strips.

2. Bring 2 cups (472 ml) water and lemon peels to a boil in a small pan for 5 minutes.

3. Drain water and repeat with 2 cups (472 ml) of fresh cold water. Perform the boiling steps five times total. This removes any bitter taste from the lemon piths and peels.

4. Drain and set peels aside.

5. Combine 2 cups (472 ml) fresh water with the sugar. Bring to a boil, stirring to dissolve the sugar. Reduce heat to low and stir in citrus peels; simmer until the white pith is translucent.

6. Strain peels from syrup and allow them to dry on a cloth or cooling rack.

7. Toss dry candied peels in sugar and store them in an airtight container at room temperature.

WAYS TO USE CANDIED LEMON PEELS

* **Baking.** Chop into small pieces and add to cakes, cookies, or muffins for a zesty twist.

* **Garnish.** Use as an elegant garnish for desserts, cocktails, or even savory dishes.

* **Gifts.** Package in pretty jars or bags for thoughtful homemade gifts that friends and family will adore.

* **Tea.** Drop a candied lemon peel into your cup of tea for a subtly sweet and citrusy infusion.

Carrot Peel Chips

Next time you're preparing carrots for canning, don't forget to save the peels for a batch
of homemade carrot peel chips. They're a delicious snack and a wonderful example of using culinary creativity
to reduce food waste.

1 cup (110 g) carrot peels (or as
many as you have)

Olive oil

Seasonings of your choice

1. Start by collecting the carrot peels. Ensure they are clean and
   dry. It's perfectly fine to use the peels from carrots that you've
   already used in other canning recipes in this book.

2. In a bowl, drizzle the carrot peels with a bit of olive oil. This
   will help the seasonings adhere and promote crispiness. Toss
   the peels to coat them evenly in the oil.

3. Sprinkle your choice of seasonings over the carrot peels.
   Common options are salt and pepper, paprika, rosemary,
   or thyme. You can also try sweet chips with a little sugar
   and cinnamon.

4. Toss the peels again to ensure the seasonings are distributed
   evenly. The key is to have each peel coated in a light, even
   layer of flavor.

BAKING OR AIR-FRYING

* **Baking.** Preheat your oven to around 350°F (175°C). Spread
  the seasoned carrot peels on a baking sheet in a single layer.
  Bake for approximately 10 to 15 minutes, or until the peels turn
  golden brown and crispy. Flip halfway through for even baking.

* **Air-frying.** Preheat your air fryer to a similar temperature.
  Arrange the seasoned peels in the air fryer basket, making
  sure they're in a single layer. Air-fry for about 5 to 7 minutes, or
  until they become crispy and golden.

  *NOTE: Once they're done, let the carrot peel chips cool for a
  few minutes. They will become even crispier as they cool down.
  Enjoy them as a healthy and satisfying snack.*

Candied Jalapeño Peanut Brittle

Makes approximately 4 cups (588 g)

If you've saved your homemade candied jalapeño syrup (see note on page 103), it's time to transform it into something delightful: candied jalapeño peanut brittle. This fusion of sweet, spicy, and nutty flavors combines jalapeños, spicy charm with the crunch of peanut brittle. The result is a sweet and slightly fiery treat with the right balance of heat and sweetness, wrapped in a crispy, melt-in-your-mouth brittle.

1 pint (473 ml) candied jalapeño syrup

½ cup (118 ml) light corn syrup

1 teaspoon vanilla extract

2 teaspoons (9 g) baking soda

2 tablespoons (28 g) butter, room temperature

2 cups (290 g) peanuts, chopped

1. Spray a large baking sheet or flat pizza pan with non-stick cooking spray.

2. In a heavy saucepan, bring to a boil the candied jalapeño syrup and corn syrup.

3. Set a candy thermometer in syrup and continue to boil, stirring occasionally, until it reaches the hard crack stage (300°F/149°C). *If you don't have a candy thermometer: Test the temperature of the syrup by drizzling a little from a spoon into some ice water. It should turn brittle in the ice water.*

4. Remove syrup from heat and quickly add vanilla, baking soda, butter, and peanuts. Do this quickly before it hardens.

5. Pour quickly onto baking sheet/pizza pan and use two forks to stretch and pull brittle. Use extreme caution: the syrup is very hot.

6. Once brittle is cool, break into pieces.

7. Store brittle in airtight containers.

Homemade Apple Cider Vinegar from Scraps

Makes approximately 1 quart (946 ml)

Making apple cider vinegar at home can be fun and rewarding, but it may take some time to achieve the flavor you prefer. Patience is key, and experimentation is encouraged to find the perfect balance for your taste buds.

Apple peels and cores (enough to fill a quart-sized jar)

Granulated sugar (2 tablespoons [26 g] per 1 quart [946 ml] of water)

Warm water

EQUIPMENT

A quart-sized glass jar

A piece of cheesecloth or a coffee filter

A rubber band or string

1. Gather apple peels and cores from your canning recipes. They can be from a mix of varieties or a single type of apple.

2. Thoroughly wash and sanitize a quart-sized glass jar. Make sure it's completely dry before you start.

3. Stuff the jar with the apple scraps, leaving about 2 inches (5 cm) of space at the top.

4. Dissolve 2 tablespoons (26 g) sugar per 1 quart (946 ml) water. Use warm water to help the sugar dissolve more easily. Allow the solution to cool to room temperature.

5. Pour the sugar-water solution over the apple scraps in the jar, ensuring they are fully submerged. Leave about 1 inch (2.5 cm) of space between the liquid and the top of the jar.

6. Cover the jar's opening with a piece of cheesecloth or a coffee filter, securing it with a rubber band or string. This will allow air to flow while keeping out debris and insects.

7. Place the jar in a warm, dark place, like a pantry or a cupboard. Stir the mixture briefly every day for the first week. This helps kick-start the fermentation process.

8. Allow the mixture to ferment for several weeks. It typically takes around 3 to 4 weeks, but you can let it ferment longer for a stronger flavor.

9. After a few weeks, start tasting your apple cider vinegar. When it reaches your desired level of acidity, it's ready to use.

10. Once your apple cider vinegar is ready, strain out the apple scraps, and pour the liquid into a clean, airtight container for storage.

Celery Cider Vinegar

Makes approximately 1 quart (946 ml)

Celery cider vinegar is easy to make at home, and it's an excellent way to reduce food waste. By using celery scraps—and with a little patience—you can create your own unique vinegar, perfect for salad dressings, marinades, or even as a natural cleaning solution.

½ cup (100 g) celery, pulped

4 cups (944 ml) white vinegar

2 teaspoons (36 g) salt

2 tablespoons (26 g) granulated sugar

EQUIPMENT

A quart-sized glass jar

A piece of cheesecloth or a coffee filter

A rubber band or string

1. Place celery tops and leaves in a food processer, and chop to a pulp consistency. You may need to add a little water to the celery to get it to a pulp.

2. In a medium saucepan, boil vinegar, salt, and sugar for 1 minute, or until sugar is dissolved.

3. To a quart jar, add celery pulp and pour in vinegar brine.

4. Cover with a cheesecloth or coffee filter, secured with a rubber band or string.

5. Let the vinegar infuse for 2 or 3 weeks, shaking or stirring the jar often.

6. When infusion is complete, strain out the pulp in the jar and pour the vinegar into an airtight bottle or container for storage.

Homemade Onion Vinegar

Makes approximately 1 pint (473 ml)

Homemade onion vinegar, crafted from kitchen scraps, is a flavorful staple for budget-conscious home cooks. Enjoy its rich essence drizzled over salads; used in marinades, vinaigrettes, and savory sauces; or as a complement to roasted vegetables, grilled meats, and crusty bread.

2 cups (320 g) onion scraps or 2 large onions, sliced

2 cups (472 ml) white wine vinegar

1 tablespoon (13 g) granulated sugar

1 teaspoon salt

2 to 3 sprigs of fresh thyme (optional)

1. In a saucepan, combine the onion scraps or sliced onions, vinegar, sugar, salt, and fresh thyme sprigs if desired.

2. Heat the mixture over low heat and allow it to simmer for approximately 5 to 7 minutes, or until the onions become tender.

3. Remove the saucepan from the heat and let the mixture cool to room temperature.

4. Carefully pour the onion and vinegar mixture into a jar or glass container. Ensure that the container's lid is airtight, as this will help preserve the vinegar.

5. Seal the container with a lid and place it in a cool, dark location.

6. Let the vinegar infuse 2 to 4 weeks.

7. After the infusion period, strain the onion vinegar to remove the onion slices and any thyme sprigs. Transfer the vinegar back to the container and seal it tightly.

Homemade Tarragon Vinegar

Makes approximately 1 pint (473 ml)

Homemade tarragon vinegar is a delightful infusion that captures tarragon's unique peppery flavor. I've used this vinegar to make amazing refrigerator pickled peppers. This aromatic vinegar adds a touch of sophistication and herbaceous charm to your menu creations. Use it to enliven salad dressings, add depth to seafood dishes, or drizzle over roasted vegetables.

½ cup (32 g) fresh tarragon leaves

2 cups (472 ml) white wine vinegar (or your vinegar of choice)

1. Begin by washing and thoroughly drying the fresh tarragon leaves. To jump-start the infusion, cut the leaves into smaller pieces.

2. Boil the vinegar in a small saucepan. Remove from heat.

3. In a clean, dry pint jar or glass container, layer the tarragon leaves. Pour the vinegar over the tarragon, ensuring it covers the leaves entirely.

4. Seal the container with an airtight lid, and place it in a cool, dark location.

5. Allow the tarragon and vinegar to infuse for at least 2 weeks. Shake the container gently every few days to encourage the infusion.

6. After the desired infusion period, strain the tarragon vinegar to remove the leaves, ensuring you're left with a clear and aromatic vinegar. Transfer the vinegar back to the container and seal it tightly.

Honey-Fermented "100-Year Garlic"

*Makes approximately
1 pint (473 ml)*

I call this recipe "100-Year Garlic" because it can last hundreds of years. The tradition of fermenting garlic in honey dates back thousands of years, as ancient Egyptian tombs have revealed—a captivating narrative that transcends borders and cultures. But you don't have to wait a century to enjoy this time-honored treat.

PER WIDE-MOUTH PINT JAR

20 to 30 peeled whole garlic cloves, approximately 1 cup (136 g)

1 cup (340 g) raw honey

1. Place the peeled whole garlic cloves in a pint-sized, wide-mouth Mason jar, ensuring they are evenly distributed. To quick-peel garlic, place cloves in a microwave dish and microwave for 10 to 12 seconds. The garlic peels will slip right off.

2. Pour enough raw honey into the jar to completely cover the garlic cloves. Ideally you want the jar no more than two-thirds full, allowing air space for the garlic to bubble (ferment) in the honey.

3. Place a canning lid and ring on the jar, leaving the ring loose. Place the jar on a countertop or shelf.

4. Every couple of days for 2 to 4 weeks, unscrew the ring and "burp" the garlic to release the gases in the jar from the fermentation process.

5. Tighten the ring securely, and flip the jar upsidedown to recoat the garlic cloves.

6. When turning the jar upright again, loosen the ring before returning it to the counter or shelf.

7. When the honey no longer contains gas bubbles (around 1 month), the garlic has finished fermenting and is ready to enjoy. The longer it sits on your shelves, the darker the garlic will become and the more infused the flavors.

8. For long-term storage, keep the jar in a cool, dry environment away from direct sunlight. Enjoy for the next hundred years!

WHAT IS NORMAL DURING FERMENTATION?

* Bubbles in the honey. These are gases related to the fermentation process.

* Hissing or whooshing sounds when burping the jar every day.

* Honey becoming runny. Honey is hydrophilic and will draw the water from the garlic, thinning the honey.

* Garlic cloves with a bluish or greenish hue during fermentation. While this may look unusual, it's not harmful and the honey garlic remains usable.

IMPORTANT THINGS TO KNOW

* It is crucial to use *raw* honey for this recipe, as it contains the necessary bacteria and wild yeast for fermentation. This recipe is unsafe to consume unless you use raw honey.

* Do not give any part of this recipe—honey or garlic—to infants or children under two years of age.

* Place a plate or napkin under the jar during fermentation. The mixture may bubble up as part of the process, causing some honey to drip out.

* To address concerns about botulism, use a pH test strip. Botulism spores cannot thrive in an environment with a pH below 4.6. Honey typically has a pH of around 3.9, though this can vary.

* Do not add more honey or garlic to the jar after fermentation. If you are running low, start a brand-new jar with new ingredients. Reusing honey can lower the pH to unsafe thresholds.

HOW TO USE FERMENTED GARLIC HONEY

* Straight from the jar. A teaspoon of garlic honey with one fermented clove is a wonderful treat, and it also has good medicinal properties. Take at the first sign of a cold or as a routine immune booster for health maintenance.

* In cooking. Use in condiments, salad dressings, fruit and pizza drizzle, and marinades.

Variations for Fermenting in Honey

Ginger Honey

INGREDIENTS PER PINT JAR

1 cup (100 g) peeled and sliced ginger

1 cup (340 g) raw honey

Add all ingredients to the jar and follow steps for "100 Year Garlic."

Figs and Dates Honey

INGREDIENTS PER PINT JAR

½ cup (75 g) figs, quartered into ½-inch (1.25-cm) slices, stems removed

½ cup (89 g) dates, sliced in half

1 cup (340 g) raw honey

2 teaspoons (10 ml) water

Add all ingredients to the jar and follow steps for "100 Year Garlic."

Pomegranate Honey

INGREDIENTS PER PINT JAR

1 cup (174 g) pomegranate arils (seeds or pips)

1 cup (340 g) raw honey

½ teaspoon ground ginger

½ teaspoon ground cloves

Add all ingredients to the jar and follow steps for "100 Year Garlic."

Tepache: A Zesty Pineapple Brew

Makes approximately 2 quarts (1.9 L)

Tepache is rooted in Mexican culture, a testament to reducing waste while making a slightly tart fruit drink that's ideal for sipping on warm days. Tepache has a similar fermenting process as that for kombucha—and the fizzy tang of tepache is comparable to kombucha as well.

Pineapple peels, cores, and rinds, enough to fill jar

1 cone piloncillo (raw cane sugar), cut into pieces (found in Latin American or Spanish groceries) Alternatively, you can substitute 1 cup (150 g) brown sugar if you cannot find piloncillo.

1 cinnamon stick

3 whole cloves

2-inch (5 cm) knuckle of fresh peeled ginger

Water

EQUIPMENT

Gallon jar

Cheesecloth or breathable cloth

Rubber band or string

1. Add pineapple scraps to the jar until it is full.

2. Add piloncillo pieces or brown sugar to the jar.

3. Add spices to the jar and cover all jar contents with water to the top of the jar.

FERMENTING

1. Add cheesecloth or breathable cloth to the top of the jar and secure with a rubber band or string.

2. Let the tepache set at room temperature for 2 to 3 days, or until froth forms on the top.

3. Strain food out of the tepache liquid and ladle liquid into glass jars for drinking.

4. Refrigerate and enjoy within 2 to 3 weeks.

My Most Beloved Canning Recipe

This is more than just another canning recipe to me: it's my heritage preserved in a jar, a culinary homage to the enduring love and dedication of my ancestors.

This recipe dates back five generations, spanning over 130 years, and it all began with my great-great-great-grandmother, Mattie "Annie" Pool. Born in 1873, she married at a young age and lovingly canned food to sustain her husband and six children. The warmth of her kitchen, the aroma of simmering pots, and the skillful preservation of harvests have left an indelible mark on our family.

This tradition would have been lost to history had it not been for my Great-Aunt Madgie. In 1975, she generously shared this ancestral recipe with my grandmother, Marie. With quick hands and determination, Marie transcribed Annie's precious canning knowledge on a flimsy piece of 3-by-5 notepaper with the insignia "Gary Vault Company." My mother, Patty, still has the paper she inherited from her mother.

The legacy of this canning recipe lives on, passed down through generations to me. I grew up eating these sweet pickle chips like candy, not knowing the deep history they held. The aromatics boiling in the brine instantly transport me back to my childhood.

With my mother's blessing, we've decoded the antiquated language to present this heritage canning recipe for you to enjoy. As you enjoy the flavors, you're not just cooking, you're participating in an enduring story of love, devotion, and the joys of canning. This is the summation of my canning history, offering a taste of my heritage to you and all who gather around your table.

Annie's Sweet Pickle Chips

Makes approximately 5 to 9 pint jars. Recipe can be doubled or tripled.

28 pickling cucumbers (Kirby), 4 to 5 inches (10 to 13 cm) long

Water

2 tablespoons (12 g) whole allspice

1 quart (946 ml) white vinegar

8 cups (1.6 kg) granulated sugar

2 tablespoons (36 g) salt

The number of jars needed depends on the size and cut of the cucumbers, including the cucumbers' water content, which may cause shrinking. Have plenty of extra pint jars available while canning.

9-DAY PICKLE PROCESS

DAY 1

1. Wash cucumbers and place in a deep container (a water bath canner works well). Cover cucumbers with boiling water (no salt) and cover.

DAY 2

1. Drain and discard water from cucumbers. Cover cucumbers with fresh boiling water (no salt) and cover.

DAY 3

1. Drain and discard water from cucumbers. Cover cucumbers with fresh boiling water (no salt) and cover.

DAY 4

1. Drain and discard water from cucumbers. Cover cucumbers with fresh boiling water (no salt) and cover.

DAY 5

1. Drain and discard water from cucumbers.

2. Slice cucumbers into ½-inch (1.25-cm) coin shapes, discarding both ends of cucumbers (butt end and blossom end).

3. Wrap whole allspice in a cheesecloth bag. You can cut a square piece of cheesecloth and secure it with kitchen twine if you do not have a bag.

4. In a large saucepan, bring vinegar, sugar, salt, and cheesecloth bag of allspice to a boil. Stir until sugar is dissolved. Pour boiling brine and spice bag over sliced cucumbers and cover.

DAY 6, DAY 7, DAY 8

1. Strain brine liquid from cucumbers into a large saucepan and reboil. Pour over cucumber slices and cover.

DAY 9

1. Strain brine liquid from cucumbers into a large saucepan and reboil. Pour over cucumber slices and let sit for 30 minutes.

2. Place canning jars in a canning pot filled with water and bring to a simmer (180°F/82°C) to heat the jars.

3. Strain brine liquid from cucumbers into a large saucepan and reboil. Discard cheesecloth spice bag and remove from heat.

CANNING (HOT PACK)

1. Retrieve hot jars from canner.

2. Place a canning funnel on top of a jar and, using a slotted spoon, drain pickles away from brine and pack into pint jars, leaving ½-inch (1.25-cm) headspace.

3. Use a bubble remover tool to remove air bubbles. Add more brine to correct headspace if needed.

4. Wipe the jar rim with a clean, damp towel or a vinegar-dampened towel to remove any residue.

5. Place the lid on top of the jar and secure with a band, screwing it on until finger light.

6. Place the filled jar back into the canning pot using a canning rack and repeat process until all jars are in the canner. Ensure the jars are covered with at least 1 inch (2.5 cm) of water.

7. Bring the water to a boil and, once boiling, start the timer for 5 minutes for pints or 10 minutes for quarts. Adjust processing time for altitude as needed.

Appendix

A Glossary of Canning and Food Preservation Terms

Canning and food preservation involve a unique set of terms and techniques. This glossary provides definitions and explanations for key terms to help you navigate the world of home food preservation.

Altitude adjustments. The process of adjusting canning recipes and processing times to account for variations in altitude, as pressure and boiling points change with elevation.

Boil. The rapid bubbling and vaporization of a liquid when heated to its boiling point.

Boiling point. The temperature at which a liquid turns into vapor and bubbles form, typically 212°F (100°C) at sea level for water.

Brine. A vinegar solution used in pickling to preserve and flavor vegetables or other foods.

Canning jar. A glass container designed for preserving food through canning. Jars come in various sizes and shapes.

Canning lid. A flat metal lid with a sealing compound used to create an airtight vacuum seal in canning jars.

Canning ring. A screw-on metal ring used to hold the lid on a canning jar in place during processing but should be removed after sealing.

Cantry. The author coined this phrase as a term of endearment for her pantry of canned goods. She refers to this storage area, often a dedicated pantry or shelf, where home-canned goods and preserved foods are kept.

Cold pack. A canning method in which unheated food is packed into jars and then covered with liquid.

Conserve. A type of fruit preserve made with a mixture of fruits, nuts, and sugar, often with added spices.

Dial gauge. A type of pressure gauge used on pressure canners to measure the pressure inside the canner.

Dry pack. A method of canning where dry food items are placed directly into jars without added liquid.

Finger light. The author's term for the method of lightly adding the ring to the jar using three fingers to secure the lid prior to processing. Once the ring engages with the jar and the jar begins to spin, the ring is secure. Also known as finger tight.

Flat sour. An unappealing but avoidable flavor in canned goods. Caused by keeping just-processed foods at a warm temperature for extended periods of time by either leaving jars in the canner or covering them with towels instead of letting them cool naturally.

Food mill. A kitchen tool used to purée or strain fruits and vegetables for canning, removing seeds and skins.

Funnel. A kitchen tool used to easily transfer foods into canning jars without spillage.

Gasket. A rubber or silicone seal used to create an airtight closure in a pressure canner.

Gel stage. The point during jelly or jam making when the mixture thickens and reaches the desired consistency.

Headspace. The empty space left between the food or liquid and the top of a canning jar, allowing for expansion and a proper seal during processing.

Hermetic seal. An airtight, vacuum seal achieved in canning that prevents the entry of spoilage organisms.

Hot pack. A canning method in which food is heated before packing into jars.

Jam. A fruit preserve made from fruit, sugar, pectin, and acid (usually lemon or other fruit juice). Distinct from jelly in that jam contains pieces of the fruit used in its production.

Jar lifter. A specialized tool used to safely lift and remove hot canning jars from a boiling water bath or pressure canner.

Jelly. A fruit preserve made from fruit juice, sugar, and pectin, resulting in a clear, firm product.

Jelly bag. A cloth bag used to strain fruit juices when making jelly.

Jiggler/weighted gauge. A pressure regulator on some pressure canners that jiggles or rocks to indicate and maintain the desired pressure.

Marmalade. A type of fruit preserve made from citrus fruits, typically containing both juice and peel.

Nut milk bag. A fine-mesh bag used to strain nut milks and juices, or to remove solids from liquid mixtures during canning.

Open-kettle canning. A method of canning where hot food is poured into jars and sealed immediately without further processing.

Oven canning. A discouraged method of canning that involves sealing jars in the oven, which is not considered safe by modern canning standards.

Parcook (par-cook). A culinary technique involving the partial cooking of food to a specific point before it is finished or used in a final recipe, often to achieve desired textures or reduce cooking times.

Pectin. A naturally occurring substance found in many fruits, particularly in their skins and cores. It acts as a thickening agent when heated with sugar and acid, forming a gel-like texture. This natural thickening property is what makes jams and jellies set and become solid.

Pickling. The process of preserving foods in an acidic solution, often vinegar or brine, to create pickles or other preserved products.

Pickling lime. A food-grade chemical used in pickling to firm and crisp fruits and vegetables. Also used to water-glass eggs for long-term storage.

Preserves. A type of fruit preserve made with whole or large pieces of fruit, often in a syrup or gel.

Pressure canner. A specialized canning device that uses steam pressure to safely preserve low-acid foods by destroying harmful microorganisms.

PSI (pounds per square inch). A unit of pressure used to measure the pressure inside a pressure canner.

Siphoning. When liquid from inside the jar escapes out of the jar and into the water in the canner.

Venting canner. An action allowing steam to escape from the canner before sealing it during the pressure canning process.

Water bath canner. A large, deep pot with a rack used for hot-water-bath canning, designed to hold jars that are submerged in boiling water to process high-acid foods.

References

National Center for Home Food Preservation

Website: nchfp.uga.edu

* Canning science information

* Altitude adjustments

* Time and pressure charts

* Temperature parameters

Pomona's Pectin

Website: www.pomonapectin.com/faqs

* Troubleshooting suggestions

* Information about pectin

Michigan State University Extension School

Website: www.canr.msu.edu/foodpreservation

* Preserving safety information

* Home food preservation courses

About the Author

In the few short years since she launched her TikTok channel @PeeliesNPetals, **Sarah Thrush** has become a widely popular personality in the world of canning and food preservation. The go-to canning enthusiast for time-honored and efficient canning methods, Sarah is a master creator of canning and preserving recipes to create contemporary and innovative foods for a well-stocked pantry. Sarah is an in-demand teacher on the subject in the media and for trade shows, consumer-education events, and manufacturer- and retailer-sponsored appearances. A leader in both canning and food preservation, Sarah's focus on food independence and food security has helped families and individuals eat well even when money is tight. Living with her husband and children in the Upper Peninsula of Michigan, Sarah, in addition to canning and preserving, is an avid gardener and homesteader, raising chickens and creating a robust, organized pantry to live as self-sufficiently as possible. Teaching about food preservation to help others with food insecurity is her passion. @PeeliesNPetals can also be followed on Facebook, YouTube, and Instagram.

Acknowledgments

To my family, for enduring my endless nights in the kitchen working on this project. Thank you for enjoying every canned creation with gratitude, even when you secretly yearned for pizza.

Thank you to my pressure canners Effie, Sunny, and Ginger. You are the real MVPs.

Special shoutout to my supporters for demanding a book, not accepting no for an answer, and providing me with endless moral support on this journey.

To my friends: You turned what could have been a solitary pursuit into a shared adventure. Thank you for being a pillar of support both in and out of the kitchen.

Index